LOCATING THE SACRED

LOCATING THE SACRED

THEORETICAL APPROACHES TO THE EMPLACEMENT OF RELIGION

edited by

Claudia Moser and Cecelia Feldman

Oxbow Books
Oxford and Oakville

Joukowsky Institute Publication 3

General series editor: Prof. John F. Cherry
Joukowsky Institute for Archaeology and the Ancient World
Brown University, Box 1837/60 George Street, Providence, RI 02912, USA

© Brown University, Oxbow Books and the individual contributors 2014

ISBN 978-1-78297-616-5

A catalogue record for this book is available from the British Library

Library of Congress Cataloguing-in-Publication Data

This book is available direct from
Oxbow Books, Oxford, UK
(Phone: 01865-241249; Fax: 01865-794449)
and
The David Brown Book Company
PO Box 511, Oakville, CT 06779, USA
(Phone: 860-945-9329; Fax: 860-945-9468)

www.oxbowbooks.com

*Front cover: Detail of a petroglyph representing people engaged in a dance or performance (Heishan
site, Gansu, China).*
*Back cover: Sacrificial procession on the frieze of the monument of Domitius Ahenobarbus (Rome,
end of the 2nd century B.C.).*

Printed by
Berforts Information Press, Eynsham, Oxfordshire

Contents

List of Figures

List of Tables

Notes on Contributors

Chih-hua Chiang is Assistant Professor in the Department of Anthropology in the National Taiwan University. She received her Ph.D. from the Anthropology Department at the University of California, Berkeley. Her research interests include household archaeology, intrasite spatial analysis, landscape archaeology, and the politics of archaeology, and the archaeology of East Asia and Southeast Asia.

Paola Demattè is Professor of Chinese Art and Archaeology in the Department of History of Art and Visual Culture at the Rhode Island School of Design. She holds a *Laurea* in Chinese Language and Literature from the Università degli Studi di Venezia (Italy), and a Ph.D. in archaeology from the University of California, Los Angeles. Dr. Demattè specializes in the Neolithic and Bronze Age archaeology of China and has written on the origins of Chinese writing, early urbanism, archaic jades, and on the rock art of China. She has also a keen interest in religion and East-West contacts. In this context, Dr. Demattè has curated an exhibition at the Getty Center and co-authored a volume on Sino-European exchanges from the 16th through the 19th centuries (*China on Paper*, Getty Publications 2007).

Cecelia Feldman received her Ph.D. from the Joukowsky Institute for Archaeology and the Ancient World at Brown University in 2011 and is currently a Lecturer in the Department of Classics at the University of Massachusetts Amherst. This chapter arises from her dissertation, *Living Fluidly: Uses and Meanings of Water in Asia Minor (2nd century B.C.E. – 2nd century C.E).* Her research interests include urban development, ritual landscapes, and the economic and cultural implications of technological developments, particularly those pertaining to water.

Yi-chang Liu is a Research Fellow at the Institute of History and Philology, Academia Sinica, where he specializes in Taiwanese archaeology. His research interests are the cultural history of Taiwan and its surrounding areas, transportation and exchange systems, early production technology and resource management.

Robert N. McCauley is William Rand Kenan Jr. University Professor of Philosophy and the Director of the Center for Mind, Brain, and Culture at Emory University. His two principal areas of research are the cognitive science of religion and the philosophy of science. His most recent book is *Why Religion Is Natural and Science Is Not* (Oxford University Press, 2011).

Isaac Morrison is an anthropologist and internet-media analyst who studies culture networks between the US and the Middle East. He received an M.A. in Anthropology at the George Washington University in 2009 and he currently works as an independent consultant and program evaluator in the International Development sector. In addition to his research and consulting work he is an adjunct lecturer in Anthropology at Ashford University and a freelance ceramic artist.

Claudia Moser is in the final stages of her doctoral research at the Joukowsky Institute for Archaeology and the Ancient World, Brown University. She is currently working on a dissertation on the archaeological record of sacrifice at the altars of Republican Rome and Latium. Her research interests include the materiality of Roman religion, the intersection of text and material culture, and the relationship between place and ritual.

Chryssanthi Papadopoulou received her Ph.D. in Classical maritime archaeology from King's College London in 2010 and is currently involved in underwater excavations in Greece. Her research interests include several aspects of ancient Greek religion, issues of past maritime identities, and the development of maritime cults.

Ian Straughn is Joukowsky Family Middle East Studies Librarian, and former Postdoctoral Fellow at the Joukowsky Institute for Archaeology and the Ancient World, both at Brown University. His research examines the landscapes and material transformations of the Muslim world in its formative periods, issues which serve as the basis of his current monograph in progress, *Islam Emplaced: The Landscape of an Emerging Religious Tradition*. His fieldwork has largely centered on the Levant and currently focuses on the Petra region of Jordan. He also serves as an editor of the journal *Archaeological Dialogues.*

Christina Williamson received her Ph.D. in Ancient History and Mediterranean Archaeology from the University of Groningen in the Netherlands in 2012. Her research applies an interdisciplinary approach as it seeks to interpret the role of major rural shrines in civic development in Hellenistic Asia Minor. The article here draws in part on her current post-doctoral project on monuments, perception, and state formation processes in the landscape of Pergamon. She received a grant from the Dutch government to conduct this research at the Joukowsky Institute for Archaeology and the Ancient World, Brown University.

Contributor Addresses

Cecelia Feldman
Department of Classics, Herter Hall
University of Massachusetts Amherst
Amherst, MA 01003
cfeldman@classics.umass.edu

Claudia Moser
Joukowsky Institute for Archaeology and the Ancient World
Brown University
Providence, RI 02912
Claudia_Moser@brown.edu

Chih-hua Chiang
Department of Anthropology
No.1 SEC. 4 Roosevelt RD.
National Taiwan University
Taipei, Taiwan, 106
Chihhua@ntu.edu.tw

Paola Demattè
Department of History of Art and Visual Culture
Rhode Island School of Design
Providence, RI 02903
pdematte@risd.edu

Yi-chang Liu
Institute of History and Philology
Academia Sinica
Taipei, Taiwan 115
liuyc@mail.ihp.sinica.edu.tw

Robert N. McCauley
Center for Mind, Brain, and Culture
Emory University
Atlanta, GA 30322
philrnm@emory.edu

Isaac Morrison
1312 Guilford Ave. #314
Baltimore, MD 21202
isaac@gwmail.gwu.edu

Chryssanthi Papadopoulou
The British School at Athens
Souedias 52
10676 Athens
Greece
c.papadopoulou@bsa.ac.uk

Ian Straughn
Brown University Library, Research and Outreach Services
Brown University
Providence, RI 02912
Ian_Straughn@brown.edu

Christina Williamson
Joukowsky Institute for Archaeology and the Ancient World
Brown University
Providence, RI 02912
cgwilliamson@gmail.com

— 1 —

Introduction

CLAUDIA MOSER AND CECELIA FELDMAN

To practice ritual is to be *emplaced*. Religious ritual cannot be studied as a disembodied event or series of events – removed from its location and separate from the physicality of its performance. Instead, the ritual must be examined in its specific material and topographical context in which ritual action impacts its physical setting while, simultaneously, the location in which the ritual is enacted informs and guides the religious practice. The critical importance of the interconnection between ritual action and place is the basic premise on which this book rests and is the thread that ties this collection of papers together. This reciprocal relationship between ritual and place can be approached from a variety of perspectives and manifested in a multiplicity of ways. Sacred space does not exist *a priori* but is the outcome of actions, intentions, and recollections – it is the result of past and present interactions among humans, material implements, architecture, and landscape. Each paper included in this collection presents a specific case study in which this interrelationship between ritual and its setting is explored and unpacked, investigating the numerous ways in which the sacred can be located.

The past scholarship investigating ritual has tended to rely on written sources and ethnographic accounts to investigate religious practice. Such approaches that draw primarily on written and verbal transmission of ritual practice not only tend to privilege a single perspective or account of the event, but also fail to consider both material and topographical aspects of religious ritual. In other words, both literary and anthropologically-based approaches to the study of ritual generally disassociate the religious practice from its material and spatial context. Moreover, these studies tend to offer accounts of ritual that are limited to the period of time governed by verbal or textual transmission, and thus are subject to the inherent biases of these types of record keeping. Therefore, such approaches lack strategies for investigating ritual action in the deep past or within societies lacking written records.

Complementing the standard literary and anthropological approaches to the study of religious ritual, an examination of the material record incorporates the element of temporal depth. Such a material-based approach allows for a view of ritual as a *process* through consideration of the ritual's relationship to its material setting over time. It is with this ability to examine the overall character of invariance and change in a ritual over time, taking into account its material and topographical nexus, that the discipline of archaeology offers critical tools to the study of religious ritual.

An increasing awareness of ritual theory within archaeology and other disciplines concerned with material culture has been accompanied by a similarly burgeoning interest in conceptions and theories of 'place.' Every human action must occur in the physical world and therefore ritual events – deliberate and repetitive movements and interactions with materials in time – must be linked to the places in which they occur. All of the papers in this volume approach ritual as firmly situated within a material and topographical matrix, taking as a foundation the co-constitutive relationship between ritual and place (cf. Smith 1987). Whether focused on Buddhist China, the Greco-Roman Mediterranean, or present-day Israel, each paper investigates how religious practices are imprinted on and preserved within a location, and how that specific place may inform and guide ritual. We hope that the papers in this volume, with their geographic and chronological diversity, will serve as a resource for a theoretical approach to the study of ritual practice that may have broad cross-cultural application and provide new insight into the relationship between ritual and place.

Ritual and Place in the Scholarly Landscape

In the last 20 years, scholars have paid increasing attention to religious ritual. Among the most notable of these scholars is Catherine Bell. In two separate books, *Ritual Theory, Ritual Practice* (1992) and *Ritual: Perspectives and Dimensions* (1997), Bell has developed a theory of ritual practice focused on the human body. For Bell, ritual at its core is a human action, manipulated and differentiated from other actions. Bell defines ritual as a practice that is non-habitual and repetitive, an action that, when compared to other actions, appears singular; for "ritualization…distinguish[es] and privilege[s] what is being done in comparison to other, usually more quotidian, activities" (1992: 74). This characterization of the uniqueness of ritual closely parallels the tendency in the archaeological study of ritual to rely on unusual, extraordinary, material artifacts (cf. Insoll 2004; McCauley and Lawson 2002).

Bell draws on the ethnographic present in developing her understanding of the "non-everyday;" but how might her theory be explored beyond ethnographic examples or applied to the ancient past? The study of the mutually-constitutive relationship between place and ritual finds its beginning in Bell's examination of the environment as an agent which can "impress these schemes upon the bodies of [ritual] participants" (1992: 99). But in this statement, Bell considers the environment in which ritual is practiced only insofar as it impacts the bodies of ritual participants, failing to regard how ritual itself might, reciprocally, impart its action on the environment, imprinting the physical landscape with the traces of its action. Bell's approach to ritual is crucial in its recognition of ritual practice as incorporated – literally, as actions that were performed by and based in the human body. However, while Bell makes significant contributions to the discussion of the location of ritual as a setting for action, she does not fully address the extent of the relationship between ritual and place, between the actions of ritual practitioners and the locations in which they are carried out.

J.Z. Smith in *To Take Place: Toward Theory in Ritual* (1987) gives setting a greater role in his attempt to place ritual. For Smith, place is the setting where ritual action is realized, the locus of attention. Like Bell, Smith considers place to be a critical component in religious ritual, viewing setting as the instrument through which the divine creates the sacred (cf. Eliade 1957). Smith sees place and ritual as intertwined; but for Smith, place is not a fixed geographic location, but rather a more flexible, almost non-materially contingent abstraction. Each specific site is only potentially bound up with a particular practice, temporarily imprinted by the "here" and "now" of ritual (1987: 105, 110). With this variability, the practice of ritual is not given the opportunity to impress itself on a particular geographic location, or to be temporally situated. While Smith advances the idea of sacrality as a "category of emplacement" (1987: 104), his focus on the "religions of the book" does not allow for an easy transfer of his concept of place to a material-based, archaeological study of ritual practice.

Bell's emphasis on the embodiment of ritual, and Smith's focus on an abstract place as a variable determinant in creating the sacred, highlight the need for a study of the materiality of ritual, of how such religious practice affects and is affected by a particular, specific place. Ritual, as embodied practice and repetitive human action, can have a direct influence on both materials and landscape, allowing the dialogue between ritual and place to be examined through physical remains and through the architectural and/or topographic disposition of space. Colin Renfrew has been most influential in investigating the material aspects of religious practice. First addressing these questions of materiality in his 1985 book, *Archaeology of Cult: The Sanctuary at Phylakopi*, Renfrew asks how one might recognize the archaeological evidence of religious behavior or cult practice. Noting the

definitive importance of the repetitious nature of ritual, Renfrew, similar to
Bell and Smith, recognizes the possible existence of a corresponding physical
patterning over time that would allow archaeologists to trace these practices
in the material record.

The four, interconnected aspects of ritual practice that Renfrew identifies
as having possible correlates in the archaeological record may serve to
illustrate the common theme underlying the diversity of subjects and
approaches represented by the articles in this volume. Renfrew proposes
that (1) ritual as an attention-focusing practice can be evidenced in the
physical record (see, for example, Williamson's study of the processional
routes of sanctuaries in Western Asia Minor and their purposeful, symbolic
manipulation by ruling dynasts; Dematte's discussion of the strategic location
of landscape modification in northern China; McCauley's analysis of the
connection between human cognition and hazard precaution systems as they
are manifested in ritual actions); that (2) special aspects of liminal zones
have their material correlates (Chiang and Liu's discussion of the mortuary
rituals within the domestic spaces of the Wansan society in prehistoric
Taiwan; Papadopoulou's argument that the liminal location of sanctuaries was
linked with and mirrored by the initiation rites that occurred in those very
locations); that (3) the presence of the transcendent and its symbolic focus is
evident in the physical record (Feldman's examination of the ways in which
the Egyptian gods were incorporated into a sanctuary in Western Asia Minor;
Morrison's discussion of the site of Megiddo as a particularly sacred node
in Christian tourist itineraries of the Holy Land); and that (4) the relations
between participation and offering is available through archaeological
evidence (Moser's discussion of the material memory imprinted on sacrificial
altars in Republican Italy).

The study of the archaeology of ritual has continued to receive significant
attention nearly 20 years after Renfrew's seminal work. In his book *Archaeology,
Ritual, Religion,* Timothy Insoll (2004) emphasizes the importance of the
archaeology of ritual by suggesting that all material culture can be structured
by religious consideration. Insoll therefore makes ritual a focusing lens for the
sacred, an approach that recalls the work of J.Z. Smith. Insoll underscores the
material implications of ritual practice and, like Bell, looks to physical traces
of the extraordinary to explain ritual. This attention to the singular, however,
often results in highlighting one particular aspect of religious practice evident
in the archaeological record – focusing on, for example, votive deposits,
sacrificial remains, donative statuary, or monumental architecture – at the
expense of the larger context and location of the ritual action.

Several recent volumes devoted to the topic of archaeology and ritual
demonstrate a burgeoning interest in studying religious ritual through the

material record. Though this developing interdisciplinary synthesis has yet to generate its own unifying approach to cross-cultural and comparative inquiry, the outpouring of new work makes an invaluable contribution to our knowledge about specific archaeological sites or case studies of the materiality of cult. These thematically-organized collections such as Kyriakidis' (2007) *Archaeology of Ritual* or Barrowclough and Malone's (2007) *Cult in Context: Reconsidering Ritual Archaeology,* D'Agata et al.'s (2009) *Archaeologies of Cult: Essays on Ritual and Cult in Crete,* or Bertemes' and Beihl's (2001) *The Archaeology of Cult and Religion,* have advanced our knowledge both of the material specifics of ritual and the theories and methods appropriate to particular circumstances.

Among these particularized archaeological and anthropological studies of ritual, however, little attention has been paid to "place" as a basic unit of lived experience and a nexus of human praxis (Casey 2008: 44–45). The concept of "place" is gaining traction in a number of disciplines (most notably landscape archaeology, cultural anthropology, ecology and evolution, depth psychology, and philosophy) (Casey 2008: 45), but it has not yet been fully embraced by scholars concerned with ritual practice. Yet, examining ritual action through the lens of "place" offers productive inroads to the exploration of religious ritual as both impacting and being impacted by its topographic and material matrix. Theorists of place conceive of "place" and "space" as two fundamentally different orders of reality: space, in the early modern and modern sense of the term, is homogeneous, neutral, and isotropic, whereas place results from a concentration of concrete human activity in the world (Casey 2001: 404; Casey 2008: 45). In other words, space is general and homogeneous and exists purely in its capacity as a location for things, whereas place is the particular outcome of actions in a location. Initially and most explicitly articulated by Y.-F. Tuan in *Space and Place* (1977), a work which stresses the experiential features of place in its "subjective" and "lived" aspects, theories of place concentrate on the phenomenological and human dimensions of "being" in a place (Heidegger 1977). This formulation of place-making as embodied practice is echoed in Catherine Bell's approaches to ritual discussed above. Ritual is conceived of as a practice grounded in the body (Bell 1992) and place is considered to be the outcome of a density of human engagement (Casey 1993, 2001; Ingold 2007); thus, there is an interconnected and reciprocal relationship between practitioners of religious ritual and the locations in which this action occurs. Theoretical approaches to "place" and their focus on human practices and bodily engagement, which can be perceived in a variety of ways from the archaeological, literary, and ethnographic record, frees the study of ritual from its prior reliance on written sources and ethnographic material.

Focus on place in the study of ritual allows for investigation to go beyond abstract and universalizing discourse, or reliance on contemporary examples and the ethnographic present, approaches that, to this point, have impeded archaeological study of ritual and religion. For example, Doreen Massey (2005: 130) maintains that place implies its own specificity. Echoed by Edward Casey a "placescape" or "place-world" is an

> historic or prehistoric world that is anchored in a given or unique place – there in particular, nowhere else and certainly not in an abstract and universal space that tells us nothing about the character of a concrete locality, its layout as it bears on human habitation and in relation to the natural world in which it is situated [Casey 2008: 49].

This specificity of place argued by Massey and Casey not only applies to topographical locations as points or areas on a map, but also conceives of place as integrations of space and time; "as *spatio-temporal events*" (Massey 2005: 130, emphasis original). This notion of place as an ephemeral constellation of actors, location, and time – as a "time-space event" – further provides a means to investigate singular moments of activity or to trace ritual practice over time. In other words, place is a gathering that brings together people and things in the here and the now (recalling the language of J.Z. Smith discussed above); each of those singular and specific moments combines to form a collective record of practice.

Ritual practice is repeated action, and is therefore identifiable by evidence of its repetition in the material world. An archaeological perspective provides just such a means to investigate traces of these actions – actions based on a principle of continuity, actions repeated in time and space (Kyriakidis 2007: 297). The iterative action of ritual is precisely the concentration of human praxis that acts to "emplace." Ritual action necessarily occurs in place, but further, it creates place: "*Lived bodies belong to places* and help to constitute them…By the same token, however, *places belong to lived bodies* and depend on them" (Casey 1996: 24, original emphasis). In other words, just as surely as human actions and engagements are the fundamental components that make place, place also contributes to the actions of people and their engagements with the world around them. The application of this concept of "constitutive co-ingredience" (Casey 2001: 406), this interdependent relationship between ritual action and place, has yet to be fully realized by scholars of ritual or by theorists of place. The concept of "place" provides explanatory power for understanding ritual practice, while reciprocally, ritual can be examined as a mode of emplacement. This volume makes a contribution to the study of ritual practice by taking as its theme the mutually constitutive relationship between ritual and place – by considering ritual practice as both emplacing and emplaced.

Locating the Sacred:
Theoretical Approaches to the Emplacement of Religion

This archaeological approach to religious ritual, which situates practice in its topographic as well as its material context, can be illustrated by the specific case studies presented in this volume, each demonstrating such material-based approaches to the emplacement of religion "in action." Each article strives to approach ritual in its specific topographic nexus; taken as a whole, the volume creates a coherent claim about the uses and value of the study of the emplacement of ritual. Using the lens of emplacement to study ritual and the impact of ritual on place, each paper adopts a distinct theoretical framework that not only is appropriate for the specific case study to which it is applied, but might be found to be useful as well when applied to diverse examples of ritual practice from other places and times. For example, papers in this volume have adopted approaches originating in anthropological ethnography (Chiang and Liu), rational game theory (Williamson), cognitive science (McCauley), textual analysis (Morrison), studies of memory and identity (Moser), and philosophical perspectives on "place" (Demattè, Feldman, and Papadopoulou). It is impossible to offer one universal definition of "sacred" applicable to all the papers in this volume. Instead, we leave it to each author to explore how, in distinct settings, "sacred" can be both an *a priori* category and an outcome of human action. The articles in this volume cover a wide temporal and geographical range – from prehistoric Taiwan to contemporary Israel – yet all share a concern with "placing" ritual practice. A concept of the interconnectedness between ritual and place permeates the entire volume and forms a principle component of each paper.

Each article not only represents a distinct geographic and temporal setting, but also its own distinct disciplinary character. Yet, despite the pluralism in theory and methodology of the disciplinary approaches represented in this volume (e.g., anthropology, archaeology, textual analysis, art history, religious studies, cognitive science, and East Asian studies) and the diversity of the kinds of evidence each perspective employs, the studies collected here are concerned with examining both ritual action and material culture as evidence of the interaction of ritual performance and place. As is clearly expressed throughout the papers in this volume, religious ritual imprints itself in its topographical nexus and in the material record in a variety of ways: for example, through votive deposition (Moser), the architecture of temples, altars, residences (Feldman, Papadopoulou, Straughn), manipulation of the "natural" environment (Demattè), visual representations, textual transmission, pilgrimage routes (Morrison, Williamson), human remains (Chiang and Liu), and the landscape of the human mind (McCauley).

With such a temporally and geographically diverse collection of case studies, the arrangement of the papers in the volume could have taken many forms. The emergence of some broad thematic connections among the papers has served as a loose organizing framework (though the many congruencies among them could have produced a number of different, and equally legitimate, groupings). Themes recur throughout the volume, though more prominently in some papers than in others: the fundamental importance of landscape (Demattè, Feldman), movement and processions or pilgrimage (Morrison, Williamson), the connection among ritual action, memory, and identity (Chiang and Liu, Moser), and the interrelationship between the secular and sacred (McCauley, Papadopoulou). Rather than a simple temporal progression or geographic regionalization, we have organized the papers thematically, resulting in an ordering that meanders through time and place, but, nevertheless, attempts to provide a thematically coherent exploration of examples of emplaced ritual. The thematic journey begins with a concern with landscape – how ritual imprints both built and natural environments, and how architecture and the landscape are guided and informed by the specificities of ritual (Moser, Feldman, Demattè). Moving along, so to speak, we come to two papers that deal specifically with movement through the landscape as a determining factor in the construction and experience of the sacred (Morrison, Williamson). Next are papers concerned with the role of the sacred in the formation of collective identities (Papadopolou, Chiang and Liu). Fittingly, our final movement is inward, into the human mind itself, to explore how the mind's natural cognitive processes condition it to respond to rituals in a certain way, responses that can shape the very locations in which rituals occur (McCauley). By way of conclusion, many of the issues concerning the material and topographic matrix of ritual practice recurring throughout the collection of papers are expanded upon in a meditation on sacred space (Straughn). Organizing the papers in such a way provides the reader with what seems to us a convenient and cohesive thematic sorting. There is, however, nothing sacred about this particular emplacement of our authors; we leave it to the reader to explore other pathways to the rich and resonant connections offered by this collection of papers.

We begin with Claudia Moser's article, "*Linear Reflections: Ritual Memory and Material Repetition at the Thirteen Altars at Lavinium*," which explores the iterative nature of ritual and its material implications. Moser examines the implications of ritual change and ritual memory, arguing that the sequence of the thirteen altars at Lavinium, and particularly the conservation of architectural form, size, function, and orientation of the altars, can reflect in the archaeological record a sort of "material memory," that is the material reification in the physical world of the actions of religious ritual over time.

Her study proposes that the materiality of the altars and the relative stability of their natural setting provide the permanent material framework for the recollection and repetition of ephemeral ritual actions.

Cecelia Feldman next examines the way that water was employed in the sacred space dedicated to the Egyptian gods at Pergamon in her article, "*Re-Placing the Nile: Water and Mimesis in Egyptian Religion at Pergamon.*" She argues that the Selinus River, incorporated into the sanctuary, and the rain water that was employed in ritual practice were used to mimic the action of the Nile River in Egypt and to express the universal power of Egyptian gods over all water. The organization of this sanctuary reflects a broader interest in the importance of "place," and strategies for recalling and re-enacting that specific locality from a distance, both through architectural choices and ritual action.

Paola Demattè, in "*Itinerant Creeds: The Chinese Northern Frontier,*" explores the relationship among landscape, movement, and ritual practice. Focusing on China's northwest frontier zone, the author investigates how the structure of the landscape (the mountains, springs, and caves) contributes to the creation of the sacred and also allows for the co-presence of practices from different religious traditions and from different time periods. Examining the perceived sacrality of specific landscapes and the fluidity of space and religion, this article focuses on the co-incidence of prehistoric ritual centers and Buddhist sites in China.

Christina Williamson addresses ritual space as an active agent in the transmission of ruler ideology in "*Power of Place: Ruler, Landscape, and Ritual Space at the Sanctuaries of Labraunda and Mamurt Kale in Asia Minor.*" Going beyond monumental ruler self-representation, Williamson analyzes the architectural changes initiated by rulers at these two sanctuaries in terms of "concentric ritual space", creating an internal focus at the sanctuaries, and "linear ritual space", connecting the places of cult with other significant places in the landscape through processional routes and framed perspectives. Drawing from theories in cognitive science and rational game theory, she provides an interpretation of these transformations in which ruler ideology was combined with landscape, architecture, and ritual to create a common focus and thereby a shared identity for the targeted community.

Isaac Morrison, in "*The Dig at the End of the World: Archaeology and Apocalypse Tourism in the Valley of Armageddon,*" uses textual analysis of online religious tourism websites to explore Israel's Tel Megiddo (Armageddon) Archaeological Park and its role as a sacred site for Christian tourists. He demonstrates that commercial websites can be used to reveal site significance for a religious constituency and shows how the distinctive vocabulary of Biblical geography and spiritual experience surrounding Megiddo place religious visitors at the nexus of the location's Biblical past and eschatological future.

The inextricable bond between location and cult is the main theme of Chryssanthi Papadopoulou's chapter "*Transforming the Surroundings and its Impact on Cult Rituals: The Case Study of Artemis Mounichia in the Fifth Century.*" In this chapter, Papadopoulou examines how the development of the port of classical Athens converted a remote sanctuary housing initiation rites into a principle polis sanctuary, which overlooked naval facilities and housed a maritime cult. She investigates how and why changes in the topography of a Classical Greek sanctuary inevitably affected the rites performed in that sanctuary as well as the cult persona of the honored deity, showing that sacredness had a dynamic relationship with the environment that contained and surrounded it.

In their chapter "*The Sacred Houses in Neolithic Wansan Society,*" Chih-hua Chiang and Yi-Chang Liu argue that, for Neolithic Wansan society, family residences were not only places that merely housed the activities of daily life, but also were places where ancestors were domiciled. Inspired by scholarship on "house societies" and contemporary ethnographic examples, Chiang and Liu demonstrate that Wansan residential structures housed both mundane and ritual activities. The interpenetration of ritual and residential activities occurring within the houses of the Neolithic Wansan testifies to the fact that there was no separation between domestic and sacred spaces. For the Wansan, the sacred pervaded houses, a presence suggesting that there was always an element of sacrality in domestic spaces and daily activities.

Robert N. McCauley explores the cognitive by-product theory of religious belief and practice in "*Putting Religious Ritual in its Place: On Some Ways Humans' Cognitive Predilections Influence the Locations and Shapes of Religious Rituals.*" He argues that religions routinely exploit everyday cognitive systems that have developed in human minds on the basis of very different considerations from anything having to do either with religion or with one another. He suggests some ways that hazard precaution systems concerned with contamination avoidance and ordered environments influence the shapes and locations of religious rituals.

Ian Straughn concludes the volume with his article "*Aptitude for Sacred Space.*" Straughn draws together the diverse case studies presented in the collection by highlighting the idea so prominent in each paper, namely that practice – ritual or otherwise – makes its mark on the material world and that such materiality is necessarily located. By offering an example from the Islamic world, Straughn concentrates on the interrelationship between practice and place, arguing that sacred space *is* ritual practice, not merely a product of, or container for, ritual action. The author offers the area of the

Dead Cities in Syria as a religious landscape that was materially and culturally transformed over time, both through the manipulation of landscape and through the creation of multiple narratives. Straughn concludes that for the Dead Cities, as well as for the other sites and landscapes presented in this volume, place-making, as an essential force in organizing human experience, requires significant practice.

This collection of papers represents a wide-ranging and heterogeneous assortment of geographical, temporal, disciplinary, methodological, and theoretical concerns surrounding the material study of ritual, which here find common ground in their examination of the interrelation of ritual action and place. In the concept of "place," fields of inquiry closely related to the archaeology of religion have discovered a productive means of bridging the gap between the social and material components of their methods of study. We hope that this diverse assembly of papers on the theme of place in ritual studies will help bring increased attention to the archaeology of religion and to the elegance and utility of the concept of "emplacement." Moreover, we hope that this book will serve as an early contribution to a developing conversation about the place of place in future studies.

Acknowledgements

We would like to thank the Joukowsky Institute for Archaeology and the Ancient World at Brown University. In particular, thanks are due to John Cherry for all the hard work and time he put into this volume as the General Series Editor.

References

Barrowclough, David A., and Caroline Malone (editors)
    2007 *Cult in Context: Reconsidering Ritual Archaeology.* Oxbow Books, Oxford.

Bell, Catherine
    1992 *Ritual Theory, Ritual Practice.* Oxford University Press, Oxford.
    1997 *Ritual: Perspectives and Dimensions.* Oxford University Press, Oxford.

Bertemes, François, and Peter. F. Biehl
    2001 The Archaeology of Cult and Religion: An Introduction. In *The Archaeology of Cult and Religion,* edited by Peter F. Biehl, François Bertemes, and Harald Meller, pp. 11–24. Archaeolingua, Budapest.

Casey, Edward
    1993 *Getting Back into Place: Toward a Renewed Understanding of the Place-World.* Indiana University Press, Bloomington, IN.
    1996 How to Get From Space to Place in a Fairly Short Stretch of Time: Phenomenological Prolegomena. In *Senses of Place,* edited by Steven Feld and Keith Basso, pp. 13–52. School of American Research Press, Santa Fe, NM.

2001   Body, Self, and Landscape: A Geophilosophical Inquiry into the Place World. In *Textures of Place: Exploring Humanist Geographies,* edited by Paul C. Adams, Steven Hoelscher, and Karen Till, pp. 403–425. University of Minnesota Press, Minneapolis MN.

2008   Place in Landscape Archaeology: A Western Philosophical Prelude. In *Handbook of Landscape Archaeology*, edited by Bruno David and Julian Thomas, pp. 44–50. Left Coast Press, Walnut Creek CA.

D'Agata, Anna Lucia, Aleydis van de Moortel, and M. B. Richardson (editors)
2009   *Archaeologies of Cult: Essays on Ritual and Cult in Crete. Hesperia* Supplement 42. American School of Classical Studies, Athens.

Eliade, Mircea
1957   *The Sacred and the Profane: The Nature of Religion.* Harcourt, Orlando.

Heidegger, Martin
1977   Building, Dwelling, Thinking. In *Basic Writings: From Being and Time (1927) to The Task of Thinking (1964)*, pp. 343–365. Harper Collins, New York.

Ingold, Tim
2007   *Lines: A Brief History.* Routledge, London.

Insoll, Tim
2004   *Archaeology, Ritual, Religion.* Routledge, London and New York.

Kyriakidis, Evangelos (editor)
2007   *The Archaeology of Ritual.* Cotsen Institute of Archaeology, University of California at Los Angeles, Los Angeles.

Massey, Doreen
2005   *For Space.* Sage, London.

McCauley, Robert, and Thomas Lawson
2002   *Bringing Ritual to Mind.* Cambridge University Press, Cambridge.

Renfrew, Colin (editor)
1985   *The Archaeology of Cult: The Sanctuary at Phylakopi.* British· School at Athens Supplementary Volume 18. British School at Athens, Athens.

Smith, Jonathan Z.
1987   *To Take Place: Toward Theory in Ritual.* University of Chicago Press, Chicago.

Tuan, Yi-Fu
1977   *Space and Place.* University of Minnesota Press, Minnesota.

Linear Reflections: Ritual Memory and Material Repetition at the Thirteen Altars at Lavinium

Claudia Moser

Confined to a small area situated at an especially significant location in the natural landscape of Latium, a line of 13 U-shaped, adjoining altars was constructed at Lavinium over the course of the sixth to the fourth centuries B.C. (Figure 2.1). These enigmatic constructions, whether taken together or examined separately, reveal themselves as static neither in time

Figure 2.1 The Sanctuary of the Thirteen Altars at Lavinium (Claudia Moser)

nor in placement. Rather, these altars were a constantly mutating yet stable assemblage, evolving and developing within a permanent natural landscape, preserving ritual memory over generations, even as the particulars of ritual practice and function changed.

The Sanctuary of the Thirteen Altars at Lavinium, with its multiplicity of altars, offers a unique opportunity to study the relations among ritual, memory, place, and monument. In this sanctuary in Lavinium, with its successive phases of construction, each altar can be disassociated from its companions and thus studied comparatively. Such an approach allows for an examination of what is monument and what is setting, and how monuments individually and collectively may interact with each other and their setting in a mutually constitutive relationship.

The memory of the particular kind of repeatable personal and social experience we call "ritual" leaves its mark not only in the minds of the ritual participants, but also on the places and the material objects with which the performance interacts to produce the experience of ritual. Through the study of the imprint of ritual on the physical world in the material and archaeological record, we can begin to understand the inherent stability of ritual experience over time.

The continuities of place have their temporal counterparts in ritual. The sustained material attention over three centuries to the site at Lavinium and the repetition of form, style, and orientation of the altars there necessarily promoted memories of past ritual practice. The landscape and the altars themselves must have played some part in reinforcing ritual memory over time and in the construction, preservation, or reinvention of ritual practice. The relative fixity of the natural features of the site set against the dynamic, ongoing, repetitive construction of the altars over time presents the opportunity to recall, reenact, and reinterpret past ritual practices occurring within the space defined by the landscape and by earlier monuments.[1] And conversely, the iterations of architectural form question the accompanying reconfiguration and evolution of ritual and change in religious practice. The rituals performed at these altars likely reproduced remembered practices, continued and repeated, their very continuation mirroring the repetition of the architectural forms of the altars.

I argue that the sequence of the Thirteen Altars at Lavinium, and in particular their conservative form, size, function, and orientation, can reflect in the archaeological record a sort of "material memory," that is, the material reification in the physical world of the actions of religious ritual over time. The ritual repetition that helps encode and inscribe mental memory mirrors, as well as is mirrored by, the material repetition at the altars in Lavinium.

Grounding Ritual Theory: Archaeology Finds its Place

Ritual theory, although very good at explaining the details of ritual action and placing ritual in a broader religious or social context, for the most part fails to integrate its organizational abstractions usefully into the details of what these explanatory principles are supposed to discuss or study. All too often, ritual theory serves merely as a tool for bringing ritual into some larger argument: ritual is the key element of social cohesion (Durkheim 1995); ritual enacts belief (Geertz 1973); ritual is repeated and learned (McCauley and Lawson 2002); ritual involves a network of interactions and social meanings (Turner 1977); ritual is a mode of communication (Rappaport 1999). This distancing of theoretical methods from the observable nature of ritual is further magnified by the tendency in the scholarship of ritual theory to focus on the ethnographic present or near-present. Scholars concentrate on the interactions among the participants, or on a few generations of verbal transmission of a particular ritual, or on the ritual's meaning, thus neglecting the human dimensions of the interaction of ritual performance with place and time.

The concern for finding an explanation for ritual can be seen throughout the various disciplines of social, historical, and cultural study – in anthropology, religious studies, cognitive science, as well as in the social, intellectual, art, and literary history of the ancient world. But perhaps this concern to find an explanation, this overwhelming preoccupation with deciphering the meaning of a particular ritual, distracts us from an understanding of the actual ritual performance itself and its relation to its material instruments and its physical and temporal setting. The invariant material and temporal character of ritual that set it apart from ordinary actions is largely ignored. The implementation of archaeological methods can strengthen and extend the knowledge base upon which all theory must depend. Archaeology, by giving material and temporal depth to the physical record, can make an important and novel contribution to the contextualization of ritual theory. In suggesting the practical value of a comprehensive theoretical framework, I do not mean to imply that the archaeology of ritual is a heretofore unexamined field of research. In fact, in recent years many scholars of archaeology have investigated ritual and its material remains and many different avenues of study have developed from such research (Barrowclough and Malone 2007; Bertemes and Biehl 2001; D'Agata et al. 2009; Insoll 2004; Kyriakidis 2007; Renfrew 1985).

I understand ritual practice to be one component of the human phenomenon of religion. Just as the sacred and the secular necessarily interact, so too do ritual and belief. For the historical archaeologist, these interactions take place over time and the character of the corresponding changes in the material remains is a principal question of study. Nevertheless, the conservative nature of ritual practice may also be noted – within a society, some elements of practice tend to remain relatively fixed in the face of other evidence for general social change and shifts of religious belief. From a methodological point of view, making a distinction between ritual and belief can be quite useful. In line with this concept, I do not attempt to explain and reconstruct Roman beliefs or belief systems, but rather I study a repeated ritual practice and how it may inscribe itself on a particular sacred place.

Perhaps the pervasive quest for meaning and symbolism in ritual should be put on hold and, as Dan Sperber puts it quite neatly, we should ask not *what* rituals mean but *how* they mean (1975: 51). For the archaeologist, this program would entail seeking not *what* rituals might mean in the behaviors and verbal representations of individuals and groups, but rather asking *how* a ritual means, that is, how its action can be represented in material objects and how these representations can take on meaning. The study of religious rituals should give priority to the action, the setting, the instruments, and the relations among these components of ritual action. These material things and ephemeral actions do not merely serve as background to describe what "really happened" mentally or socially, but rather provide a foundational structure to bridge the gap between matter and mind, an empirical basis for sound theoretical interpretations of the implications or symbolism associated with these actions, settings, and instruments.

Lavinium:
Landscape and Setting of the Sanctuary of the Thirteen Altars

From the time of the first excavations at Lavinium in the 1950s, many different hypotheses have been proposed for the significance of this line of altars, for the relevance of the number 13, and for the divine associations with the individual structures. But within this concern to uncover the all-embracing symbolism of these altars, the physical structures of the altars have been largely ignored in the scholarship; the altars are not treated as entities in their own right but rather are taken to be abstract manifestations of a society, a culture, or an institution (Holloway 1994; Torelli 1984). The altars at Lavinium need to be considered as active participants in the formation and preservation of the memory of the ritual actions occurring at the sanctuary – their form, structure, style, material, and orientation must all be seen as part of how communal religion recorded, recalled, and reenacted previous rituals.

Lavinium is situated about 27 km from Rome and its Sanctuary of the Thirteen Altars lies 300 m to the south of the city center, within sight of the city walls, and about 60 m from the sea (Figure 2.2).[2] Eighth and seventh

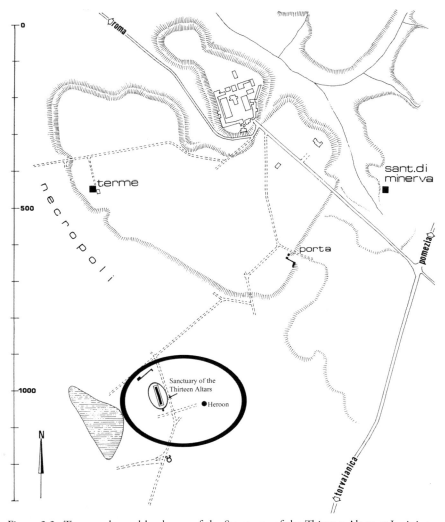

Figure 2.2   Topography and landscape of the Sanctuary of the Thirteen Altars at Lavinium
(after Castagnoli 1981, modified)

centuries B.C. fragments of funerary objects, *instrumentum domesticum,*
and evidence of Iron Age huts, a protohistoric tomb, as well as a nearby
seventh-century B.C. tumulus attest to an early occupation of the site. In
the first half of the sixth century B.C., the altars dominated the site with the
construction of the first three altars (XIII, VIII, and IX) above the site of an
earlier, so-called "archaic" altar (as termed by Castagnoli 1975: 122). These
constructions were followed in the late sixth century B.C. by an auxiliary

service building to the northeast of the sanctuary. All of the sixth-century structures respected the orientation of the archaic altar. A second phase of construction (altars I–V) in the mid-fifth century B.C. altered the orientation slightly, while later building campaigns – altars VI and VII in the middle of the fifth through the end of the fourth century B.C., and altars X–XII at the end of the fourth century B.C. – returned to the original orientation. The site was abandoned and deliberately buried at the end of the second century B.C. Despite some variations in the articulation of the transition between architectural elements, the 13 altars share a common, fundamental tripartite form: each is a rectangular construction with antae flanking an entrance to a U-shaped cavity on the front side. Each altar is seated on a large platform, above which rests a projecting rounded inverted echinus, rising in a shaft-like neck crowned with an echinus and projecting abacus (Shoe 1965: 95).

Not only the altars but also their setting would have played a role in material memory. Apart from archaeology's concern with the material aspects of ritual over time, there is a substantial body of scholarship that addresses questions of place in ritual (Alcock and Osborne 1994; Basso 1996; Bell 1992; Casey 1996; Cole 2004; Smith 1987). Landscape serves not only as background context for material constructions, but natural topography itself plays a major role in the selection of sites for the placement of sacred monuments, these privileged features of the surrounding natural physical world, in effect, interacting with man-made structures (cf. Demattè, Feldman, and Williamson in this volume).

Landscape and monuments at Lavinium, working together, localize and maintain the sacred character of the site. As the foci for worship and sacrifice, the altars interact with their physical surroundings, claiming the site for the sacred, creating a stage for ritual action where "a ritual object or action becomes sacred by having attention focused on it in a highly marked way" (Smith 1987: 104). The altar cannot be interpreted as the means by which a physical site becomes sacred, nor can the site be said to confer sanctity on the altar; rather, object and place are mutually constitutive of and dependent on each other in an interwoven set of relationships (Smith 1987: 103–104).

These modes of memory transmission between ritual action and place, between monument and landscape are compatible – the sanctification of the recurrence of ritual procedure at the Thirteen Altars may have been reinforced and reified over time both by the repetitions of the material forms of the altars and by the iteration of the altars' positioning with respect to visual features of the landscape. Moreover, their orientation may have been chosen with respect to a newly arisen need to reconcile the scheduling of festival days – traditionally determined by the annually recurring astrometeorological events of the archaic seasonal year – to the novel scheme of a year of fixed months and days introduced by the systematic civil calendars of the fifth century (Lehoux 2007; Michels 1967: 109–112; Purcell 2003: 30). But though intimately linked, structure and setting must also elicit different memories. That which has been brought into existence and that which is believed to have always been play different roles in the collective, cultural remembrance of past religious practices. The memory evident in the conservative architecture of the altars must be distinct from that called to mind by the seemingly fixed, unchanging physical setting. The first type of memory can be seen only through evidence of development and evolution, the change in fact highlighting not what is different in form, but what remains the same; the memory evoked by the landscape, in contrast, can occur only as a result of belief in the invariance of the natural topography, its presumed immutability over time.

The monuments and quasi-monumental utilitarian structures in the area of the Thirteen Altars add a particular, specialized character to the site, creating their own "disembodied voices, immanent though inaudible" (Basso 1996: 56). The landscape actively acquires a lived, storied aspect, interacting in a "roundly reciprocal and incorrigibly dynamic" way with the community and the monuments that it houses (Basso 1996: 55). The continuous attention to this one particular area over many centuries ensures the embedding of this specific topography in memory, for in such a setting "the physical landscape becomes wedded to the landscape of the mind, to the roving imagination, and where the mind may lead is anybody's guess" (Basso 1996: 55).

One hundred meters to the east of the site of the Thirteen Altars, the seventh-century B.C. tumulus stood, a form not known to occur elsewhere in the region. This unique Lavinian tomb structure followed contemporary Etruscan models, like those at Tarquinia or Cerverteri (Pallattino 1968; Romanelli 1951). The original tumulus – it was substantially altered some 300 years later – consisted of an earth barrow 18 m in diameter, surrounded by an external wall. Inside the structure was the rectangular grave of an individual of great importance, as evidenced by the rich deposit of grave goods found in the excavation of the site. The objects date to as early as the sixth century B.C. (*oinochoai* made of heavy bucchero, for example), indicating that the tomb was the locus for some form of cult from this early date (Sommella 1972). The tumulus, no doubt a monumental incentive to locate the altars in its vicinity, at a later time came to be revered as the tomb of the legendary Aeneas (Castagnoli 1981; Sommella 1972). The developing mythological significance of the tumulus encouraged its reconfiguration in the fourth century B.C. into a small building with a *cella* and *pronaos*. The new structure's monumentality and the presence of a large number of votives mark this building as a sacralized burial site, a *heroon*.

The structure, visible from the ancient city center 300 m to the north, must have stood out within the landscape of Lavinium. Its conspicuous presence and its relation to the neighboring site of the earliest altars suggest a dialogue between these two complexes, extending some share of their sacrality to the whole of the area between the natural bounds of the *heroon* and the sanctuary. The major road separating the tumulus from the line of Thirteen Altars, a feature of the urban infrastructure serving as a virtual *temenos* to the sanctuary of the altars, visually distinguishes the city within the walls from the landscape without and, within this world of nature beyond the city, the sanctuary of the living from the tombs of the dead. The altars are not only connected to the tumulus, but also topographically to other tombs, to an inhumation perhaps of an infant under the earliest altar IX, and to a protohistoric tomb directly to the south of altar I (Castagnoli 1975: 13). The presence of these tombs in the area of the Sanctuary of the Thirteen Altars should not necessarily be read as evidence for an intimate relationship between the altars and the cult of the dead, but rather as an indication of the sacrality embedded in the immediately surrounding terrain.

Shortly following the construction of the first altars at the end of the sixth century B.C., in fact often viewed as nearly contemporary building projects, directly to the northeast, a large rectangular edifice was built in *cappellaccio tufa* and sandstone, roughly 25 m by 15 m, having the same orientation as the altars. This building most likely did not have a specific cult function apart from its orientation with respect to the altars, but rather seems to have had some utilitarian purpose. This is inferred from the remains of a large hearth on the south side of the building, which may have been used for the fabrication of votives for use at the sanctuary. The building was destroyed by a fire in the mid-fifth century B.C. and subsequently reconstructed. During this second building phase, a structure consisting of two contiguous hearths, one hearth larger than the other, was set up (Castagnoli 1981: 169). After the fire, the ground level of the area surrounding the sanctuary was raised and the terrain leveled. The ground on which the Thirteen Altars stood did not need to be raised since the monuments already rested on high ground.

The choice of location for the sanctuary seems likely to have been related to the earlier habitation on the site and to its topographic situation directly outside the city, near a confluence of streams, in a direct line between the acropolis and the coast. Natural features often determine a sacred space, lending agency to the landscape, taking on a "special significance by virtue of their geographical location" (Bradley 2000: 11). At Lavinium, a stream ran along the north side of the sanctuary and was later converted to a canal, allowing the southward expansion of building in the area. The main road connecting the center of Lavinium to the sea runs along the southeast edge of the sanctuary. No *temenos* has been found for the sanctuary; these preexisting natural and architecturally topographical features can be seen to have formed the boundaries of the *area sacra*. This northern canal, however, eventually dried up and perhaps was used more for drainage, as a *compluvium*. Another drainage canal, probably also a successor to an earlier stream, ran north to south, along the east face of the line of altars; the canal turned the north corner of altar XIII at an obtuse angle, and perhaps joined the canal that ran east-west directly to the north. The canal would have brought water from the nearby hills to the city and afterwards would have passed the eastern face of the altars. The western side of the canal has a smooth, sloping profile which would have carried away the ritual water that had been poured onto the front platforms of the altars (Castagnoli 1972: 75, 28). Evidence for this drainage canal is most visible between altars V and VI, and between XII and XIII.

The Thirteen Altars at Lavinium

In this topographically and monumentally charged landscape, the first of the Thirteen Altars, altar XIII, was constructed in the first half of the sixth century B.C. (Figure 2.3). Considered a later phase of the building program that began with altar XIII, a pair of adjoining altars, VIII and IX, which have the same orientation as the first altar, was constructed a short distance south of altar XIII (Castagnoli 1975). In form, dimension, and detail, the first, sixth-century versions of altars XIII and VIII seem to correspond closely to each other architecturally, while the contemporary altar IX seems to be a more elaborate variation. The design of the slightly later altar VIII echoes that of the first altar, altar XIII – each altar rises on its own individual platform and its inverted echinus rests directly on the platform without any intermediary molding. Altar IX, which at a later phase is made to share a platform with altars X–XII, has a more ornate profile: the altar rises from platform to echinus through a half-round molding, plinth, and small torus. The entrance at the front of the altar accommodates this increase in height with the addition of two steps leading up to the plinth level. Altar IX was originally placed on top of an older altar.[3] This "archaic" altar has the same orientation as the later altars but was made from more common materials which were later reused (along with beaten earth) for the foundations of altar IX (Castagnoli 1975: 122). Perhaps altars XIII and VIII should be linked as well to this older, "archaic" altar, suggesting that the early sixth-century three-altar complex respects or amplifies in some specific way an earlier ritual function of the site (Castagnoli 1975: 145). However, this "archaic" altar is at such a lower level than altars XIII, VIII, and IX that such a hypothesis remains purely speculative. But whatever the precise relationship between altars XIII, VIII, and IX and the earlier archaic altar may have been, it is clear that all subsequent altar construction at the sanctuary seems to respect and reinforce the importance of this earliest altar in architecture, in orientation, and in the concentration of votive deposits around the site of this archaic altar, even in subsequent periods.

In the next phase of construction, around 450 B.C., a line of five more altars (I, II, III, IV, and V) was added, similar in dimension to the earlier three altars but at a slightly different orientation. These later altars, related in design, display new developments in style as well as recall the form of the earlier structures. For example, the curved bases of altars I, III, and V all recall that of altar VIII. Altars I and II have projecting fillets directly above their plinths instead of a torus like that found on altar IX. Closest to the sixth-century altars and the last built of the sequence, altar V rests, most conservatively, directly on its platform, in the manner of altars VIII and XIII (Castagnoli 1975). A study of the platforms and the joins between the altars of this group establishes a chronology of construction: altar IV as the first of the group, then III, then altars II and I, and finally altar V (Castagnoli 1975: 105).

After the second half of the fifth century but before the end of the fourth century B.C., two more altars were added (VI and VII), sharing a platform. These altars return to the orientation of the earliest altars (XIII, VIII, IX, and the "archaic" altar below IX), altar VI meeting altar V at an angle of about three or four degrees. Altars VI and VII are similar in form – each has two steps and decorative moldings on its echinus base (Shoe 1965: 101). The inclusion of a shared platform between altars VI and VII imposes some sort of regularization onto the complex as a whole, connecting the seven altars on the east side of the complex (I–VII) with an extended platform sequence.

And finally, at the end of the fourth century B.C., coinciding with the reconfiguration of the seventh-century tumulus into the *heroon*, three more altars were inserted between altar IX and altar XIII, all on a single platform and sharing the orientation of the earlier altars. Altars X, XI, and XII are similar in form, each having two steps in the center and each possessing substantially curved bases with elaborate molding. Altar X has a decorative molding where the plinth meets the platform and an elaborate echinus resting on a small torus. Altars XI and XII, considerably larger than altar X and identical to each other in form, are perfectly aligned, and recall the style of altar VII, with an elaborate crowning molding and echinus. Also in this phase, the original altar IX was reconstructed and perhaps altar XIII was abandoned.

Memories in Stone

As I hope to have shown from this brief survey of the construction of the altars at Lavinium, over the course of the three centuries of ongoing building and rebuilding, slight variations in form and style occurred as the sanctuary evolved and the number of altars increased. Variations of this kind are unsurprising and can be accounted for by normal changes in architectural fashion during the centuries of construction. But the experience of the archetypal persistence of the basic design and orientation of the non-Italic, U-shaped, "archaic" altar, the echoing and mimicking of earlier altars in details down to the molding and curvature of the monument, the expansion and enlargement of platforms to include older altars, and the reconstruction of earlier monuments would have resonated with, amplified, and channeled the conscious and deliberate operations of cultural and architectural memory. This imprint of the past on the interaction of materials and their forms would then serve, in extra-physiologically-based extensions of the concept of memory, as a kind of analog of unconscious or automated memory (McCauley and Lawson 2002: 49; Whitehouse 2004: 6). The "material memory" residing in the interaction of materials, forms, and placements of the altars would necessarily call to mind ritual practices or other associations of the monuments with religious actions.

This stability and continuity expressed in the repetition of the form of the altars would naturally evoke corresponding memories of architectural function, suggesting an accumulation of meaning and value borne by these monuments over time. The style of the altars may vary with changing fashions, but the altars, acting as material witnesses to ritual practice over the centuries would be imprinted with a form of material memory of reoccurring religious practice. It is as representatives of the past that the altars at Lavinium become dynamic, inherently active, and, in effect, *social* structures, acquiring an agency that both lends sacrality to the space itself and establishes a tradition of ritual and religious action – a physical account of past practices. In the example of Lavinium, it is the materiality of the altars and their setting more than verbal transmission or mental representation of action that serve as the media that give shape and form to the scripted recollection of past practices. Represented jointly in the mind of the participant and in the material of the altar, the action of sacrifice, repeated and scripted, becomes automated, guiding participation in the ritual.

I do not intend to argue that the Lavinian altars had a single, uniform religious significance or associated ritual practice over three centuries, and I recognize that objects and spaces are interpreted and perceived in a multiplicity of ways over time. Nevertheless, close examination reveals a careful replication of underlying forms, a continued attention to the orientation of the original "archaic" altar, and a concern for preservation and rebuilding. The altars at Lavinium would have necessarily evoked a cultural and, in particular, an archaeological memory – a thematically coherent complex of material and topographical memory associated with the survival of the earliest altar as a paradigmatic form.

Actions Imprinted on Altars

In the late 1960s, Castagnoli carefully excavated and documented the area around each altar, recording the finds that could be associated with each structure based on their placement in the strata and in the foundation layers (1975). Such a strategic and detailed excavation record allows us to study the finds related to each specific altar. By distinguishing patterns and consistencies within the finds, noting certain privileging of altars through select artifacts, we can perhaps begin to approach an understanding of the details of the process by which ritual might imprint its material memory on a monument.

Votives, fine ceramics (imported and local), bronze or terracotta statuettes, and tiles were found at many of the altars. Of the rarer finds, ash, carbon, or bones (i.e., organic evidence of sacrifice) were only recorded at altars VIII, IX, and X; definitive representations of or dedications to specific gods only at altars I, X, and between VIII and IX; coins were recorded only at altars V, VI, IX, and X; whole or fragmentary *lamellae* (bronze sheets commonly used for inscriptions) were documented only at altars III, IV, and between VIII and IX; jewelry was recorded at altars IX (a ring) and III; and architectural antefixes were recorded at altars IV and IX (Castagnoli 1975).

If it were purely the untouched nature of the place, the landscape of the Sanctuary of the Thirteen Altars, that defined the type of ritual enacted at the altars, then the artifacts around the altars, the materialization of ritual, would arguably be uniform, controlled and determined by the fixed, unchanging setting. Some variations might be expected, especially over time, with materials related to performance styles and techniques, modifications in ritual practice, or the use of individual artifacts changing over the three centuries. But allowing for fashion, the majority of the finds would most likely fall into the same range of basic forms, the same types of representations, the same ritual implements. Instead, specific types of dedications seem to be linked to specific altars or groups of altars and not to the more general setting. The presence of the more unique objects, although dispersed in no clearly discernable pattern, but nevertheless evident only at certain altars throughout all phases of construction, suggests some particularly valorized category of repeated ritual practice, some method of signaling or marking specialized practice, distinguishing such practice from the more ordinary practices represented by the more typical finds.

Perhaps these hypothetically exceptional practices, suggested by the privileged distribution of artifacts, can be seen as an attempt to recall, reiterate, and memorialize previous models and modes of ritual. Perhaps one altar was seen as preeminent and its assemblage of ritual objects set a sort of precedent, a model, a standard that was repeatedly emulated and re-enacted over the centuries. Every kind of the more distinctive artifacts or remains listed above (coins, *lamellae*, jewelry, representations of specific gods, antefixes, ash, bone, and carbon) was discovered around altar IX, the early sixth-century successor to the "archaic" altar lying beneath. Aside from the normal finds of terracotta votives, ordinary black-glaze ceramic wares and tiles, the excavations around altar IX produced, in addition to a large amount of bone and ash, a *patera* (a sacrificial bowl), extremely fine miniature ceramics, an inscribed cup, bronze *koroi*, an iron spear-point, silver and bronze rings, coins, and a votive model of a temple. In addition to these finds, one of the only two full inscriptions[4] associated with the Sanctuary of the Thirteen Altars was found between altars VIII and IX; this inscription, written in an archaic Hellenized Latin, was to Castor and Pollux (Castagnoli 1975: 441–443). The stratum in which the *lamella* to Castor and Pollux was discovered postdates the original construction of altar VIII and therefore may be associated with the construction of altar IX (or the later rebuilding of altar VIII). The continued focus of attention on altar IX over three centuries creates the leading figure in a sort of "master narrative" of ritual practice, a mythical history that "stresses the continuity of the past and present…the past is moved forward closer to the present" (Alcock 2002: 16; Bernbeck et al. 1996: 140). This clear privileging of altar IX can be seen to engage the materiality of memory, a memory that is "deliberately designed" to be intimately linked to the physical structure of the altar (Alcock 2002: 28).

The memory evoked by altar IX, the memory inscribed or imprinted, so to speak, onto the physical monument of the altar itself, the memory that subsequently encompasses the form of the other structures in the sanctuary, does not originate in the overall natural landscape setting of the Sanctuary of the Thirteen Altars but is rather, to some extent, linked to the specific circumstances of the placement of altar IX. Perhaps, therefore, J.Z Smith's discussion of place and ritual, of their mutually constitutive relationship, or Catherine Bell's concept of ritual creating an "arena," must be narrowed and particularized when considering the "topography of remembrance" (Bell 1992; Alcock 2002: 7). It may not be simply the general, panoramic considerations of landscape that invoke the memory of ritual practice, but

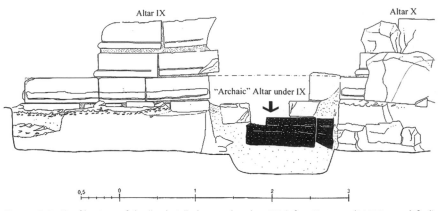

Figure 2.3   Profile view of the "archaic" altar under altar IX (after Castagnoli 1975, modified)

rather, first and foremost, the specific placement of a structure, the material interaction of monument and site, its seating, in an almost literal sense of the word, that supports cultural and religious reminiscence. At Lavinium, the specificity of the location and orientation of altar IX, and not the general topography of the area, is what defines and determines the sacrality of the sanctuary.

The early "archaic" altar under altar IX would have been the determining consideration in prescribing the location, the form, and the orientation of the site as a whole (Figure 2.3). This earlier altar has a similar form and characteristics as altars XIII and VIII and helps to explain the specification of a common alignment and a non-astronomically canonical orientation to this earliest row of altars. Altar XIII, the first of the early sixth-century altars, is the model that the later altars would emulate. But while the date of the "archaic" altar under IX is as yet undetermined, the monument necessarily predates altar XIII and is certainly the first religious structure built on this site (Castagnoli 1962). This sequence explicates altar XIII's seemingly complex relationship to the edifice to the northeast of the sanctuary. While altar XIII is thought to have been constructed slightly before the edifice, the exact coincidence of the orientation of the two structures raises the question of the extent to which the edifice is utilitarian or extraordinary, secular or sacred. Furthermore, the edifice seems to block the view of the sunrise from altar XIII (a view that was likely intended by the design of the altar); this subsequent obstruction of its sight lines by the later edifice lessens the strength of the claim for the preeminent sacrality of this eldest altar implied by its placement. Altar IX, on the other hand, has an unobstructed view in its direction of orientation. While the edifice respects the orientation of the altars and may have had some secondary association with the sanctuary, the building itself almost certainly did not play a direct role in cult. Altar XIII, perhaps demoted in importance by the construction of the new altar IX on the privileged site of the "archaic" altar, would have had to surrender ground to the practical need of the expanding sanctuary for a service building.

Following Richard Bradley's model of place as proactive and determinative, which argues that certain sites are maintained as sacred over time for a reason, that "particular places were especially important in allowing communication" between humans and the divine, sacrality can be seen as inherent to and demonstrative of the specific location of altar IX – from the primal "archaic" altar, to the construction of an altar directly on top of it, to later altars and related constructions mimicking, accommodating, and incorporating altar IX, and to the reconstruction of the altar itself (Bradley 2000: 11). Within the Sanctuary of the Thirteen Altars at Lavinium, altar IX is repeatedly singled out as the most sacred of the sacred structures, not only by the uniqueness and abundance of the finds associated with the altar but also by the respect the later monuments pay to the traditional style and orientation of this archetypal monument.

The concentration of attention on the form and alignment of altar IX can perhaps best be seen in the slight shifts in orientation over the three centuries. In the first phase of construction, altars XIII, VIII, and IX, and the rectangular edifice shared the same orientation (following that of the earlier, "archaic" altar) (Figure 2.4, Phase 1). In the next phase of construction, altars I, II, III, IV, and V shared an orientation altered by 4.3 degrees from that of altar IX (Figure 2.4, Phase 2). Most tellingly, the two further building phases (altars VI and VII, and then later X, XI, XII) dropped the orientation changes of the second phase and returned to the original orientation of altar IX (Figure 2.4, Phases 3 and 4).

This sequence clearly reveals the significance of the religious and cultural memory attached to the original altar. If fifth or fourth-century B.C. builders of the sanctuary's third phase were just indifferently adapting their constructions to the practical economies and constraints of the site, imitating form without recalling the inherent meaning and religious significance of the structures, or if they were merely fine-tuning adjustments of the sanctuary to the landscape in an effort to enhance the importance and sacrality of the general setting, then presumably the orientation of these later altars would have followed that of the altars of the second phase of construction rather than returning to the first.

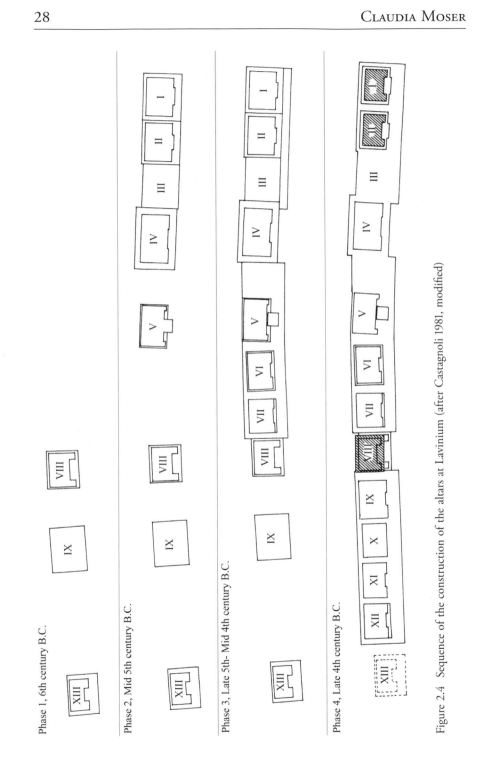

Phase 1, 6th century B.C.

Phase 2, Mid 5th century B.C.

Phase 3, Late 5th- Mid 4th century B.C.

Phase 4, Late 4th century B.C.

Figure 2.4 Sequence of the construction of the altars at Lavinium (after Castagnoli 1981, modified)

Community of Ritual

At Lavinium, the practice of sacrifice at the Thirteen Altars that would persist for over three centuries must have indeed abided over the generations by some form of "ritual coherence" (Assmann 2006: 121). These altars, however, were not mere static bystanders but rather dynamic material entities intended to be interacted with, indispensible members of the sacrificial community. Much recent work has emphasized the important role that socialization plays in the process of creating extra-generational, collective, so-called "cultural" memory (Van Dyke and Alcock 2003). As Jan Assmann (2006: 11) notes in *Religion and Cultural Memory: Ten Studies*, "whenever people join together in larger groups they generate a connective semantics, thereby producing forms of memory that are designed to stabilize a common identity and point of view that span several generations." The concept of an enduring, verbally communicated, societal memory is both elegant and useful; however, I see no reason why matter and individual mind should be excluded from playing their appropriate parts in the construction of a more comprehensive and properly material model of "cultural" memory. Minds interpret the experience of things – even words are transmitted physically. However much the cognitive representation of experience may be mediated by social circumstances – memory and matter remain inextricably bound. Material memory, then, should be recognized as playing its own part in a multi-dimensional cognitive universe which enables the individual in society to "orient himself in the entire expanse of his memory spaces" (Assmann 2006: 21).

I would suggest, therefore, that it is through the study of the material remains which themselves attest to the heightened experience of repetitive sacrificial ritual, in other words, through the examination of the archaeological record of the ritual participants' interaction with the setting of the sacrifice, that we can most easily come to a greater understanding of how material memory is stored and transmitted. Assmann divides collective memory into communicative and cultural forms, a distinction between present and past which, paradoxically, helps to provide the link between the cognitive science study of memory in the anthropological present (McCauley and Lawson 2002; Richert et al. 2005; Whitehouse 2004; Whitehouse and Laidlaw 2004) and the potential uses of memory in the study of the material record of archaeological past. According to Assmann, communicative memory is the first-hand experience of the recent past; it is related by word-of-mouth into the present. Cultural memory, on the other hand, relates to the traditional and ancient, as well as, arguably, to the archaeological record: for "with cultural memory the depths of time open up" (Assmann 2006: 24). Cultural memory might easily be said to be preserved over time not only by verbalized communications about the past but also by repetitive sub-communicative cultural activities like ritual. I would argue further that permanent materials communicate, that the imprint on a sanctuary of material memory is as much a mental representation of an action of the past on the present as would be the imprint of the narration of a religious myth – the stones speak (MacKendrick 1983).

The sacrifice itself, incorporating, at least in some representative fashion, the whole community (whether through direct participation or more passive observation), might be preserved principally neither through verbal memory nor through the mimetic, motor, or collective performance memory of its ritual participants but rather, over a great span of time, through the memory evoked by the physical experience of the sanctuary. It is ritual's enactment in a particular, permanent, physical setting, and its interaction with specific, authoritatively designated, enduring natural topography and material structures, that conserve the form of the sacrifice and valorize the importance of the preservation of the act, both for the present community and for the "maintenance of…[the] universe" (Assmann 2006: 37). For as Assmann (2006: 153) says in a revealing exercise in reification, "ritual as a form of thought is an *officium memoriae*, a cultic memory service that daily sets a vast store of knowledge of the world in motion. Its purpose is not just to interpret the world, but to take the meaning it has elicited and to feed it back into the world to strengthen, foster, and rejuvenate it." Translating terminology and point of view from Assmann's cultural memory of performance to the concept of a materially cultural memory more appropriate to archaeology, I would take the reification further and say that the material manifestation of cult gives form to both ritual thought and the performance of ritual actions, storing permanent knowledge of ritual in the stone of the altars for the changing community at Lavinium.

Conclusion

At Lavinium, the Thirteen Altars resist the evolution of time. Despite changes in decorative fashions over three centuries, the three phases of architectural variation are minimized and passed over in favor of the memory of ritual experience stored in the iteration and permanence of architecture, materials, and landscape. Perhaps even in its very abandonment in the late second century B.C., the site maintains its preoccupation with the preservation of ritual memory. When the urban center at Lavinium was abandoned, instead of leaving the Sanctuary of the Thirteen Altars to the uncertainties of future time, the departing inhabitants intentionally strew numerous ex-votos on the tops of altars and then buried the entire monumental complex. While this deposition of votives and the interment of the altars can perhaps be considered an additional, and novel, final act of ritual, it underscores as well the concern to preserve the altars as structures inherently tied to a past ritual and religion, as structures that defy the changes of time, as structures embedded with memory. And with this final phase of the Sanctuary of the Thirteen Altars, the memory of the original, "archaic" altar under altar IX is once more recapitulated, with its 13 successor altars being ritually buried just as it itself had been ritually buried centuries earlier.

Acknowledgements

I would like to thank my co-editor Cecelia Feldman for making this volume a fun and enjoyable process. I also owe much gratitude to Michelle Berenfeld for her helpful comments and suggestions on earlier versions of this paper. Any remaining errors are my own.

Notes

1   I do not mean to imply here that the landscape is completely static. Rather, the landscape does change, but it does so in geological time, on a scale generally imperceptible to humans.

2   The information about the site of Lavinium and the Sanctuary of the Thirteen Altars is taken from Castagnoli 1972 and 1975.

3   This altar has parallels in form to those at S.Omobono sanctuary in Rome; see Castagnoli 1975: 126. The significance of this placement will be discussed later in this chapter.

4   The other inscription was found in the general area of the altars, also inscribed on a *lamella,* and is thought to address Ceres (though there has been much debate over the meaning of this inscription). See Castagnoli 1975: 444 for bibliography.

References

Alcock, Susan E.
   2002 *Archaeologies of the Greek Past: Landscape, Monuments, and Memories.* Cambridge University Press, Cambridge.
Alcock, Susan E., and Robin Osborne (editors)
   1994 *Placing the Gods: Sanctuaries and Sacred Space in Ancient Greece.* Clarendon Press, New York.
Assmann, Jan
   2006 *Religion and Cultural Memory.* Stanford University Press, Stanford.
Barrowclough, David A., and Caroline Malone (editors)
   2007 *Cult in Context: Reconsidering Ritual Archaeology.* Oxbow Books, Oxford.

Basso, Keith
    1996   *Wisdom Sits in Places: Landscape and Language among the Western Apache.* University of New Mexico Press, Albuquerque.

Bell, Catherine
    1992   *Ritual Theory, Ritual Practice.* Oxford University Press, Oxford.

Bernbeck, Reinhard, and Susan Pollock
    1996   Ayodha, Archaeology and Identity. *Current Anthropology* 37: 138–142.

Bertemes, François, and Peter. F. Biehl.
    2001   The Archaeology of Cult and Religion: An Introduction. In *The Archaeology of Cult and Religion,* edited by Peter F. Biehl, François Bertemes, and Harald Meller, pp. 11–24. Archaeolingua, Budapest.

Bradley, Richard
    2000   *An Archaeology of Natural Places.* Routledge, London.

Casey, Edward
    1996   How to Get From Space to Place in a Fairly Short Stretch of Time: Phenomenological Prolegomena. In *Senses of Place*, edited by Steven Feld and Keith Basso, pp. 13–52. School of American Research Press, Santa Fe NM.

Castagnoli, Ferdinando
    1962   Sulla Tipologia degli Altari di Lavinio. *BullCom* 77: 145–174.
    1972   *Lavinium I: Topografia generale, fonti e storia delle ricerche.* Consiglio Nazionale delle Ricerche, Rome.
    1975   *Lavinium II: Le Tredici Are.* Consiglio Nazionale delle Ricerche, Rome.
    1981   *Enea nel Lazio: archeologia e mito.* Edited by Ministero per I Beni Culturali e Ambientali Soprintendenza Archeologica per il Lazio. Fratelli Palombi Editori, Rome.

Cole, Susan
    2004   *Landscapes, Gender, and Ritual Space: The Ancient Greek Experience.* University of California Press, Berkeley.

D'Agata, Anna Lucia, Aleydis van de Moortel, and M. B. Richardson (editors)
    2009   *Archaeologies of Cult: Essays on Ritual and Cult in Crete. Hesperia* Supplement 42. American School of Classical Studies, Athens

Durkheim, Emile
    1995   *The Elementary Forms of Religious Life.* The Free Press, New York.

Geertz, Clifford
    1973   Religion as a Cultural Symbol. In *The Interpretations of Cultures: Selected Essays*, pp. 87–125. Basic Books, New York.

Holloway, Ross
    1994   *The Archaeology of Early Rome and Latium.* Routledge, London.

Insoll, Tim
    2004   *Archaeology, Ritual, Religion.* Routledge, London.

Kyriakidis, Evangelos (editor)
    2007   *The Archaeology of Ritual.* Cotsen Institute of Archaeology, University of California at Los Angeles, Los Angeles.

Lehoux, Daryn

    2007 *Astronomy, Weather, and Calendars in the Ancient World: Parapegmata and Related Texts in Classical and Near Eastern Societies.* Cambridge University Press, Cambridge.

MacKendrick, Paul

    1983 *The Mute Stones Speak: The Story of Archaeology in Italy.* W.W. Norton, New York.

McCauley, Robert, and Thomas Lawson

    2002 *Bringing Ritual to Mind: Psychological Foundations of Cultural Forms.* Cambridge University Press, Cambridge.

Michels, Agnes Kirsopp

    1967 *The Calendar of the Roman Republic.* Princeton University Press, Princeton.

Pallattino, Massimo

    1968 *La necropoli di Cerveteri.* La Libreria dello Stato, Rome.

Purcell, Nicholas

    2003 Becoming Historical: The Roman Case. In *Myth, History and Culture in Republican Rome: Studies in Honour of T.P. Wiseman,* edited by David Braund and Christopher Gill, pp. 12–40. University of Exeter Press, Exeter.

Rappaport, Roy

    1999 *Ritual and Religion in the Making of Humanity.* Cambridge University Press, Cambridge.

Renfrew, Colin (editor)

    1985 *The Archaeology of Cult: The Sanctuary at Phylakopi.* British School at Athens Supplement 18. British School at Athens, Athens

Richert, Rebekah A., Harvey Whitehouse, and Emma Stewart (editors)

    2005 Memory and Analogical Thinking in High-Arousal Rituals. In *Mind and Religion: Psychological and Cognitive Foundations of Religiosity*, edited by Harvey Whitehouse and Robert M. McCauley, pp. 127–149. Alta Mira Press, New York.

Romanelli, Pietro

    1951 *Tarquinia: La Necropoli e il Museo.* La Libreria dello Stato, Rome.

Shoe, Lucy T.

    1965 *Etruscan and Republican Roman Mouldings.* Memoirs of the American Academy XXVIII. American Academy at Rome, Rome.

Smith, Jonathan Z.

    1987 *To Take Place: Toward Theory in Ritual.* University of Chicago Press, Chicago.

Sommella, Paolo

    1972 Heroon di Enea a Lavinium, recenti scavi a Pratica di Mare. *Atti della Pontificia Accademia romana di archeologia, Rendiconti* XLIV: 47–74.

Sperber, Dan

    1975 *Rethinking Symbolism.* Cambridge University Press, Cambridge.

Torelli, Mario

    1984 *Lavinio e Roma: Riti iniziatici e matrimonio tra archeologia e storia.* Quasar, Rome.

Turner Victor

    1977   *The Ritual Process: Structure and Anti-Structure.* Cornell University Press, New York.

Van Dyke, Ruth, and Susan E. Alcock (editors)

    2003   *Archaeologies of Memory.* Blackwell, Oxford.

Whitehouse, Harvey

    2004   *Modes of Religiosity: A Cognitive Theory of Religious Transmission.* Alta Mira Press, New York.

Whitehouse, Harvey, and James Laidlaw (editors)

    2004   *Ritual and Memory: Toward a Comparative Anthropology of Religion.* Alta Mira Press, New York.

Re-Placing the Nile: Water and Mimesis in the Roman Practice of Egyptian Religion at Pergamon

Cecelia A. Feldman

The Nile River formed the backbone of ancient Egyptian life and culture and its annual flood was celebrated in Egypt with the festivals to the divine pair Isis and Osiris. As Egyptian-inspired religion spread throughout the Greco-Roman world, the Nile was invoked in the layout of sanctuaries and in the instruments of ritual practice, and water was incorporated into ritual action in a variety of new ways. By the second century A.D., Egyptian religion enjoyed broad popularity across the Roman Empire. Information about the diverse practices associated with Egyptian-inspired religion has been gleaned from material remains of the spaces in which these rituals took place and the few ancient *testimonia* that describe them. The visual culture and religious practices derived from Egypt were subject not only to a general *interpretatio romana* but were also thoroughly grounded in the particular geography and temporality in which they were situated.

The sanctuary of the Egyptian gods (the so-called Red Hall) at Pergamon, in northwestern Asia Minor, is one of the largest and most impressive religious complexes from the Greco-Roman world. Within the Red Hall, special attention was paid to capturing and channeling water in and around the sanctuary in a manner that significantly differed from other complexes dedicated to the Egyptian gods. The relationships among these water features, the monumental architecture of the Red Hall complex, and possible ritual practices, however, have been significantly underexplored. The sanctuary was partly excavated by Otfried Deubner and Oskar Ziegenaus in the years 1934–1938, but many of the records and plans of the site were destroyed during World War II. The excavators moved on to other projects, and the complex has since remained unsystematically studied (Koester 1998: 78). Deubner (1977), one of the original excavators of the sanctuary, published an overview of its architectural layout, stylistic details, and the few artifacts uncovered. The complex has been the subject of several recent architectural studies (e.g., Brückner 2005;

Hoffmann 2005; Lembke 2005) and Ulrich Mania has recently undertaken some targeted excavation and published several articles on the architecture of the sanctuary (Mania 2005, 2008). A few, but significant, secondary treatments of the sanctuary have been published in the past three decades. The most thorough study is Robert Wild's 1981 analysis of the sanctuary complex in light of evidence for water use; this study was part of his larger investigation of the role of water in cultic worship of Isis and Sarapis in the Greco-Roman world and, therefore, the evidence from the Red Hall was interpreted in light of his broader thesis. In addition, Salditt-Trappmann (1970) discusses the sanctuary within the context of her investigation of temples to Egyptian gods in Greece and on the western coast of Asia Minor. A handful of subsequent general architectural studies have been carried out by Koester (1995) and Nohlen (1998), and Radt (1988, 1999) discusses the sanctuary within the framework of his larger work on the art and archaeology of Pergamon.

Building on the limited archaeological evidence, my own observations of the sanctuary complex, and through the adoption of a theoretical framework that will allow more effective use of the available information, this chapter seeks to answer why there was such a focus on capturing, channeling, and diverting water at the Red Hall and what the organization of this sacred space may reveal about how Egyptian-inspired religion was practiced at Pergamon. In what follows, I suggest that the Egyptian gods and the Nile River were invoked through the manipulation of water so that water in the sanctuary served as a metonym for Egypt – that the ability to be 'emplaced' in Pergamon and to simultaneously recall Egypt is related to the role of the Nile in the conceptual geography of the cult of the Egyptian gods and the efficacy of the Egyptian gods to act through water.

Informed by ritual theory (McCauley and Lawson 2007; McCauley, this volume; Smith 1987) and philosophical perspectives on place (Casey 1996, 2001, 2008; Ingold 2007; Massey 2005), this chapter investigates how the intersection of place and water played out in the temple to the Egyptian gods at Pergamon. If place is considered to be a basic unit of lived experience and a nexus of human practice (Casey 2008: 44–45), it follows that any location in which there is a density of engagement can be considered "place" (Ingold 2007: 96). Ritual action serves as a mode of emplacing because, as J.Z. Smith (1987: 103) argues, ritual is a mode of *paying attention* to place (and, reciprocally, place directs attention to ritual). Ritual action has the ability to make space sacred, and conversely, sacred spaces lend legitimacy to ritual action. To participate in ritual is to be emplaced through the reciprocal, attention-focusing nature of both ritual *and* place. Smith (1987: 109) also suggests that the power of ritual lies in the fact that it consists of ordinary activities situated within an extraordinary setting. A cognitive approach to religious ritual can begin to explain how the power of ritual action performed within sacred spaces can transform the ordinary into the extraordinary (Malley and Barrett 2003; McCauley and Lawson 2002, 2007; McCauley, this volume).

Since the Red Hall was never systematically excavated, there is little material evidence for the types of ritual practices and activities that occurred in the sanctuary. Its substantial architectural remains, however, provide information about choices made in the organization of space, which, in turn, demarcate the appropriate setting for the worship of Egyptian gods. The sanctuary complex, being a carefully constructed sacred space, was necessarily distinct both from secular spaces and from built environments sacred to other deities. The Red Hall contains several permanent water installations as well as large water storage facilities, and it is clear that much care was taken to capture and channel rainwater in the sanctuary. Yet, only rainwater was utilized within the sanctuary itself, offering an opportunity to investigate a clear articulation of the importance of the source of water for certain ritual practices. Moreover, the Selinus river was literally incorporated into the cult space by means of the siting of the sanctuary complex, in which part of the *temenos* (the sacred precinct) actually bridged the river. A close examination of the organization of the sanctuary itself, in combination with the ancient literature attesting to practice and belief pertaining to Egyptian religion under the Roman Empire, provides a means by which to investigate the uses of water within this sacred space.

The organization of this sanctuary reflects both an ancient conception of the importance of "place" and strategies for recalling and re-enacting a specific location from a distance. At the same time, the use of local water sources within the complex grounds the sanctuary in its particular topographical nexus. The arrangement of the sanctuary and the manipulation of water provide a context that refers to Egypt, the Nile, and the Egyptian gods while nonetheless being connected to its location in Pergamon. This multivalence was accomplished through mimesis achieved both architecturally and spatially, and by means of translations of Egyptian religion through a specifically Greco-Roman lens.

Water in the Red Hall at Pergamon: Nile and the Gods

The Red Hall complex in Pergamon, so-called because of the red bricks of which it is built, is one of the largest and most impressive structures in the Roman East. Ceramic material found in a construction trench now definitively dates the complex to the second century A.D., during the reign of Hadrian (117–138 A.D.) (Brückner et al. 2008: 183). In addition to being associated with the Egyptian gods, Brückner et al. (2008) have speculated that the construction of this monumental temple was undertaken in connection with the Imperial cult (Brückner et al. 2008: 183; Grewe et al. 1994: 349; Mania 2008).[1] The building complex was located in the "lower city" at the base of the Pergamene Acropolis, an area that was probably a residential zone prior to the sanctuary's construction. Core civic, religious, and administrative activity continued on the Acropolis as it had since the city's foundation in the third century B.C.; but an increase in population during the Roman Imperial period probably impelled settlement expansion down the slope and into the valley below. The uniqueness of the sanctuary's architecture and layout is illustrated by early, yet conflicting, attempts by several scholars to identify its function. For example, Conze (1912: 284) saw in it a Roman bath complex, Schazmann (1910: 385–88) refused to describe the function of the building, referring to it as "basilica," and Smith (1956: 146–47) interpreted it as a *Praetorium Trajani* (as noted in Nohlen 1998: 79–80). Unfortunately, no ancient literary descriptions of this building or its use survive (Wild 1981).

The monumental *temenos,* which extends approximately 270 m from east to west and approximately 100 m from north to south (Figure 3.1, d), encloses the entire sanctuary complex including a main temple building (Figure 3.1, a), two smaller buildings flanking the central temple (Figure 3.1, c), courtyards, and porticoes (Figure 3.1, b). The dimensions of the whole complex dwarf even those of the Temple of Jupiter in Baalbeck and the Temple of Ba'al in Palmyra, making it one of the largest in the ancient world (Deubner 1977; Koester 1995: 266; Nohlen 1998).

Indeed, while identification of the complex with the Egyptian gods is widely accepted, there is very little concrete evidence to support it.[2] This identification is largely limited to small finds and architectural decoration which blended Egyptian with Roman design, creating a stylistically hybrid product. Deubner (1977: 248) points out that no other temple to the Egyptian gods in the Greco-Roman world exhibited such interpenetration of stylistic choices. For example, fragments of several double atlantid figures (male sculptural column supports) found in the south portico are adorned with Egyptian *klaft* headdresses (a typical Egyptian headdress of the Third Dynasty) and may have been fitted with black marble signifying the dark skin by which Egyptians were characteristically described in antiquity (Nohlen 1998: 95–98). A few small finds also indicate that this sanctuary was associated with the Egyptian gods – a small terracotta head wearing what appears to be a *klaft* headdress, and a small terracotta head of Isis were both found in the courtyard (Salditt-Trappmann 1970: 24 Abb. 25, 24; Wild 1984). On the basis of the figurine of Isis, who was depicted wearing a headdress with clear Hellenistic iconographic traits, Deubner (1977: 245) argued that there may have been an earlier temple dedicated to Isis in the

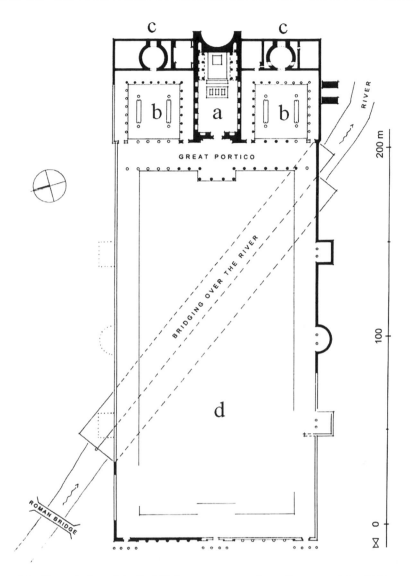

Figure 3.1   Ground plan of the Red Hall sanctuary complex at Pergamon (after Nohlen
1998: Figure 1, modified)

western part of the Red Hall *temenos*. Salditt-Trappmann (1970: 23) suggests
that the Roman-period sanctuary may have been a Sarapeum.[3] Wild (1984:
1806) however highlights the fact that, while Egyptianizing materials akin
to those found at Pergamon have been found at several Roman-period Isis
temples outside of Egypt (Cyme, Pompeii, Rome Campus Martius, Rome

Regio III, Soli Temple D), none have been discovered at Sarapaea outside the Nile valley; Wild therefore also assigns this temple to Isis. Although the determination of which deity was worshipped at this sanctuary has occupied much previous scholarly discussion, for the purposes of this paper, the answer to this particular question is not essential. It is possible to investigate the role of water in this sanctuary and the strategies for using it to recall "Egyptianness," the Nile River, and the power of the Egyptian gods without determining specifically to which god the temple was dedicated, because each was connected to water in some way.

Water, Mimesis and the Nile River

Mimetic invocation of the Nile within the Red Hall complex may have occurred in a variety of ways, including the possible recreation of the annual flood. In Egypt, the Nile's inundation took place annually in early summer. This event was celebrated with a great festival to the goddess Isis, who was held to be responsible for supplying the fertile waters of the Nile flood (Merkelbach 1963; Wild 1981). Outside of Egypt, the Nile and its annual flood became closely associated with Egypt and integral to the Greco-Roman perception of the country, its people and, significantly, its gods. The etiology associated with Isis and Osiris, connecting them to Nile River and its annual flood, formed a focal point for the Greco-Roman practice of Egyptian religion (Plutarch *de Is. et Os.*).[4] Though there were several variations, by the Roman Imperial period, the central kernel of the myth was the episode of the death and resurrection of Osiris. The myth, as narrated by Plutarch, conveys that Osiris, killed by his brother, Typhon (Seth), was dismembered and then thrown into the Nile River. Grieving for her husband/brother, Isis searched for, found, and re-animated Osiris, thereby bringing him back from the dead. Considered to be congruent entities, Osiris was thought to inhabit the Nile such that the fates of the god and the fates of the River were believed to be fundamentally intertwined. Isis' power over the River is evident in her ability to resurrect the god, and in so doing, to ensure the continued fertility promised by the Nile's annual inundation.

As water and the Nile River figured prominently into the etiologies of the cult, provisions for water were furnished by permanent water facilities within sanctuaries to the Egyptian gods. The monumental sanctuary complex of the Red Hall provided a grand setting in which the water facilities were situated (Figure 3.1). The Red Hall itself is the central building within a much larger sanctuary complex. The main temple building is flanked on both sides by smaller, Round Buildings, possibly also temples. On both sides of the main building, and positioned on axis with the Round Buildings, are two square

Side Courts. Each Side Court was covered by porticoes around its edges, its open center outfitted with two identical water basins. These three structures – the Red Hall and the two Round Buildings with their associated courtyards – stand at the far eastern end of the monumental *temenos*. Perpendicular to the main temple buildings and stretching north to south along the width of the *temenos*, the Great Portico separates the outer court from these main temples. At the western end of the sanctuary complex and opposite the cult buildings, the northwest corner of the *temenos* wall, reaching a height of 13 m, is still standing today in the midst of the old part of Bergama. In the massive space created by the *temenos* one might imagine, perhaps, altars or an avenue of sphinxes (akin to Sarapeion C on Delos) (Nohlen 1998: 85); there may also have been a Hellenistic temple to Isis here (Deubner 1977: 248), as well as surrounding stoas along the outer walls which were common in Alexandria and on Delos (Nohlen 1998: 85).

The Red Hall sanctuary complex at Pergamon exhibited a complex arrangement of water infrastructure and storage facilities. A canal system runs throughout the Great Portico and the Side Courts, channeling water in and around the sanctuary complex. In my personal investigation of the canal system, I identified two forms of canals, differentiated in both construction technique and material. The visible canals in the Side Courts are primarily rubble-built, vaulted channels. On account of the vaulting, therefore, these canals must have been covered. In contrast, many of the channels in the Great Portico are preserved as parallel walls constructed of andesite blocks. In particular, two channels in the Great Portico run parallel to the main axis of the sanctuary, their walls comprised of andesite ashlars. Marble slab paving as high as the former *crepidoma* of the temple was laid over the floor of the Great Portico (Nohlen 1998: 87), remains of which are patchily preserved near the entrance to the main temple building. Due to the level of the marble slab paving which is probably several centimeters higher than the top of the channels in the Great Portico, it is likely that these channels were probably also covered with a layer of rubble foundation and marble paving stones. Therefore, although an unlikely scenario, it is yet an interesting proposition that there may have been a steady flow of water running through the portico in uncovered channels, in the style of the channels of water in the garden of the House of Loreius Tiburtinus at Pompeii (Figure 3.2) (Regio II.2.2, also known as the House of Octavius Quarto: Tran 1964; Zanker 1998: 145–48). Also designed to invoke the Nile River, the arrangement in the House of Loreius Tiburtinus consists of one long and narrow basin that runs the length of the garden which meets another basin arranged perpendicularly, forming a T-shape (Maiuri and Pane 1947). According to Tran (1964: 45), these channels were constructed so as to allow the production of an artificial inundation which would submerge

Figure 3.2 The garden in the House of Loreius Tibertinus in Pompeii (Cecelia Feldman)

plants, flowers, and statues placed in them. While a great leap geographically from central Italy to western Turkey, and from garden to sanctuary, perhaps this formal similarity in the arrangement of open canals suggests a common way of architecturally re-presenting the Nile.

The Side Courts on either side of the central axis were each outfitted with two large water basins. Only one basin in each courtyard is currently visible but the axial symmetry of the complex suggests a second basin in each Courtyard. Clad in white marble, the floors and walls of these water features measure approximately 1 m deep. The basins are outfitted with double-round ends and separate circular basins, approximately 0.85 m deep, crown each end (Deubner 1977: 236; Nohlen 1998: 95). Deubner (1977: 237) posits that the separate round basins were covered, but the long basins were left open. The inlet/outlets for these basins are still extant today and probably were connected to the extensive canal system running underneath the courtyard and the portico.

To the north and immediately before the entrance to the main building is a deep basin clad in white marble. It is unclear what purpose this basin served, though based on similarities to other water basins in the sanctuary, in its shape, size, and marble facing, it is likely that it contained water. No inlet/outlets are presently visible, making it impossible to determine how this basin was filled and drained.

The arrangement for the flow of water within the main temple building directed attention to the presence of water (Smith 1987: 103). Rectangular and constructed of massive brick walls, the interior space of the Red Hall was roughly divided into two sections: from the entrance, niches (five on each side) divide up the lower section of the side walls, while the axis of each niche corresponds to a window in the wall above; this section, illuminated by natural light, gives way to a darker portion of the temple where walls are flat and there are no windows (Nohlen 1998: 91). The arrangement of water features within the interior space of the temple corresponds to the emphasis on light and darkness that is created by the interior architectural design. The transition from a light to dark interior space is marked by a deep, alabaster-clad water basin set into the temple floor. Beyond the water basin is the high podium on which the cult statue stood. Approximately halfway between the entrance of the basilica and the platform for the cult statue (Figure 3.3, c) is a depression in the floor that may have served as a shallow basin (Figure 3.3, a). It measures approximately 11.30 m from north to south, 5.20 m from east to west and has a depth of 22 cm – enough to hold 15–20 cm water (Wild 1981: 58). No inflow pipe or drain has been associated with this depression. Located approximately 2 m beyond the shallow depression and marking the

Figure 3.3   Interior of the Red Hall Main Temple building: a) shallow depression, b) alabaster-clad water basin, c) platform for the cult statue (Cecelia Feldman)

transition from the bright end of the main hall closest to the entrance to the darker, galleried section where a platform for the cult statue was located, is the deep basin (1.37 m), originally lined with Egyptian alabaster (Figure 3.3, b) (Nohlen 1998:91; Salditt-Trappmann 1970: 5; Wild 1981: 57). This basin is of equal width to the shallower one (ca. 11.3 m) but is much narrower, measuring 1.40 m. The single inflow or outflow point within this basin is located in the center of its west wall. This opening is quite large, measuring 1 m high and 0.45 m wide. From this opening, Salditt-Trappmann (1970: 6) was able to trace a channel running west toward the entrance of the temple. However, she provides no additional description.

This deep basin was certainly intended to hold water and there are signs that suggest the water contained within it was associated with, or used for, the mimetic invocation of the Nile. Unlike all of the other water features which were clad in marble, this basin was faced with Egyptian alabaster. This stone, quarried in Egypt itself, may have conveyed both a physical and semiotic connection with its place of origin. The choice to adorn *only this* basin with Egyptian alabaster differentiates it and marks it as more significant than the other water features within the sanctuary complex. The position of the basin within the main temple building – at the place where light gave way to darkness and just in front of the cult statue – also suggests that this water feature was the focus of ritual attention. Indeed, this basin may have been designed to overflow, mimicking the Nile flood. Wild (1981: 58) points out that such a large channel (1 m high and .45 m wide) is incongruous to the size of the basin with which it is associated. The basin had a capacity of only 21 m^3, a small volume incommensurate with such a large water line. Wild (1981: 58) suggests that the large size of this channel may have served to convey considerable quantities of water from outside the temple into the basin, filling it perhaps to the point of overflowing.

If the water from the Selinus River were channeled into the sanctuary, there may have been a direct connection between the flooding of the Selinus and the filling of this alabaster-clad basin, connecting the action of the Egyptian and Pergamene rivers by their similar action (although the evidence at present seems to point to the contrary [see below, and Trexier 1849]). Considered by Wild (1981: 58) to be a more likely possibility, the basin may have been filled when a thunderstorm sent water coursing through the drains in the courtyard. This particular suggestion may be bolstered by Deubner's (1977: 246) cursory study of the flow of water through the sanctuary. The system for draining water from the roof is still extant (Nohlen 1998: 87), indicating that the rainwater that fell on the roof of the temple, the Great Portico, the smaller Side Courts, as well as the rain that fell into the open space created by the *temenos*, was all channeled through a series of variously-sized canals and eventually into two cisterns (located in the substructure of the foundations of the south Round Building).

Significant provisions for the storage of rain that fell into the sanctuary complex further indicate the importance of rainwater. An additional cistern over 4 m deep is located under the cult platform in the area in front of the base for the cult statue (Nohlen 1998: 92; Salditt-Trappmann 1970: 15; Wild 1981: 57).[5] On the south side of the cult platform, Salditt-Trappmann discovered an arched opening through which she could not only see the water in the cistern but also a similar arch with two outlets below it in the interior wall on the opposite side (Salditt-Trappmann 1970), indicating an extensive system of underground conduits. The considerable facilities for capturing and storing rainwater within the sanctuary suggest that rain was the primary source of water used in the ritual practice that took place within the sacred enclosure. Therefore, the action of the rainwater as it flooded into the basin in the main temple and its simultaneous contact with the stone from Egypt itself may have served to ritually transform the rainwater into Nile water. The significance of rainwater for cultic practice within the sanctuary will be discussed in further detail below.

The Selinus River and the Nile River

One of the most striking features of the sanctuary complex is the bridging of the Selinus River in order to create the level platform for the *temenos*.

Figure 3.4   Vaulted tunnels bridging the Selinus River (Cecelia Feldman)

The Selinus River was channeled into two vaulted tunnels, over which the *temenos* platform was built (Figure 3.4). A bridge at the southern extent of the tunnel is still in use today. Each barrel-vaulted channel is nearly 10 m wide and would have been able to provide ample drainage for even the most severe floods (Öziş 1987: 59).[6] The tunnel then passes diagonally underneath the *temenos* from the southeast to the northwest for a distance of approximately 150 m (Grewe et al. 1994; Koester 1995: 268). This feat of engineering was exceptional both in terms of the double-tunnel and the distance that it covered (Grewe et al. 1994).

Because no systematic study of these tunnels or the channel system in the courtyard of the temple complex has been undertaken, it is impossible to say with certainty if these tunnels served only to direct the river under the sanctuary, if they provided drainage for the water from the surface of the *temenos*, if they were utilized to channel water for some cultic purpose inside the courtyard, or if they served any combination of these purposes (Nohlen 1998:84). Charles Trexier (1849: 2, 224) walked the length of the tunnels running beneath the *temenos* to view their construction and did not seem to have discovered any water outlets or connections to the sanctuary complex within the tunnels (Wild 1981: 220, n. 12).

A few theories have been offered to explain the impetus for constructing a sanctuary that required such a massive feat of engineering in the bridge and tunnel system for the Selinus River. Radt (1988: 230–231) identifies the bridging of the Selinus River as the principal problem in the construction of the sanctuary. Drawing an analogy to the Trajanum on the Pergamene Acropolis, which necessitated the construction of a massive terrace, Radt (1988: 230–231) suggests that instead of serving a symbolic or ideological purpose, the motivation for building the sanctuary in such a demanding location sprang from a desire to overcome engineering challenges, which he identifies as a mentality typical of Roman engineers. Koester (1995: 268) proposes that the reason for constructing the water tunnels was most likely that the patron of the building wanted to situate the sanctuary in the center of the city rather than in an outlying district. Therefore, Koester suggests that using the area over the river would have reduced the number of houses that had to be torn down in order to create sufficient space for this massive project. Echoing Koester's proposition, Nohlen (1998: 84–85) also supposes that the community directing the construction of the sanctuary would have wanted an impressive site for the cult complex. He suggests that at the time of construction, spacious building plots were only available on the outskirts of town, so the fact that they succeeded in constructing the sanctuary in the midst of urban habitation attests to the influence of the sponsors of the sanctuary.

Indeed, while not in the monumental civic center of town, the location of the sanctuary was certainly not in the far outskirts of Pergamon, and irregularities in the layout of the complex indicate that this area was already significantly built up at the time of the sanctuary's construction. Ulrike Wulf (1994: 157) suggests that the pre-existing urban grid determined the alignment of the sanctuary complex. Indeed, observing the unusual position and spacing of the two main gates on the far western extent of the *temenos*, Wulf posits that the reason for this arrangement must be that the gates correspond to the end points of two pre-established streets. Therefore, if the gridded city plan served both to direct and constrain building, the Red Hall complex must have been constructed in the center of considerable urban habitation. If, as Wulf suggests, the placement of the gates was modified to align with these two streets, it would imply that these routes pre-dated the construction of the sanctuary complex. All of this evidence points to the suggestion that dense urban settlement had extended as far as this area of the lower city by the time the Red Hall complex was built, and its construction would probably have supplanted considerable numbers of pre-existing buildings whether or not it also spanned the river. Therefore, if neither available open space nor concern for displacing large numbers of people were primary considerations for siting the sanctuary in this location, then the choice to build here, over the river, should be regarded as significant. The question remains: if the monumental complex could have been constructed anywhere in the lower town, why build in a place that necessitated bridging the river?

With the Nile River, in effect, serving as a synonym for Egypt, the construction of the sanctuary complex with the great local river flowing through it may have served to re-present and re-place the Nile River in a different locality. Strangely, however, of all the known Greco-Roman temples to Egyptian gods located outside of Egypt, only the Red Hall complex at Pergamon and Serapaeum A on Delos were constructed so that a local river flowed as part of the sanctuary complex.[7] In Pergamon, through the incorporation of the River into the sacred space of the sanctuary complex, the attention-focusing nature of sacred space and the action of the Selinus River were able to create a relationship of equivalence, such that the Selinus could act as the Nile (Smith 1987). Thereby, by bringing the river

> within the temple, the ordinary (which to any outside eye or ear remains wholly ordinary) becomes significant, becomes 'sacred,' simply by being there. A ritual object or action becomes sacred by having attention focused on it in a highly marked way [Smith 1987: 104].

By incorporating the Selinus River into the sacred precinct, the River ceases to be itself; and through the attention focused on the River by means of its inclusion in sacred space, the Selinus River can simultaneously become the Nile. The Selinus River is both itself and not itself, both in Pergamon and evoking Egypt.

Mimesis is a mode of representation in which there is an imitative relationship between the thing that does the representing and the thing in the world that is represented (Feldman 2005: 503). I argue that a number of strategies were employed to invoke the Nile in the Red Hall through mimesis, both architecturally and through the action of water. J.Z. Smith says of built ritual environments, and most particularly those intentionally crafted structures, such as temples:

> When one enters a temple, one enters a marked-off space (the usual example, the Greek *temenos*, derived from *temno*, "to cut") in which, at least in principle, nothing is accidental; everything, at least potentially, demands attention. The temple serves as a focusing lens, establishing the possibility of significance by directing attention, by requiring the perception of difference [1987: 104].

The reciprocal attention-focusing nature of both ritual and place serves to direct awareness of the ritual action and the places in which it occurs (Smith 1987: 103). Within the space delimited by the *temenos* of the sacred precinct, water was able to take on new meaning and significance by means of the attention focused on these sacred spaces. Smith expands upon the notion of difference in a ritual setting, one that underscores the differentiation between ritual time and space:

> Ritual is a relationship of difference between "nows" – the now of everyday life and the now of ritual place; the simultaneity, but not the coexistence, of "here" and "there." One is invited to think of the potentialities of the one "now" in terms of the other; but the one cannot become the other [1987: 110].

At Pergamon, not only was there a distinction made between ritual time and space as discrete from all other time and space, but in making a connection to Egypt and the Nile through architectural choice and ritual practice, there was a distinction from, yet simultaneous association with, these very places.

It appears, however, that river water was not frequently utilized to supply built water features in temples to Egyptian gods, but rather that rainwater was the preferred source (Wild 1981: 64). Pergamon receives around 70 cm of rain annually, three quarters of which accumulates during the winter months (Wild 1981: 64). While it is impossible to make any secure claims about how the water in the sanctuary was supplied without thorough study of the canal system (which has yet to be undertaken), it was also most likely the case at Pergamon that the majority of water used in ritual practice was rainwater. Trexier's (1849) exploration of the tunnels through which the Selinus River was channeled revealed no definitive outlets into the sanctuary and therefore it seems likely that the river ran through and under the sanctuary but was not actively used in ritual practice.

Rainwater collected from the roof and stored in cisterns, therefore, was most likely used to supply the sanctuary with water for cult purposes (Deubner 1977), while the Selinus River running through the sacred precinct served as a visual connection to the Nile River in Egypt. Greco-Roman epistemology of Egyptian religions held rainwater and the Nile River to be somewhat equivalent (Wild 1981: 63–65), both by means of the benefactions they each bestowed and the association between these sources of water and the action of the Egyptian gods. Exploration of these relationships will shed further light on the accommodations for water in the Red Hall complex.

Water and the Egyptian gods

In the conceptual scheme of Egyptian religion as practiced in the Roman Empire, the question remains whether water was considered to be inherently sacred, and what, if any, was the connection between the rainwater used in cult practice and the Nile River itself.

Wild (1981: 64–65) convincingly argues that the Egyptian gods Isis, Sarapis, Osiris, and their consorts were considered to have provided for lands outside of Egypt through their power over the elements – in Egypt this took the form of the annual Nile inundation, while in the Mediterranean fertility was assured by sufficient rainfall. In support of this notion, one of the most popular literary *topoi* that focused on the Nile was the "rivalry between the Nile and the Rain" (Sauneron 1952; Wild 1981: 88). Sauneron (1952) identified passages from 12 ancient authors who addressed this theme, to which Wild suggests 11 other examples could be added (Wild 1981: 64). The ancient literary *testimonia* identified by Sauneron that address this theme extend from the fifth century B.C. to the early first century A.D. and include authors writing in both Greek and Latin.[8]

Sufficient rainfall was critical for agricultural productivity in the Mediterranean. It seems that the fact that Egypt did not need to rely on rain for its agricultural success, as was the case across the Mediterranean, was a source of intellectual fascination during classical antiquity (Wild 1981: 88). An example of this sense of wonder is Aristanetus' description in *de Nili bonis* of the Nile festival as it was celebrated in Egypt (cited in Eudocia, *Violar.* 698). He relates that, in the course of the festival, hymns customarily sung in honor of Zeus were chanted to the Nile because the Nile does equivalent work to Zeus and waters the land (Wild 1981: 230, Note 18). Interestingly, this recounting of the Nile festival conveys the reciprocal influence of Greco-Roman culture on religious practice in Egypt.

The conflation of hymns to Zeus with the Nile River furnishes an example of the syncretism that occurred as a result of the intersection of religious traditions, and suggests that Zeus and the Nile River were considered to do the same work in providing for the land and its people. The frequency with which the comparison between rainfall and the Nile was made in ancient literature suggests a widely held belief that considered the provision of Nile for Egyptian well-being and that of rainfall for the agricultural success of the Mediterranean to be somewhat equivalent.

Many ancient literary accounts comment on the relationship among the Egyptian gods, the Nile River, and natural phenomena, particularly water. However, literary attestations about the Nile River (and water in general) rarely come from actual participants in the cult; therefore, these testimonies cannot necessarily be taken as true reflections of the opinions of practitioners (Wild 1981: 86). For example, Plutarch describes how Osiris himself was considered to have been found within Nile water, and as king of the realm of the dead he was credited with power over water, especially over the Nile's inundation, and over vegetation generally (Plut. *de Is. et Os.* 32; Griffiths 1970: 36; Salditt-Trappmann 1970: 15). Aelius Aristides describes Sarapis as he who "brings the Nile in summer and he who recalls it in winter" (*Or.* 45.32, translation by Behr 1981). According to theology expressed during the Greco-Roman period, the Nile River's annual inundation was both caused and controlled by Isis herself (Bianchi 2007: 504). However, Isis, the "mistress over the rivers and the winds and the sea," was also connected with sources of water aside from the Nile River (Isis Aretology of Cyme, 39; Wild 1981: 68). From these few ancient *testimonia*, it is clear that the Greco-Roman conception of Egyptian religion allowed for the power of the Egyptian gods to extend over many different sources of water, not only the Nile River in Egypt.

While there has been debate among scholars about whether the Egyptian gods were considered to have exerted their power over water or were thought to be contained within it (Frankfort 1948; Wild 1981), it seems that relationships to natural phenomena and the gods associated with these phenomena in Greco-Roman cosmological epistemology were more complex and nuanced than can be expressed by the structuralist dichotomy within/without – that is, whether the gods acted through or resided in water. It is not important here to determine whether divine forces were acting *on* natural phenomena or, in contrast, were present *within* them. Rather, it seems clear that the Egyptian gods were *associated with* natural phenomena, water in particular, and that their power was thought to influence these phenomena – whether externally or from within.

How does this epistemology relating to natural phenomena impact the organization of sanctuaries to the Egyptian gods throughout the Roman Empire and the rituals practiced therein? The presence of water in Roman sanctuaries to Egyptian gods has been noted as integral by a number of scholars, either in-depth or in passing (Deubner 1977; Salditt-Trappmann 1970; Wild 1981), and permanent water facilities in a large number of Hellenistic and a few Roman sanctuaries of Isis and Sarapis attest to this importance. For example, Wild (1981: 9) estimates that approximately 60 percent of the known sanctuaries dedicated to Egyptian gods contained a permanent water facility. If the presence of the gods was considered to be manifest in natural phenomena, and particularly in water, it follows that the presence of water in sanctuaries could serve as vessels for the presence of the gods.

The Nile River, specifically, was brought into sanctuaries to Egyptian gods by means of mimesis. As mentioned above, it appears as a general trend that in sanctuaries outside of Egypt river water was not typically used to supply permanent water containers in temples to Egyptian gods, but rather that rainwater was the preferred source (Wild 1981: 64). Significantly, evidence suggests that water within the Red Hall at Pergamon was neither supplied by the municipal water system through urban aqueducts, nor by means of river water channeled into the sanctuary, but rather by rain that fell directly within the complex. The use of rainwater for the Red Hall sanctuary in Pergamon suggests the recognition of the importance of rainwater for agricultural and economic success as analogous to the role of the Nile River in Egypt. The power of the Egyptian gods over all sources of water allowed their efficacy to be felt in Egypt while also, simultaneously, in other places. By bringing rainwater into the sanctuary for cult purposes, the organization of the Red Hall suggests an appreciation for the variety of ways in which the power of the gods was made manifest through water.

Conclusion

A sense of "Egyptianness" within the Red Hall sanctuary complex was conveyed by means of employing water from various sources (i.e., river water and rain water) in both the sacred space and in ritual practice. "Egypt" and the presence of the Egyptian gods invoked by means of the architectural and spatial organization of the sanctuary, the provision of both rain and river water, and the actual setting in which the ritual actions took place, became equally instrumental in the creation of that sense of place – both the "here" and the "not here" of J.Z. Smith's definition of sacred space (1987: 110). The Nile served as a metonym for Egypt itself, and the power of Egyptian gods over the Nile, perhaps, was considered to have extended to all the waters over which the gods were given reign. Therefore, through mimetic action, through a concentration on the "associative dimensions of place," the sanctuary at the Red Hall was formulated so that the action of the Nile and the action of the Egyptian gods could be replicated away from Egypt (Smith 1987: 94). The Nile and Egypt were translated and trans-located through the medium of architectural organization, and were therefore able to be re-placed at the sanctuary in Pergamon (e.g., Law 2002; Witmore 2006).

Ritual action and sacred space, therefore, have the power to make both place and water sacred through the assertion of difference and their ability to focus attention (Smith 1987). In the context of the sacred space of the Red Hall in Pergamon, the ordinary was turned into the extraordinary (McCauley and Lawson 2007; Smith 1987); the Selinus River was turned into the Nile and rainwater served as a vessel through which the Egyptian gods could act.

Acknowledgments

Much of the work for this paper was conducted during a research trip in August 2010, and I would like to thank Felix Pirson and the DAI Istanbul for their support in Turkey, and the Joukowsky Institute for Archaeology and the Ancient World at Brown University for their travel grant which helped me to get there. I owe a great debt of gratitude to Michelle Berenfeld and Jennifer Gates-Foster for their helpful comments on earlier versions of this paper and to my co-editor, Claudia Moser, for her great eye for commas (among many other things). Any remaining errors are entirely my own.

Notes

1   Ceramic material found in a construction trench now definitively dates the complex to the second century A.D. (Brückner et al. 2008: 183). However, the sanctuary was always dated to the Hadrianic period based on stylistic grounds. Conze mentioned this building in the initial volume of *Altertümer von Pergamon* (1912: 284), and dated it to the reign of Hadrian. A Hadrianic date has also been argued on stylistic grounds by Klaus S. Freyberger (1990: 131) and Jens Rohmann (1995: 109–21, on the capitals of the Red Hall, see especially pp. 112–113). A Hadrianic date seems to be further supported by the phenomenon of 'Egyptomania' during the Second Sophistic and the spreading popularity of so-called 'mystery cults', particularly those of Isis and Sarapis (Wild 1981: 7) in the second century A.D.

2   On the basis of architectural analogies and similarities in stylistic execution, Brückner et al. (2008) argue that, in addition to being dedicated to the Egyptian gods, the Red Hall sanctuary complex was a locus for the Imperial cult.

3   Salditt-Trappmann's assignation of the sanctuary as a Sarapaeum rests largely on an inscription (*Inschriften von Pergamon* 336) that names Sarapis first among many gods (including Isis, Anubis, Harpokrates, Osiris, Apis, Helios, Ares, and the Dioskuroi, among others).

4   In general, Malaise (2007: 38–39) rejects the use of the word *aegyptiaca* in the broad sense of "evoking an association with Egypt." Rather, he argues for a more precise definition that allows room for differentiating between pharaonica, nilotica, and products of aegyptomania. This differentiation provides specificity in the perception and reception of the Nile over and against other means of invoking Egypt among people living under *imperium Romanum*.

5   Salditt-Trappmann (1970: 15) noted that the cistern's water level remains constant at approximately 2 m in winter and summer, but provided no other dimensions and did not indicate the location of the cistern on her plan of the sanctuary.

6   Indeed, Grewe et al. (1994: 351–52) stress the capacity of the tunnels to support 720 m^3 of water per second (Nohlen 1998:84).

7   Serapaeum A on the Cycladic island of Delos dates to the Hellenistic period. It was constructed at the east end of a narrow courtyard, approximately 11 m west of the Lower Reservoir of the Inopus River (Roussel 1916; Wild 1981: 35). A tradition attested by the Alexandrian poets viewed the Inopus River as physically linked with the Nile itself (Wild 1981: 35; Strabo 6.2.4; Pliny, *HN* 2.229; Pausanias 2.5.3). In this way, the river was incorporated into the sanctuary, both through its proximity to the complex and by means of the inlet that (probably) channeled river water into the basin below the temple.

8   The authors identified by Sauneron are: Herodotus (2.13), Euripides (*Hel.* 1–3), Aristophanes (*Thesm.* 855–856), Isocrates (*Bus.* 13), Tibullus (*Elegies* 1.7.21–26), Pomponius Mela (*De Chorographia* 1.9), Seneca (*Q Nat.* IV a, II, 2), Martial (*Epigrams* 1.61), Pliny the Younger (*Tra.* 30), Philo (*De Vita Mosis* 2.36), Heliodorus (*Aeth.* 9.9.3), and Claudian. To these Wild would add Deut. (11: 10–12), Theophrastus (*Caus. Pl.* 3.3.3), Apollonius Rhodius (*Argon.* 4.270), Theocritus (*Id.* 17.77–80), Schol. Pindar (*Pyth.* 4.99), Ovid (*Ars. Am* 1.645–52), Lucan (8.445), Aelius Aristides (*Or.* 36.123), Aristaenetus (*De Nili bonis*, cited in Eudocia, *Violar.* 698), Himerius (*Disc.* 1.8) and Schol. Lucan (8.826) (Sauneron 1952; Wild 1981: 222, note 37).

References

Behr, Charles (editor and translator)
    1981   P. *Aelius Aristides: The Complete Works*. Brill, Leiden.

Bianchi, Robert Steven
    2007   Images of Isis and Her Cultic Shrines Reconsidered: Towards an Egyptian Understanding of the *Interpretatio Graeca*. In *Nile into Tiber: Egypt in the Roman World. Proceedings of the IIIrd International Conference of Isis Studies, Faculty of Archaeology, Leiden University, May 11–14 2005*, edited by Laurent Bricault, Miguel J. Versluys and Paul G.P. Meyboom, pp. 470–505. Brill, Leiden and Boston.

Brückener, Corinna
    2005   Die Rote Halle aus bauhistorischer Sicht – Neue Dokumentationsarbeiten. In *Ägyptische Kulte und ihre Heiligtümer im osten des römischen Reiches*, edited by Adolf Hoffmann, pp. 35–46. *Byzas* 1. İstanbul: Ege Yayınları.

Brückener, Corinna, Adolf Hoffmann, and Ulrich Mania
    2008   Die Erforschung der Roten Halle in Pergamon. *Das Altertum* Band 53: 179–189.

Casey, Edward

    1996   How to Get from Space to Place in a Fairly Short Stretch of Time: Phenomenological Prolegomena. In *Senses of Place*, edited by Steven Feld and Keith H. Basso, pp. 13–52. School of American Research Press, Santa Fe, NM.

    2001   Body, Self, and Landscape: A Geophilosophical Inquiry into the Place-World. In *Textures of Place: Exploring Humanist Geographies,* edited by Paul C. Adams, Steven D. Hoelscher and Karen E. Till, pp. 403–425. University of Minnesota Press, Minneapolis.

    2008   Place in Landscape Archaeology: A Western Philosophical Prelude. In *Handbook of Landscape Archaeology*, edited by Bruno David and Julian Thomas, pp. 44–50. Left Coast Press, Walnut Creek CA.

Conze, Alexander, Otto Berlet, Alfred Philippson, Carl Schuchhardt, and Friedrich Gräber

    1912   *Stadt und Landschaft. Altertümer von Pergamon* 1.2. Walter de Gruyter, Berlin.

Deubner, Ottfreid

    1977   Das Heiligtum der Alexandrinischen Gottheiten in Pergamon Gennant 'Kizil Avli' ('Rote Halle'). *Istanbuler Mitteilungen* 27–28: 227–50, pls. 58–72.

Feldman, Carol Fleisher

    2005   Mimesis: Where Play and Narrative Meet. *Cognitive Development* 20: 503–513.

Frankfort, Henri

    1948   *Ancient Egyptian Religion: An Interpretation.* Columbia University Press, New York.

Freyberger, Klaus S.

    1990   *Stadtrömische Kapitelle aus der Zeit von Domitian bis Alexander Severus.* Philip von Zabern, Mainz am Rhein.

Grewe, Klaus, Ünal Oziş, Orhan Baykan, and Ayhan Atalay

    1994   Die antiken Flußüberbauungen von Pergamon und Nysa (Türkei). *Antike Welt der Technik* VII: 348–52.

Griffiths, J. Gwyn (editor and translator)

    1970   *Plutarch's De Iside et Osiride.* University of Wales Press, Cambridge.

Hoffmann, Adolf

    2005   Die Rote Halle in Pergamon – Eine komplizierte Forschungsgeschichte mit Zukunftsperspktiven. In *Ägyptische Kulte und ihre Heiligtümer im osten des römischen Reiches*, edited by Adolf Hoffmann, pp. 3–20. *Byzas* 1. İstanbul: Ege Yayınları.

Ingold, Tim

    2007   *Lines: A Brief History.* Routledge, London.

Koester, Helmut

    1995   The Red Hall in Pergamon. In *The Social world of the First Christians: Essays in Honor of Wayne A. Meeks*, edited by L. Michael White and O. Larry Yarbrough, pp. 265–274. Fortress Press, Minneapolis.

Law, John

    2002   *Aircraft Stories: Decentering the Object in Technoscience.* Duke University Press, Durham NC.

Lembke, Katja
  2005   Kolossalität und Monumentalität: Zur Größe und Ausdehnung der Roten Halle. In *Ägyptische Kulte und ihre Heiligtümer im osten des römischen Reiches*, edited by Adolf Hoffmann, pp. 47–58. *Byzas* 1. Istanbul: Ege Yayınları.

Ling, Roger
  1991   *Roman Painting*. Cambridge University Press, Cambridge.

Maiuri, Amedeo, and Roberto Pane.
  1947   *La Casa di Loreio Tiburtino e la Villa di Diomede in Pompei*. La Libreria dello Stato, Rome.

Malaise, Michel
  2007   La Diffusion des Cultes Isiaques. In *Nile into Tiber: Egypt in the Roman World. Proceedings of the IIIrd International Conference of Isis Studies, Faculty of Archaeology, Leiden University, May 11–14, 2005*, edited by Laurent Bricault, Miguel J. Versluys and Paul G.P. Meyboom, pp. 19–39. Brill, Leiden and Boston.

Malley, Brian, and Justin Barrett
  2003   Can Ritual Form Be Predicted from Religious Belief? A Test of the Lawson-McCauley Hypothesis. *Journal of Ritual Studies* 17(2):1–14.

Mania, Ulrich
  2005   Neue Ausgrabungen – neue Aspekte in der Erforschung der Roten Halle. In *Ägyptische Kulte und ihre Heiligtümer im osten des römischen Reiches*, edited by Adolf Hoffmann, pp. 21–46. *Byzas* 1. İstanbul: Ege Yayınları.
  2008   Hadrian, Ägypten und die Rote Halle in Pergamon. In *Austausch und Inspiration: Kulturkontakt als Impuls architektonischer Innovation*, edited by Felix Pirson and Ulrike Wulf-Rheidt, pp. 184–201. Philipp von Zabern: Mainz am Rhein.

Massey, Doreen
  2005   *For Space*. Sage, London.

McCauley, Robert, and Thomas Lawson.
  2002   *Bringing Ritual to Mind*. Cambridge University Press, Cambridge.
  2007   Cognition, Religious Ritual, and Archaeology. In *The Archaeology of Ritual*, edited by Evangelos Kyriakidis, pp. 209–254. Cotsen Institute of Archaeology, University of California, Los Angeles, Los Angeles.

Merkelbach, Reinhold
  1963   *Isisfeste in griechisch-römischer Zeit: Daten und Riten*. A. Hain, Meisenheim am Glan.

Nohlen, Klaus
  1998   The "Red Hall" (Kizil Avlu) in Pergamon. In *Pergamon, Citadel of the Gods: Archaeological Record, Literary Description, and Religious Development*, edited by Helmut Koester, pp. 77–110. Harvard Theological Studies 46. Trinity Press International: Harrisburg PA.

Öziş, Ünal
  1987   Ancient Water Works in Anatolia. *International Journal of Water Resources Development* 3 (1): 55–62

Radt, Woflgang

   1988   *Pergamon: Geschichte und Bauten, Funde und Erforschung einer antiken Metropole.* DuMont Buchverlag, Köln.

   1999   *Pergamon: Geschichte und Bauten einer antiken Metropole.* Primus Verlag, Darmstadt.

Rohmann, Jens

   1995   Ininge Bemerkungen zum Ursprung des feingezackten Akanthus. *Istanbuler Mitteilungen* 45: 109–21.

Roussel, Pierre

   1916   *Les cultes égyptiens à Délos du IIIe au Ier siècle av. J.-C.* Berger-Levrault, Paris.

Salditt-Trappmann, Regina

   1970   *Tempel der Ägyptischen Götter in Greichenland und an der Westküste Kleinasiens.* Brill, Leiden.

Sauneron, Serge

   1952   Un thème littéraire de l'antiquité classique: le Nil et la pluie. *Bulletin de l'Institut Français d'Archéologie Orientale* 51: 41–48.

Schazmann, Paul

   1910   Die römischen Bauwerke der Unterstadt. In Die Arbeiten zu Pergamon 1908–1909, edited by Wilhelm Dörpfeld. *Mitteilungen des Deutschen Archäologischen Instituts, Athenische Abteilung* 35: 385–388.

Smith, Earl Baldwin

   1956   *Architectural Symbolism of Imperial Rome and the Middle Ages.* Princeton University Press, Princeton.

Smith, Jonathan Z.

   1987   *To Take Place.* University of Chicago Press, Chicago.

Tran, V. Tam Tinh

   1964   *Essai sur le culte d'Isis à Pompéi.* E. de Boccard, Paris.

Trexier, Charles

   1849   *Description de l'Asie Mineur, faite par ordre du gouvernement français.* Didot, Paris.

Wild, Robert

   1981   *Water in the Cultic Worship of Isis and Sarapis.* Brill, Leiden.

   1984   The Known Isis–Sarapis Sanctuaries from the Roman Period. *Aufstieg und Niedergang der römischen Welt* Band II 17.4, pp. 1739–1851. Walter de Gruyter, Berlin.

Witmore, Christopher

   2006   Vision, Media, Noise and the Percolation of Time: Symmetrical Approaches to the Mediation of the Material World. *Journal of Material Culture* 11(3): 267–292.

Wulf, Ulrike

   1994   Der Stadtplan von Pergamon. *Istanbuler Mitteilungen* 44: 135–175.

Zanker, Paul

   1998   *Pompeii: Public and Private Life.* Harvard University Press, Cambridge.

— 4 —

Itinerant Creeds: The Chinese Northern Frontier

Paola Demattè

The use of particular types of sacred places in different religious practices is often the means by which belief systems are analyzed and distinguished from each other. For this and other reasons, ancient and modern beliefs variously described as shamanistic or animistic, but better understood as ancestor and spirit worship, are presented as inherently *different* from organized or "high" religions. This spurious distinction is enabled by (among other factors) a dichotomous analysis of the place where the sacred is enacted: is it a cultural or a natural landscape? Built or wild?

The implications are obvious. Belief systems that are seen as less structured, such as ancestor and spirit worship, are presented as *natural* or spontaneous practices centered on individual spirituality, mobility, and, most importantly, the natural landscape as the privileged ritual setting. To the contrary, organized religions, like Buddhism, Christianity, or Islam, are seen as urban practices that inhabit the constructed or domesticated landscape and are bound by clergy, defined rituals, and fixed (constructed) places of worship. As a consequence, places of worship of organized religion are carefully distinguished from those locations where participants in loosely structured beliefs systems enact their rituals, even though both may occupy the same area, contiguous locations, or structurally similar spaces. Geographers and philosophers have discussed at length the issue of place and space, trying to disentangle the presumed differences that distinguish the two. In general, most researchers, such as Tuan (1977), see space as more open and less specific than place; though some later scholars have problematized this distinction (Casey 1996). I would like to move beyond this and other dichotomies and focus on a more unifying term, such as landscape, because I prefer to highlight similarities rather than differences. Nonetheless, I want to clarify that, as opposed to Tuan (1977), I interpret space archaeologically, that is, as physically confined or enclosed.

In China, culturally constructed distinctions about the nature of sacred places are very pronounced, as the size of the country and its ethnic and cultural variety invite many separations and classifications of beliefs and places. Differences are assumed about the nature of a sacred place based on its position in the territory, its stylistic or structural qualities, as well as the ethnic and cultural affiliation of the local inhabitants. Notwithstanding the creation of these artificial separations, it is clear that, aside from cultural peculiarities, there is little difference in the ways the various religions identify, obtain, and use sacred places. Landscape and movement have consistently played a major role in all belief systems, no matter the complexity of their organization. Indeed, if the place of landscape in worship is prominent in cultures where mobility is a mode of life (hunter-gatherers, pastoralists, merchants, travelers), the sacrality of particular places and the necessity for believers to go on spiritual journeys to reach them is likewise a constant in the organized religions of settled cultures. Thus, Buddhist, Muslim and Christian believers are often expected or even required to participate in ritualized movement to sacred places or on ritual routes to fulfill their religious duties or to acquire a deeper understanding of their faith (Coleman and Elsner 1997).

Furthermore, locations that embody the sacred often are important through time for different religions, either in succession or simultaneously. These continuities and contiguities are easily recognized for well-known places, such as, for instance, Jerusalem or Mecca, or for the countless pagan temples, synagogues, mosques, and churches that over the centuries have been acquired and transformed for use within a new religion. Unfortunately, these phenomena are not as readily recognized in other contexts, particularly if the religions involved in the sharing are thought to be fundamentally different. For these reasons, it is worth exploring the issue of sacred continuity and contiguity with particular regard to prehistoric ritual centers and Buddhist sites in China.

Cults of Place: Mountains, Rivers and Beyond

China is an ideal place to study the interaction of the sacred within the land, as many of its belief systems from the state and ancestral rituals associated with Confucianism, Taoism, Buddhism, and related folk practices have consistently placed great emphasis on the spiritual valence of natural features and on the role of human interaction with the landscape (Lewis 2006; Munakata 1991). These practices include both the worship of landscape elements, like mountains, rivers, and their spirits, as well as the analysis and coding of spatial relationships (*fengshui*), and structured movements, such as cosmological or ritual pilgrimage (Naquin and Yu 1992).

Often, the epicenter of all these spiritual concerns is the mountain, which can be either an actual physical entity where the sacred is found or enacted, or a representation, realistic or symbolic, of a sacred peak (Munakata 1991). If the mountain is the obvious fulcrum of sacrality, the river and water in general are constant counterparts. Sacred sites are always in the vicinity of water, be they rivers, creeks, lakes, or waterfalls. Powerful spirits were thought to inhabit water; foremost among them was the Yellow River, a spiritual entity worshipped at the imperial level (Dodgen 1999). This concern for the territory and its natural and sacred features is well reflected in the *Shanhaijing* (Classic of Mountains and Seas, or more properly Lakes), an ancient text that offers systematic descriptions of places, peoples, and spirits and can be understood as a spiritual geography of China (Yuan Ke 1985).

In China, cults associated with mountains, rivers, and even lakes and seas can be traced back to the most ancient times. Sacred mountains abound and figure prominently in worship, where they are associated with a variety of cults, from ancient spirit and nature worship, to state rituals of Confucian nature, to Buddhism and Taoism (Little 2000). Originally, some mountains, such as Mount Tai (Taishan) in Shandong, were probably centers of worship for local cults, which originated in the prehistoric period. However, with the centralization of political power by the early empire in the third century B.C., these sacred mountains entered the national spiritual geography, acquiring further cosmological significance. Eventually, the most important were organized in groups, such as the Five Marchmounts (*wuyue* 五岳), which mark the five cardinal directions (north, south, east, west, and center) of Chinese imperial ideology (Kleeman 1994). In Taoism, mountains were seen as the abode of immortals or the seat of something akin to a paradise. Among the best-known legendary seats of immortals are the Kunlun Mountains, home to the immortal Xiwangmu (Mother Queen of the West) and her grove of longevity peaches. Another abode of immortals is Penglai, a mountainous island floating off the eastern coast of China where those who had achieved deathlessness subsisted on morning dew (Cahill 1993).

When Buddhism reached China around the first century of the common era, new concepts became attached to this native stratum of nature cults. Thus, the mountain as the center of Taoist and other Chinese spiritual concerns was blended into Mount Sumeru, the sacred mountain of Buddhism that functioned as *axis mundi* and as the abode of some Buddhist deities (Sadakata 1997: 26, 38). As a consequence, many of the mountains that were originally dedicated to the worship of local gods and spirits also acquired a Buddhist spiritual dimension and often also a prominent temple.

With time, the mountain (and landscape in general) became the locus of a representational and literary tradition that signals the progressive idealization of a lost landscape by both urban elites and agricultural communities. In landscape painting from the Song dynasty (960–1279 A.D.), the mountain often appears imposing and remote, overlooking a river. In a successful attempt to convey the power of the sacred, tiny human figures are represented roaming in the scene, but they appear completely overpowered by the peaks and rivers and the collective force of nature (Munakata 1991). The creation of landscape replicas in city gardens or even on trays, which became popular in the Ming (1368–1644) and Qing dynasties (1644–1911), points to further idealizations of the sacred character of the mountain and of the "natural" landscape in general (Ledderose 1983).

Physical reminders of these ancient and modern practices and beliefs are found throughout the Chinese territory, from the heart of China in the Yangzi and Yellow river valleys to the most remote locations at the northern, western, or southern margins. This interconnection between different cults and belief systems suggests that there is uniformity in the choice of places between organized religions and less codified expressions of belief. As I will show below, this is confirmed by the material evidence in the landscape.

Case Studies:
Rock Art, Nomads, and Buddhism on China's Northern Frontier

The weaknesses of the primitive-civilized dichotomy are effectively exposed on China's frontiers. The northwest zone, which includes the provinces of Ningxia, Gansu, and Inner Mongolia, is a case in point. In the deserts and canyons of this large area, rock art of Iron Age pastoralists mingles with Buddhist caves and temples, prehistoric petroglyphs are paired with official edicts of the late empire dynasties (Ming and Qing), and recent route markers intersect with the historic system of travel routes known as the Silk Road. Mountains and springs, inscribed and worshipped by pastoralists, carved to be the abodes of Buddha and Bodhisattvas, annexed by the writing of the Chinese empire, or dotted with the nomads' route markers, are transformed into a large palimpsest that defies a single religion, ritual, or political practice. Among these myriad ritual sites, three rock art locations and their surroundings may serve as useful examples: the Yinshan area of Inner Mongolia, Helankou in Ningxia province, and Heishan in Gansu.

Inner Mongolia: Yinshan

The Yinshan or Yin mountains of central Inner Mongolia, an autonomous region of the People's Republic of China that stretches from the northeastern grasslands bordering Manchuria to the western Gobi desert south of the Republic of Mongolia, runs east-west, separating the deserts and steppes of

Figure 4.1 The hill site of Bu'erhan Shan in the Yinshan; in the foreground are some burials. Urad Rear Banner, Inner Mongolia, China (Paola Demattè)

inner Asia from the agricultural lands of northern China. Positioned in the midst of north-south migration routes, for millennia the Yinshan ranges have been the location of movements, confrontations, and exchanges between inner Asian populations and the Chinese world. Their canyons served both nomads and Chinese as links to each other's lands, but also as sanctuaries, spiritual retreats, or safe havens in what was a challenging physical and political environment. The peaks and ravines of these mountains are littered with thousands of petroglyphs, which are interspersed with the remains of Chinese defensive walls and watchtowers, nomads' tombs and ritual sites, and Buddhist temples (Gai 1986).

For instance, in the gullies, hills, and open spaces on the north side of the Yinshan in Urad Rear Banner (Wulate Houqi, Bayannur League), a desert territory in north-central Inner Mongolia, nomads' tombs, rock art, and stone cairns share space with Buddhist temples and even historic Chinese walls. All these sites are in some proximity to each other and generally concentrate in high places, near water sources, or at the intersection of travel routes. At Bu'erhan Shan, a rock-art hill site on the northern edge of the Yinshan just south of Saiwusu Town in Urad Rear Banner, petroglyphs are engraved on the flat surfaces of boulders or rock slabs darkened by desert patina (Figure 4.1). The motifs, which include animals (mainly horses and mountain goats), people (some carrying bows and arrows), and abstract symbols, reach the highest concentration at the summit of the hillock. The hill, though not extremely high, emerges clearly from the undulating desert plateau standing at a relative height of ca. 50 m (total height 1630 m asl). At the base of the hill are a number of burials that, though still unexcavated, have been attributed to the Tujie, a Turkic population active in this area around the 8th century A.D. Bu'erhanshan is also on a travel route and within reach of water sources. The concentration of carved imagery at the summit, the presence of tombs and other remains in the vicinity, as well as the link with roadways and water sources are typical elements of sacred sites. This evidence suggests that the place had some ritual significance. Though we cannot establish with certainty what beliefs were involved in shaping the place, rock-art iconography and burial style indicate that the area was associated with the activities of pastoral nomads. Not far from Bu'erhanshan there are also stone cairns, locally known as *ovoo* (Chinese: *aobao*) – large and sometimes elaborately decorated piles of stones used by inner Asian nomads since prehistoric times as markers of routes, intersections, and sacred places, but also as symbols of cosmic mountains and altars to heaven (Mongolian *Tängri*) (Baldick 2000). Though today the *ovoo* are decorated with Buddhist Lamaistic symbols, their origin is linked to the pre-Buddhist beliefs of nomads and pastoralists, for whom travel was a way of life and the open landscape was sacred. As they moved in this vast territory, they left these symbols in the landscape to mark their routes and to signal their spiritual appropriation of the land.

Historical records and archaeological remains indicate that in the first centuries of the common era, this land was contested between the expanding Chinese empire and the mobile nomads (Demattè 2004). Though this place is today very dry and forbidding, in the past (particularly two thousand years ago) it was more fertile and its routes were of strategic importance (Hong et al. 2000). Evidence of this strife can be seen north of Buerhanshan and of Saiwusu Town where there are miles of a ruined Chinese Han dynasty (206 B.C.–220 A.D.) wall associated with a system of watchtowers and garrisons. This modest barrier of stones, sand, and pebbles, which originally stood about 2 m high, was not designed to block the mounted warriors, but to stall them, allowing time for Chinese troops at nearby garrisons to arrive. However, beyond its function as a powerful symbol of the boundaries of the settled empire, the wall was also a cultural marker in the landscape; this line that arbitrarily divides the land is also a signal of the connections between people on its different sides (Di Cosmo 1999).

Ningxia: Helankou

The diversity of religions and cultures found at some Yinshan locations is documented elsewhere along China's northwest frontier. An emblematic place is Helankou, a site in Ningxia province that is rich in both petroglyphs

Figure 4.2   A panel with face motifs and Xixia Buddhist inscriptions at the site of
Helankou in the Helanshan, Ningxia, China (Paola Demattè)

and Buddhist motifs and is linked to a nearby Buddhist temple and an
imperial cemetery. Helankou is one of the numerous canyons that dissect
the eastern foothills of the central Helan Mountains (Helanshan), a range
that, like the Yinshan, separates the Asian steppes from the greener fields of
northern China. Petroglyphs are found at eight major loci in the canyon,
but are concentrated at the eastern opening of the gorge on smooth cliffs
and on boulders disseminated in the alluvium. The Helankou petroglyphs
are difficult to date, but various elements indicate that they were produced
over a long time, probably from the late first millennium B.C. to the later
imperial period during the time of the Ming and Qing dynasties (Xu and
Wei 1993).

Helankou exhibits a diversified imagery that goes beyond the more
predictable animal representations and includes face outlines, hand prints,
human figures, symbols, and even inscriptions (Xu and Wei 1996) (Figure
4.2). The site is known for the variety and complexity of its face and/or
mask imagery, but the inscriptions are also very significant. The earliest
inscriptions are in Xixia, a script developed for the language of the Tangut

Danxiang, the founders of the Xixia dynasty (1038–1227 A.D.), which was centered in Ningxia. These inscriptions relate mainly to Buddhism, the religion patronized by the Xixia. Some of the inscriptions comment on the petroglyphs' spiritual meaning and associate them with the Buddha, showing that though devoted to Buddhism, the Xixia were in awe of the pre-existing rock engravings. Other inscriptions are repetitions of the name "Buddha," as if the words were an offering (like the Buddha icons found at countless cave sites), or an actual representation of the Buddha (as is the case at some Chinese Buddhist sites). These inscriptions indicate that Helankou was also a Buddhist site and that some of its later imagery may be connected to that religion. More recent inscriptions are official edicts or records in Chinese dating to the Ming dynasty. Whether in Xixia or in Chinese, these written records must be considered an integral part of the site (Demattè 2011). Their presence in the midst of, and in dialogue with, petroglyphs highlights the interconnectedness of all sign-making and other practices performed at the site.

This evidence links Helankou to a number of nearby sites that the Xixia dedicated to Buddhist or ancestral devotion. The closest is Baisikou, a Buddhist temple at the opening of a canyon situated few kilometers south of Helankou. Baisikou includes two pagodas, the ruins of a temple and of a third pagoda, the ancient burial grounds for monks, and a more recent temple building (Ningxia Institute of Archaeology and Cultural Relics 2005). Farther south, but still on the route to Helankou, is the Xixia imperial cemetery, an extensive area (ca. 50 km²) on the eastern foothills of the Helan (Han Xiaomang 1995; Steinhardt 1993) that holds the tombs of nine Xixia emperors and over 300 elite burials. The proximity and alignment of these and other smaller sites on the road to Helankou suggests that in the past the entire area may have been akin to a pilgrimage route dedicated to devotional and ritual activities (Xu and Wei 1993).

Gansu: Heishan

Rock art with Buddhist elements is known elsewhere in western China, such as at sites in the Heishan mountains of Gansu province. Even though the Heishan, like the Yinshan, appear rocky and desert-like, its canyons are rich in water and other resources necessary for human survival. Here, rock art locations number in the hundreds and are mostly concentrated in three canyons: Mozi gou, Hongliu gou, Sidaoguxing gou. These are approximately 20 km northwest of Jiayuguan, a Chinese military garrison and outpost at the western end of the Great Wall. This position is significant since Jiayuguan was established during the Han dynasty (206 B.C.–220 A.D.) to guard a key access pass to the east-west caravan route (i.e. the Silk Road), then threatened by bandits and nomad attacks.

At Hongliugou, petroglyphs were carved at different heights on both sides of the canyon's walls and often appear in groups. Most clusters include just a few engravings of animals that are sometimes barely visible, but some larger panels show more elaborate scenes. The engravings feature animals, humans engaged in various activities, symbols, and inscriptions. The themes and iconography suggest that they were probably the product of the ritual and political activities of prehistoric nomads and historic pastoralist populations who successively inhabited the area (Gansu Provincial Museum 1990; Jiayuguan City Cultural Heritage Investigative Team 1972).

A small rock panel representing birds, snakes, bulls, and tigers, which are now extinct in the area, suggests that at least some of the Heishan petroglyphs date to the late prehistoric or early historic period of the Chinese northern frontier. These phases are associated with the activities of early inner Asian pastoralists who fought for control of this area up to the time of the Han expansion in the first centuries B.C. Some of these groups, such as the Qiang, Xiongnu, and Yuezhi, are mentioned in Chinese sources and are also known from archaeological remains. Metal ornaments and weapons excavated from Xiongnu burials are often decorated with representations of wild animals (particularly tigers) or of animal combat very similar to those visible in rock panels (Di Cosmo 1994; Bunker 1997). Deeper in the canyon, a large panel on a flat rock surface features an elaborate narrative that represents about 30 human figures and a few animals engaged in what could be a dance or performance (Figures 4.3 and 4.4). People appear to wear long and heavy garments tight at the waist, boots, and in some cases feathery or ornamented headdresses. These images may represent the attires of historic Tibetan or Mongolian pastoral nomads, or those of the prehistoric or historic ancestors of these ethnic groups, such as the already mentioned Qiang and Yuezhi (Gansu Provincial Museum 1990).

At a few locations in the canyons, images of camels indicate that carving continued also in later historic times, when the area became increasingly dry and the camel was introduced to substitute the horse for work and transport. These later carving activities are confirmed by engravings that can be dated with more precision. Several images represent Buddhist symbols (such as pagodas, Buddhas, or Buddhist halls) and sometimes carry inscribed prayers in old Tibetan. The images of pagodas are most instructive because, though two-dimensional, they are essentially identical to those found at Buddhist grotto sites in Gansu and beyond. This production falls well into the historic period and ranges from the early-middle Tang (618–906 A.D.) to the Song (960–1279 A.D.) and Yuan (1279–1368 A.D.) dynastic periods

Figure 4.3 A panel representing people possibly engaged in a dance or performance from
the Heishan site, Gansu, China (Paola Demattè)

Figure 4.4 Detail of the panel shown in Fig. 4.3

(Gansu Provincial Museum 1990). Interestingly, these are not the most recent marks. In the Hongliugou canyon there are also Chinese official inscriptions and Buddhist symbols dating to the Ming and Qing periods. Inscriptions ordinarily are not considered part of rock art, yet their presence here shows how people subscribing to different belief systems claimed the same surfaces and used them in similar ways.

Comparisons

In consideration of the choices that guided the selection of these sites for the construction and use of sacred or ritual places, the rock-art locations discussed above can be compared to a number of other sites. Given the themes featured in rock art, the most obvious connection is with Buddhist temples or grotto complexes, particularly those in nearby locations and similar environments. Unsurprisingly, Gansu and Ningxia are as rich in Buddhist temples and rock cut sanctuaries as they are in rock art, though these are rare in Inner Mongolia (Juliano 2002).

Though the construction and use of Buddhist temples and grottoes required specialized technical and ritual knowledge and differs considerably from the creation of rock art, these two types of sacred places share many elements. Both rock art and Buddhist grotto sites tend to make use of elevated places close to water sources or rivers, and are positioned in remote areas that are, however, within a well traveled network of roads. Like their prehistoric counterparts, which are near prehistoric migration routes and early defensive structures, Buddhist grotto sites were established along the historic Eurasian trade roads and were often in the vicinity of historic fortifications.

Inner Mongolia

For geographic and historic reasons, Inner Mongolia has few Buddhist grottoes, but important temples dedicated to Lamaistic Buddhism are sometimes associated with preexisting nomads' *ovoo* stone cairns. Often these stone constructions are near rock-art sites and are likely to have been created by the same people who carved the petroglyphs. An example of this confluence of beliefs is embodied by the Chaolu (Black Stone) *ovoo* stone cairn and Lama temple, which are north of Saiwusu Town, an area of Urad Rear Banner (Inner Mongolia) not far from the Buerhanshan rock art site. At Chaolu, the *ovoo* complex and the Lama temple share both location and symbolism. The *ovoo* is decorated with Lamaistic symbols and elements of the iconography of the temple wall paintings are comparable to that of rock art. In one panel, in addition to the Buddha, we see deer and tigers (Figure 4.5). Though related to Buddhist stories (such as the deer and tiger *jatakas*), these animals are also a nod to the local tradition of animal representation, which paid particular attention to deer and tigers. This merging of place and imagery is not surprising, because, since the introduction of Lamaistic Buddhism among the Mongols in the sixteenth century, important *ovoos* have been incorporated into Lamaistic worship and the most important have become paired with a Buddhist temple.

Ningxia and Gansu

A comparative analysis of petroglyphs and Buddhist art can be carried out by pairing rock art sites with one of the many rock-cut sanctuaries disseminated along the ancient trade routes of Ningxia and Gansu. A good example is Xumishan, a Buddhist cave complex in southern Ningxia, though other Buddhist grottoes, such as Mogao or Binglingsi in Gansu, would be equally valid.

Xumishan holds more than 130 rock-cut cave-temples spread over a 2 km area on the eastern slopes of Mount Xumi (1800 m, on the Liupangshan range) overlooking the Si River gorge, a strategic pass on a major travel route. The grottoes are clustered into eight groups (Dafolou, Zisungong, Yuanguangsi, Xiangguosi, Taohuadong, Songshugui, Sangeyao, Heishigou) following the main peaks of the mountain (Figure 4.6). Xumishan, which

Figure 4.5   The Chaolu (Black Stone) *ovoo* stone cairn and Lama temple, north of Saiwusu
        Town, Urad Rear Banner, Inner Mongolia, China (Paola Demattè)

Figure 4.6   Panoranic view of the Buddhist grottoes of Xumishan, Ningxia, China (Paola
        Demattè)

is not an uncommon name for a Buddhist mountain site, is a reference to mount Sumeru, the sacred mountain of Buddhism (*xumi* is Chinese for the Sanskrit Sumeru and *shan* is Chinese for mountain).

Carved out of the red sandstone cliffs and originally fronted by a timber structure, the caves vary in plan and in size based on use and date. Most caves used for worship have a squarish plan and are often equipped with a *stupa* pillar at the center. However, the largest tend to have side chambers and the smallest often lack the *stupa* pillar. Caves that served as living quarters for monks are simple, square or rectangular, some with side corridors. The largest cave, the Big Buddha Mansion (cave 5 at Dafolou), houses the tallest statue of the site (20 m), a seated Buddha Maitreya. The smaller ones are just a few meters wide. About 70 of these grottoes were fully adorned with wall paintings or statues of Buddhas, Bodhisattavas, and holies carved from the living rock and painted. The remainder appear to have been either unfinished or undecorated, probably serving as the living quarters of monks. Today, only 20 caves still maintain most of their statues and decorations and a few are still in use for both Buddhist and Taoist worship (Ningxia Heritage Preserving Committee & Archaeology Dept. Beijing University 1997).

The cave temples were built in various spurts of activity between the fourth and the tenth centuries under the influence of dynasties, such as the Northern Wei (386–534 A.D.), Western Wei (534–57 A.D.), Northern Zhou (557–81 A.D.), Sui (581–618 A.D.), and Tang (618–906 A.D.), which had an inner Asian or Turkish ethnic background. The main function of the Xumishan caves was as places of worship and pilgrimage. However, beyond devotion, the reasons for this protracted building and use of Buddhist cave temples in an area that is relatively arid and isolated is connected with the strategic position of Xumishan along the Silk Road, the most important Eurasian trade and spiritual route. Nearby historic and archaeological sites indicate that Xumishan had military and commercial importance over the centuries. A Qin-dynasty (third century B.C.) defensive wall near the site and the natural defensive character of the narrow river gorge (where historic battles took place) suggest that Xumishan played a considerable strategic role. Persian and Central Asian objects such as glass and silver excavated from several large burials confirm that long-distance trade was thriving on this section of the Silk Road and was vital to the continued use of the grottoes (Ningxia Heritage Preserving Committee & Archaeology Dept. Beijing University 1997).

Notwithstanding its complex sculptural and architectural program, Xumishan resembles rock art sites in many aspects. Like these places, the Xumishan grottoes were concentrated in a series of peaks overlooking a river, and were constructed over an extended period of time by a varied population that included nomad pastoralists, Chinese agriculturalists, and their mixed descendants. Though located in what appears as a physically and spiritually remote area, their connections with trade routes and strategic mountain passes indicate that the grottoes were, after all, quite accessible.

Conclusion

All the material remains here discussed are testimony of the historic role played by the landscape in the shaping of identities and spirituality of local groups, but also of the ethnic and cultural richness of the frontier area. Sacred or other remains ascribable to different groups, from the Han Chinese, to Turkish, Mongolians, and other inner Asian nations, highlight the contested nature of these places and the sacrality of the territory for diverse populations. This heritage reminds us that in antiquity, like today, this region was inhabited by a variety of people who were actively constructing their home and sacred landscapes. The impression is that, beyond any specific religion, this place could be construed as "sacred" to many peoples and in many different ways.

Indeed, more than individual beliefs, it is the structure of the landscape, real and imagined, religious, and political, with its network of routes and visually and materially significant places that creates the sacrality (Bradley 2000; Ashmore and Knapp 1999). Yet, by this very definition, it also shows that the profane is never very far from the sacred and that the "sacred," though theoretically remote and difficult to achieve, must be accessible and consumable. Elevation and remoteness are attempts at distancing from the everyday, but waterways and travel routes indicate that such distancing was always temporary and relative. No matter the structure of belief or its complexity, or whether the believers were roaming nomads who relied on the natural environment for sustenance, traveling merchants who sought respite from it, or urban dwellers who longed for lost nature, particular places acquired sacredness or sacred value because of their positions, structures, and cumulative histories.

References

Ashmore, Wendy, and A. Bernard Knapp (editors)
   1999 *Archaeologies of Landscape: Contemporary Perspectives*. Blackwell Publishers, Malden, MA.
Baldick, Julian
   2000 *Animal and Shaman: Ancient Religions of Central Asia*. New York University Press, New York.
Bradley, Richard
   2000 *An Archaeology of Natural Places*. Routledge, London and New York.

Bunker, Emma, Trudy S. Kawami, and Katheryn M. Linduff
    1997 *Ancient Bronzes of the Eastern Eurasian Steppes.* A. Sackler Foundation, New York
          & Washington.

Cahill, Suzanne Elizabeth
    1993 *Transcendence and Divine Passion: The Queen Mother of the West in Medieval China.*
          Stanford University Press, Stanford, CA.

Casey, Edward
    1996 How to Get from Space to Place in a Fairly Short Stretch of Time: Phenomenological
          Prolegomena. In *Senses of Place*, edited by Steven Feld and Keith H. Basso, pp.
          13–52. School of American Research Press, Santa Fe, NM.

Coleman, Simon, and John Elsner.
    1997 *Pilgrimage: Past and Present in the World Religions.* Harvard University Press,
          Cambridge, MA.

Demattè, Paola
    2004 Beyond Shamanism: Landscape and Self-Expression in the Petroglyphs of Inner
          Mongolia and Ningxia (China). *Cambridge Archaeological Journal* 14: 1–20.
    2011 Mobile and Settled: the Petroglyphs of Helankou, Ningxia, Western China. *Rock
          Art Research* 28(2): 197–210.

Di Cosmo, Nicola
    1994 Ancient Inner Asian Nomads: Their Economic Basis and Its Significance in Chinese
          History. *Journal of Asian Studies* 53: 1092–1126.
    1999 The Northern Frontier. In *The Cambridge History of Ancient China: From the Origins
          of Civilization to 221 B.C.*, edited by Michael Loewe and Edward L. Shaughnessy,
          pp. 885–966. Cambridge University Press, Cambridge.

Dodgen, Randall
    1999 Hydraulic Religion: 'Great King' Cults in the Ming and Qing. *Modern Asian Studies*
          33: 815–833.

Dong, Yuxiang, and Banghu Yue
    1988 Binglinsi deng shiku diaosu yishu. In *Binglingsi deng shiku diaosu. Zhongguo meishu
          quanji, Diaosu bian* vol. 9, edited by Dong Yuxiang and Yue Banghu, pp. 1–32,
          Renmin Meishu Press, Beijing.

Gai, Shanlin
    1986 *Yinshan Yanhua* (Petroglyphs in the Yinshan Mountains). Wenwu, Beijing.

Gansu Provincial Museum
    1990 Gansu Jiayuguan Heishan gudai yanhua (Ancient Rock Art of the Heishan,
          Jiayuguan, Gansu). *Kaogu* 4: 344–359.

Guyuan Museum (editor)
    2004 *Guyuan lishi wenwu. Historical and Cultural Relics from Guyuan.* Kexue, Beijing.

Han, Xiaomang
    1995 *Xi Xia wang ling* (Xixia imperial mausolea). Gansu Wenhua, Lanzhou.

Hong, Y.T., H.B. Jiang, T.S. Liu, L.P. Zhou, J. Beer, H.D. Li, X.T. Leng, B. Hong, and
X.G. Qin
    2000 Response of Climate to Solar Forcing Recorded in a 6000-year $\partial^{18}O$ time-series of
          Chinese Peat Cellulose. *The Holocene* 10(1): 1–7.

Juliano, Annette L.

2002 Buddhist Art in Northwest China. In *Monks and Merchants: Silk Road Treasures from Northwest China*, edited by Annette L. Juliano and J. A. Lerner, pp. 118–143. Asia Society, New York.

Jiayuguan City Cultural Heritage Investigative Team

1972 Gansu diqu gudai youmu minzu yanhua (Rock Art of the Ancient Pastoral Populations of Gansu). *Wenwu* 12: 42–46.

Kleeman, Terry F.

1994 Mountain Deities in China: The Domestication of the Mountain God and the Subjugation of the Margins. *Journal of the American Oriental Society* 114: 226–238.

Ledderose, Lothar

1983 The Earthly Paradise: Religious Elements in Chinese Landscape Art. In *Theories of Art in China*, edited by Susan Bush and Christian Murck, pp. 165–183. Princeton University Press, Princeton, NJ.

Lewis, Mark E.

2006 *The Construction of Space in Early China*. State University of New York Press, Albany, NY.

Little, Steven

2000 *Taoism and the Arts of China*. Art Institute of Chicago and University of California Press, Chicago & Berkeley.

Munakata, Kinohito

1991 *Sacred Mountains in Chinese Art*. University of Illinois Press, Urbana.

Naquin, Susan, and Yü Chün-fang

1992 *Pilgrims and Sacred Sites in China*. University of California Press, Berkeley and Los Angeles.

Ningxia Heritage Preserving Committee & Archaeology Department Beijing University (editors)

1997 *Xumishan shiku neirong zonglu* (Summary of Content of Xumishan Grottoes). Wenwu, Beijing.

Ningxia Institute of Archaeology and Cultural Relics

2005 *Baisigou Xixia Fangta. Xixia Quadrilateral Pagoda in the Baisigou Valley*. Wenwu, Beijing.

Sadakata, Akira

1997 *Buddhist Cosmology*. Kosei, Tokyo.

Steinhardt, Nancy Shatzman

1993 The Tangut Royal Tombs near Yinchuan. *Muqarnas* 10: 369–381.

Tuan, Yi-Fu

1977 *Space and Place*. University of Minnesota Press, Minneapolis.

Xu, Cheng, and Wei Zhong

1993 *Helanshan yanhua* (The Rock Art of the Helan Mountains). Wenwu, Beijing.

Yuan, Ke (editor)

1985 *Shanhaijing Jiaoyi*. Guji, Shanghai.

The Dig at the End of the World: Archaeology and Apocalypse. Tourism in the Valley of Armageddon

Isaac Morrison

> How can the significance of sites and the constituencies for whom the sites are
> supposedly significant be linked? (Leone and Potter 1992: 140).

Tel Megiddo is an archaeological park in the Jezreel valley of northern Israel
that serves as a destination for 120,000 to 150,000 tourists every year (Megiddo
Park Supervisor, personal communication, September 25, 2010). The number
is, unfortunately vague, because tourism to Israel fluctuates wildly depending
on the perception of security; when incidents of terrorism are up, tourism goes
down dramatically. First settled in approximately 7,000 B.C., the site features
the layered remains of 26 distinct populations and was nearly continuously
inhabited until the exhaustion of the local aquifers in 586 B.C. Because of
its strategic position at an intersection of overland trade routes from Africa,
Asia, and Europe, the city of Megiddo has been alternately controlled by
several kingdoms, including Persians, Canaanites, Egyptians, Assyrians, and
Israelites. For the past century, the location has been the subject of four different
archaeological excavations, beginning in 1903 with Gottlieb Schumacher and
the German Society for the Study of Palestine, continuing with a University
of Chicago excavation in 1925, and a Yigael Yadin-led Hebrew University
excavation in the 1960s. For the past decade, Tel Megiddo has undergone
excavation sponsored by Tel Aviv University under the leadership of Israel
Finkelstein, Eric Cline and David Ussishkin. In a country graced with an
abundance of rich archaeological sites, Tel Megiddo is regarded as a particularly
important regional archaeological treasure; it is most famous however for
its association with the apocalyptic battle of Har Megiddo, better known as
Armageddon. The site's Biblical associations and varied history leave it open
to a number of interpretations, and as a result, it is the subject of multiple
vocalities on the part of past and present archaeological excavators, the Israeli

National Parks Authority (INPA), tour companies that describe the site, and the religious tourists that visit it.

In this paper, I outline and apply a methodology for assessing the narratives surrounding Tel Megiddo Archaeological Park as a sacred site for its distinct Christian tourist demographic. The goal of this paper is twofold: first, it seeks to outline a heuristic practice whereby modern site significance for prominent archaeological destinations can be identified through quantitative and qualitative review of site descriptors from tourism websites; second, it utilizes this practice to explore the sacred significance of Tel Megiddo Archaeological Park to its Christian tourist constituency by studying its position within the larger context of the religious tourism industry in Israel.[1]

Throughout this paper, I alternate between textual review and analysis in order to ground the process in concrete examples. By highlighting points of divergence between the general descriptive narrative and the specifically targeted site descriptions, I can link the archaeological park's public presentation and its ideological significance for its visiting constituencies. As I work to answer Leone and Potter's question, quoted at the start of this chapter, my primary concern is not with the site's actual archaeological past, but rather with how it is presented and perceived; the object of study is not the archaeology of Tel Megiddo, but rather the ideological significance of the archaeological park itself. As Thomas Levy says, "preserved archaeological sites can also be seen as material components of the society that discovers and studies them" (1998: 9). In this case, Tel Megiddo Archaeological Park serves an ideological purpose that can be seen in the text used to describe the site to its potential religious visitors.

Methodology

Textual analysis is hardly a new concept; scholars and literary critics have been indulging in it for centuries (e.g., Fairclough 2003). Likewise, the textualization of the Holy Land is part of a deep tradition in Christianity wherein the geography of the Bible is learned and understood primarily through a close reading of the Bible that defers to the primacy of the text itself (Bowman 2000: 99). The advent of the internet, however, has facilitated the use of this form of analysis to a degree that was previously unimaginable. In this chapter, I review a variety of online written material intended to attract visitors to Megiddo. This includes material from the Israel National Parks Authority (INPA) and the Israeli Ministry of Tourism, along with comparable material produced by tour companies offering travel packages to Israel. In particular, the tourism websites are used in this paper as a target for site analysis through a close reading of text and context.

A few factors and assumptions underlie my basic analytical approach. The operative principle behind this analytical method is the assumption of a high level of involvement and marketing expertise on the part of a robust and developed Israeli tourism industry. The tourism industry in Israel is well-established and deeply ingrained in the public presentation of the country itself. Furthermore, it is standard operating procedure in the Israeli tourism business, and particularly the religious tourism business, to conduct tours in such a way as to ensure that the sites visited by the various demographic groups reflect the travelers' spiritual worldview rather than simply leading them from one point of general interest to another. Neither the destinations nor their descriptions are accidental; instead they are arranged in a fashion that is appropriate to specific tourist demographics so that the presentation of sites reinforces previously held beliefs (Ron and Feldman 2009: 205; Feldman 2007: 264–266).

When examining the textual information, I paid close attention to the categories of potential tourists, the presence or absence of Megiddo in the various tour itineraries, and the way in which the site is described to the different categories of tourists. Based on this information, I drew conclusions regarding Megiddo's significance to its primary constituency. My line of inquiry here is threefold: who is Megiddo's primary constituency, what do they find significant about it, and why it is significant to them?

Online Representation

To facilitate an analysis of online textual representation, it can be useful to identify a standard baseline for comparison. As mentioned above, religious and historical tourism are substantial contributors to the Israeli economy and, as such, the INPA presents archaeological sites in a way that they are accessible to a wide range of visitor narratives and interpretations while still preserving their professional credibility by adhering to historical accuracy. Although the INPA cannot be said to be truly objective, they certainly strive towards neutrality. For this reason, I have chosen to use the text from the INPA website as a starting point to explore the distinct and varied narratives surrounding Megiddo.

The Parks Authority webpage for Megiddo National Park begins by giving it the title, "Ahab's chariot city." Even this simple appellation is rich with semiotic overtones invoking Biblical history, Israelite kings, armed warfare, and ancient Jewish civilization. The 500-word description that follows gives a brief but thorough overview of the site's history and describes some of its more noteworthy features, including the remains of city gates, horse stables, and a reconstructed water system – all of which are associated with Israelite kings and Biblical heroes in the descriptions. The theological conflation of Megiddo and the Christian Battle of Armageddon is briefly mentioned, but it only merits a single sentence in a description that is several paragraphs long.[2] The second baseline text describing Megiddo, the website for Israel's Ministry of Tourism,[3] paints a similar picture. As one might expect from a tourist-oriented website, the language is noticeably more ebullient and dramatic, emphasizing "remains from the city's glorious past" and the "beautiful and impressive national park." This page also makes reference to Armageddon and the New Testament Book of Revelation, but only in a single sentence that is largely overshadowed by the material that surrounds it.

However, unlike the INPA website, the Israeli Ministry of Tourism goes so far as to match attractions and tourists by providing a variety of suggested itineraries and destinations oriented towards 17 specific categories of tourism. These categories are as follows: "General Interest," "Jewish," "Christian," "Catholic," "Culture and History," "Family," "Archaeological," "Evangelical Christian," "Jews and the Bible," "Ecotourism," "Women in the Old and New Testament," "Ethnic Communities in Israel," "Jews and the Bible," "Bicycle Tours," "Food and Wine," "Naturally Israel," and "Itineraries for People with Mobility Challenges."

Only five of these 17 categories include Megiddo as a location of interest: "Christian," "Evangelical Christian," "Catholic," "Archaeology," and "Jews in the Bible." Not one of the other suggested itineraries mentions Megiddo. The implication here seems fairly obvious: the Israeli Ministry of Tourism has concluded that Christians are the audience most likely to be interested in Megiddo, and any attraction that the site might hold for non-Christian tourists is limited to its historical and archaeological significance. The relevance and appeal of various tour themes are presumably the product of the state tourism board's experience as a facilitator of tourist traffic; it behooves them to maximize the tourist's quality of experience in order to foster continued visitation. In this case, the focus is clearly on foreign tourist appeal; the domestic market for archaeological tourism is small and may be shrinking. Several scholars of Israeli archaeology have noted a decline in archaeological interest on the part of the general Israeli population, with Bauman stating that "Israelis only visit sites once, perhaps a school trip, during one of the educational trips with the Army, or with their families. Then there is nothing left to see" (2004: 215). Nadia Abu El-Haj cites a similar indifference to archaeology as, "national-cultural practice" (2007: 271), and even the director of the Israeli Antiquities Authority (IAA) has publicly lamented Israelis' decreased public interest in archaeology on the IAA homepage.[4]

As previously mentioned, the text from these two websites provides us with a baseline against which we can compare other textual descriptions

Figure 5.1   Word cloud generated from INPA and Israeli Ministry of Tourism webpage
text on Megiddo. (Image generated at wordle.net)

of the site. Toward this end, I have converted that written material into a
word cloud (Figure 5.1) (also called a "tag cloud" or "weighted list") that
indexes and transposes the words into a random cluster where the size of the
individual words corresponds with their frequency of usage. By placing the
official state descriptions of Megiddo into a word cloud, a visual overview
of the dominant textual motifs emerges, facilitating a rapid assessment of
the primary themes (Kuo et al. 2007). As noted above, words emphasizing
the site's age, history, and physical features are dominant, overshadowing
references to religion and the battle of Armageddon. This provides a "feel"
for the tone of the Israeli government's presentation of the site.

The online representations by the INPA and the Israeli tourist board serve
as a formal state picture of the archaeological site and a baseline against which
the commercial tourist websites can be compared. Although a causal link
between the INPA presentation and the descriptive language used by private
tour companies is impossible to verify without direct conversations with the
content managers of the tourism websites in question (a task which is beyond
the scope of this chapter), the Israeli government's attitude toward demographic
subsets of foreign visitors seems to be shared by most of the tour companies
offering Israel tour experiences. With the exception of the occasional direct
scriptural quotation and two personal accounts from visitors to Megiddo, the

commercial tour websites do not present any material that is not also found on one or both of the official Israeli Megiddo pages. This shows an interesting point of congruence between the messages presented on the official websites and those offered by their private commercial counterparts.

To whom does Megiddo matter?

During the course of my research, I reviewed material from the following 19 private tour agencies: Adventures Abroad, America/Israel Tours, ArzaWorld, Biblical Israel Tours, DD Travel, Gil Travel, Globus Travel, Holy Land Escorted Christian Tours, Holy Land Sun Tours, Holy Land Tours, Israel Revealed, Jerusalem Tours, Olive Branch Tours, Pilgrim Tours, Regina Tours, Spiritual Heritage Tours, TLC Holy Land Tours, Tours to the Holy Land, and Zola Levitt Tours.

These companies cater primarily to English speaking audiences and they offer a variety of packages broadly or narrowly oriented towards specific religious and denominational categories of clientele that are quite similar to the categories used on the Israeli tourist board website. The advertised tour packages are grouped according to specific religious and denominational designations, neatly breaking down into the following five categories: Jewish, Christian, Evangelical Christian, Catholic, and Non-religious. This is particularly useful because it enables a clarification of constituencies. With these five specific categories in mind, I examined all of the current Israel/Holy Land tour itineraries offered by the 19 online tour companies. The material produced for these distinct client groups provides another tool for linking Megiddo's significance with the constituencies to whom it is significant.

This line of research seems to reveal a clear message: excepting the occasional archaeology or history enthusiast, Megiddo is assumed to hold little or no significance for non-Christian visitors to Israel and only moderate significance for Catholics. Nonreligious tours of Israel include Megiddo rarely, if at all; only half of the six "nonreligious" tour packages included the site, and those that did focused almost exclusively on its historical and archaeological features. None of the tour companies explicitly use the term "non-religious," but many of them feature a variety of tours that are heavily oriented towards science, history, archaeology, leisure, or politics. The language used in the descriptions of these tours is carefully neutral when addressing religious themes and Biblical references are few and far between.

Megiddo is also conspicuously absent from the itineraries of Jewish-oriented tour packages as well. Of the 19 tour companies that I reviewed, six offered a variety of specifically Jewish tours, often described as "heritage" or "Jewish heritage" tours. These tour companies offer dozens of distinctly

Jewish tours, but only two of those tours include visits to Megiddo. Particularly notable examples of this exclusion can be seen at AmericaIsrael.us and Arzaworld.com. AmericaIsrael offers the largest variety of Jewish-oriented tours, and Arzaworld.com offers only Jewish-oriented tours. Between these two agencies alone, there are dozens of possible Jewish-oriented tours; not one of them stops at Megiddo.

This omission of Megiddo from Jewish-oriented tours is also evident in the Taglit-Birthright program, a non-commercial Israel tour program that provides free educational trips exclusively for non-Israeli Jewish young adults between the ages of 18 and 26. Although distinct from conventional commercial tourism, the multi-week trips are structured in a tour-like fashion, traveling around the country and visiting sites of religious and nationalistic importance. The stated goal of the program is "to strengthen the sense of solidarity among world Jewry; and to strengthen participants' personal Jewish identity and connection to the Jewish people" (Birthrightisrael.com 2009). Currently there are 24 organizations licensed to run Birthright tours in Israel, and not one of those 24 organizations feature Megiddo as a destination on their current or sample itineraries.

If there is one single piece of evidence that points most clearly to Megiddo's lack of significance for its Jewish audience it comes directly from the Israeli Ministry of Tourism, whose website offers several lists enumerating "items of interest" for different tourist demographics. Megiddo is nowhere to be found on the list enumerating "items of Jewish interest."

All of this contrasts sharply with the near-ubiquity of Megiddo as a featured destination on Christian- and Evangelical Christian-oriented tour itineraries. All of the companies operating Christian tours in Israel include Megiddo in almost every single one of their itineraries, regardless of their denominational specificity (although it is sometimes excluded from the shorter versions of variable-length tours). Although there is a range of theological variation between Evangelical Christians and more traditional Protestant denominations, it should be mentioned that the Israeli Ministry of Tourism has identified Evangelicals as their prime tourist growth market, and Evangelical themes dominate the tone of the Protestant-oriented tourist narratives (Ron and Feldman 2009: 209, 214).

A few of the tour agencies only have a single broad "Christian" category, the majority of them distinguish between Christian, Evangelical Christian, and Catholic tours. Only one of the websites offered explicitly Orthodox Christian tours, none of which included Megiddo on their itinerary. In the course of my research I found only three other Christian tours that did not include Megiddo: two Catholic tours and a highly specialized Evangelical Christian tour entitled "Following the Women of the Bible."

Descriptors of Megiddo: Recurring Features and Emphases

Having identified the itineraries that include Megiddo, I grouped them along the previously specified religious lines, and reviewed their respective descriptions to reveal what aspects of the site were emphasized for each group. In the course of this review, I identified 25 recurring descriptors, themes, and features and charted their usage within the five aforementioned religious categories (Table 5.1). My priority here was to highlight the variety of descriptions among tourist categories, not within them, so multiple uses of the same description within a denominational category were only counted once.

Online descriptors used by tour itineraries visiting Megiddo	Jewish (2)	Christian (unspecified) (11)	Christian (Evangelical) (4)	Catholic (2)	Non-religious (3)	Israeli tourism ministry	INPA website
Armageddon, Biblical	**	**********	****	*	***	*	*
Armageddon, religious	*	****	*	*			
Religious activity	*		*			*	*
Archaeology/Excavation		***********	*	*		*	*
UNESCO Status						*	
Chariots/Stables/Horses		**	*	*		*	*
Water supply system		**		*		*	*
Gates			*			*	*
Granary			*				
Multiple layers	*	****	*		*	*	*
Association with Bible	*	********	****	**		*	*
Direct scriptural citation (Old Testament)		**	*				
Direct scriptural citation (New Testament)		***	***	*			*
Association with ancient Israel	*	*****	**	**	*	*	*
Association with Biblical Kings	*	****	**	**	*	*	*
Solomon		***	**	**		*	*
Ahab		**	*	*		*	*
Non-Israelite civilization		*		*	*	*	*
Specific historical event					**	*	*
Association with war	*	*****	**	*	**	*	*
Museum/Arch park		*		*		*	*
Impressive/magnificent/important	*	*****	*	*	**	*	*
Ancient/old		***		*		*	*
Restored/restoration		*					*

Table 5.1   Online descriptors for tour companies visiting Megiddo

It is important to note that many of the site descriptions are short, some only a sentence or two long, resting within a larger paragraph outlining a multi-location, all-day itinerary. Although Megiddo's presence in the Christian tours is nearly ubiquitous, the limitations of space require the tourism websites to keep their descriptions to a bare minimum – this limits those descriptions to a one- or two-sentence snapshot of each site's two or three most important and recognizable features. When dealing with sites that contain physical remains from multiple significant periods, as is the case with Megiddo, "the selection of what to represent should give clues to the imperatives of what certain social groups feel is important to a sense of identity and history" (Bauman 2004: 213).

Bauman's observation can be applied to site descriptions as well as to the sites themselves, in this case, through a close review of site descriptions. None of the individual site descriptions contain the same volume of content as the "official" descriptions found on the Israeli Tourism or INPA websites. But, as with the analysis of the itineraries, it is just as important to note what is missing as what is present. Given the small sample size, statistical analysis is not a viable option here, but a careful review shows that from a Christian perspective descriptors related to war and Armageddon dominate, with strong Biblical and archaeological associations. The physical features of the park get little or no mention, and cues suggesting that this is a curated environment (e.g., specific mention of the museum and site reconstruction) are almost entirely absent from the descriptions as are references to non-Biblical history.

Ideology vs. Marketability

The dramatic absence of present-day territorial or nationalist language surrounding the park must also be addressed. Government-operated archaeological parks can serve as valuable ideological symbols reinforcing the narratives of history and geography that are essential to ideas of national identity (Anderson 2002; Leone 1981), but as Baram and Rowan (2004: 3) have pointed out, "at the start of the twenty-first century, nationalism is not the only political force impinging on archaeology, and it may not be the most significant." Although the presentation of Israel's archaeological past to its modern constituencies is generally under the purview of government institutions, or at least institutions dependent on government funding, good will, and oversight, Israeli sites are not rigorously bound to a single, institutionalized, interpretive strategy. Whatever nationalist semiotic utility Megiddo might have, it is eclipsed by its commercial utility and it seems evident that the state has left ideological interpretation of Megiddo open to its Christian visitors in order to foster their economic patronage. In light of this, it must be stated that the projected image of Megiddo provides an abundance of rich symbolic hardware, but demands little critical deconstruction in return. This open-ended presentation is essential to making sites appealing to a Christian constituency. As Ron and Feldman state (2009: 204), "in order to be accepted into the pilgrim's itinerary, those displays and 'revelations' must accord with a world-view rooted in theologically grounded and historically transmitted Protestant ways of seeing and aesthetic values that derive from them."

Megiddo's Ideological utility for Christianity

Understanding the relationship between the site, its past, and the viewing present is the key to recognizing and identifying ideology in the public presentation of archaeology (Leone 1981: 309). Unlike the ambivalent utility of Megiddo for Israeli nationalism, the site is a remarkably powerful tool for the reinforcement of Christian theology, and by extension, ideology. This is evident in the descriptions of Megiddo that are intended for Christian tourists. Almost all of the terminology used to describe Megiddo clusters around three repeating central themes: the Old Testament (in the form of scriptural citations and the names of Biblical Kings), war (including mentions of chariots, battles, and repeated military conquest), and the eschatological apocalyptic vision of Christ's final triumph over evil. As these themes are superimposed over the geographic location, the site becomes a solid metaphor for apocalyptic triumphalism. This can be seen in the "Tour Records" section of www.biblicalisraeltours.com where the text from the 2007 travel journal of one Christian tourist is quoted as part of Megiddo's site description: "Being a place of many battles as well as the place for the battle of all battles to come (Armageddon), we read from Rev. 16 and comments were shared about God's ultimate victory in the battle against our spiritual enemy."[5]

These ideological assumptions enable Megiddo's viewing audience to retain and contextualize narrowly specific aspects of the site, despite the presence of abundant competing historical narratives. In settings of this sort, attention is a zero-sum game: "concentrating on one point of time diminishes the importance of others, halts change, and prevents comparison" (Leone 1978: 665). This is not to say that Megiddo's Biblical associations are any less real or valid than, for example, its recently excavated "pagan" temple, or academic disputes over how certain structures were used; Ron and Feldman (2009: 207), however, note that "theologically conservative Protestant groups ignore, suppress or selectively interpret archaeological findings that contradict their understandings of scripture." When confronted with an environment saturated with archaeological remains of great significance, the tourist must rely on institutionalized interpretive strategies. In this situation, however, the ideology is not produced by a state institution, but instead preexists within the audience, already provided by the tourists' own religious institutions.

This selective mix of vision and presentation, first seen on the commercial tourism websites, integrates the extensive excavations at Megiddo into an experiential validation of ideology and world-view for its Christian constituency. Assumptions of Biblical accuracy are reinforced through material objects that can be indexically linked to iconic stories and individuals from the Bible with little or no demand for critical interpretation. The descriptive titles of the tours themselves make it clear that this reinforcement is a motivating factor in taking these trips to begin with. Titles like "In the footsteps of our Lord," "Into the promised land," "The roots of your faith," "Inspirational tour for the Bible-believing Christian," "Biblical tours of Israel with a personal pastoral touch," "Journey through the holy land," "Holy land Christian roots journey," and "Holy land sacred journey," highlight the personal connection among geography, history, and religious belief. This experiential validation lies at the root of why Christian tourists want to visit Israel:

> People are interested in constructing authentic relationships with a particular retelling of the past, and that past assists in the construction or reaffirmation of a sense of identity. Contemporary Protestant pilgrims consume these religious theme sites not solely for amusement, but also to find meaningful relationships with God, Jesus, the Bible, the past, the future, themselves and each other [Baram and Rowan 2004: 263].

Without a formal visitor survey, it is beyond the capacity of a loose model of this sort to estimate the specific ratio of Christian to non-Christian among the 150,000 tourists who visit Megiddo each year; but the absence of significance for non-Christian audiences via descriptions on tourist websites implies a rather dramatic imbalance. The methods used in this paper have provided a helpful preliminary step towards identifying and linking site significance with specific constituencies. Obviously, not all of these factors are universal, which limits the applicability of this method to specific types of locations and objects of study. But the creative researcher can adapt this as a mechanism for comparing and contrasting single-audience and multi-audience locations, particularly those in which competing narratives share a single space.

Conclusion

Addressing the distinctive approach of Protestant Christians to the Holy Land, Robert Markus (1994: 271) describes the process of site sanctification as the localization of the past into the present. The case of Tel Megiddo Archaeological Park presents a fascinating alternate version of this process.

At Megiddo, the future also becomes localized in the present. The ruined structures of the archaeological park serve as an anchor between the constructed past, the experienced present, and the expected future. This, I believe, is Megiddo's prime significance as a sacred Christian artifact: it serves as a concrete location where Christian visitors can place themselves in the path of time's arrow as it flies towards destiny.

Notes

1 My choice of Tel Megiddo as an object of study stems from my own experience with the location, first as a tourist and subsequently as an archaeology student participating in on-site excavation.
2 www.parks.org.il/ParksENG/company_card.php3?CNumber=507185
3 www.parks.org.il/ParksENG/company_card.php3?CNumber=507185
4 http://www.antiquities.org.il/about_eng.asp?Modul_id=24
5 http://biblicalisraeltours.com/Web%20Pages/Tour%20Experiences/Tour%20Experiences%20-%20Nov%202007.html

References

Abu el-Haj, Nadia
  2001 *Facts on Ground: Archaeological Practice and Territorial Self-Fashioning in Israeli Society.* University of Chicago Press: Chicago.
Anderson, Benedict
  1999 *Imagined Communities.* Verso Publishing, New York.
Baram, Uzi, and Yorke Rowan
  2004 Archaeology after Nationalism: Globalization and the Consumption of the Past. In *Marketing Heritage: Archaeology and the Consumption of the Past,* edited by Uzi Baram and Yorke Rowan, pp. 3–25. Altamira Press, Lanham, MD.
Bauman, Joel
  2004 Tourism, Design, and the Past in Zippori/Sepphoris. In *Marketing Heritage: Archaeology and the Consumption of the Past,* edited by Uzi Baram and Yorke Rowan, pp. 205–227. Altamira Press, Lanham, MD.
Birthright/Taglit Israel tours
  www.birthrightisrael.com/, accessed November 9, 2009.
Bowman, David
  2000 Christian Ideology and the Image of a Holy Land: The Place of Jerusalem Pilgrimage in the Various Christianities. In *Contesting the Sacred: The Anthropology of Christian Pilgrimage,* edited by Michael Sallnow and John Eade, pp. 98–121. Illinois University Press, Urbana, IL.
Fairclough, Norman
  2003 *Analyzing Discourse: Textual Analysis for Social Research.* Routledge, New York.

Feldman, Jackie
    2007   Constructing a Shared Bible Land: Jewish Israeli Guiding Performances for
            Protestant Pilgrims. *American Ethnologist* 34: 351–374.
Israel Ministry of Tourism description of Megiddo
    www.goisrael.com/Tourism_Eng/Tourist+Information/Discover+Israel/Cities/
        Megiddo.htm, accessed December 18, 2009.
Israel Ministry of Tourism suggested Itineraries
    www.tourism.gov.il/Tourism_Eng/Tourist+Information/Suggested+Itiner ries/
        Suggested+Itineraries.htm, accessed December 18, 2009.
Israel National Parks Authority (INPA) description of Tel Megiddo Archaeological Park. www.
        parks.org.il/ParksENG/company_card.php3?CNumber=57185, accessed
        December 18, 2009.
Kuo, Byron Y.-L., Thomas Hentrich, Benjamin M. Good, and Mark D. Wilkinson
    2007   Tag Clouds for Summarizing Web Search Results. Paper presented at the 16th
            annual World Wide Web Conference, Alberta, Canada.
Leone, Mark P.
    1978   On Texts and their Interpretation. *Current Anthropology* 19: 664–665.
    1981   The Relationship Between Artifacts and the Public in Outdoor History Museums.
            In *The Research Potential of Anthropological Museum Collections*, edited by Anne-
            Marie Cantwell, James B. Griffin, and Nan Rothschild, pp. 301–313. Annals of the
            New York Academy of Sciences, New York.
Leone, Mark P., and Parker B. Potter, Jr.
    1992   Legitimation and the Classification of Archaeological Sites. *American Antiquity* 57:
            137–145.
Levy, Thomas
    1998   *The Archaeology of Society in the Holy Land.* Continuum Books, New York.
Markus, Robert A.
    1994   How on Earth Could Places Become Holy? Origins of the Christian Idea of Holy
            Places. *Journal of Early Christian Studies* 2: 257–271.
Ron, Amos S., and Jackie Feldman
    2009   From Spots to Themed Sites — The Evolution of the Protestant Holy Land. *Journal
            of Heritage Tourism* 4: 201–216.

— 6 —

Power of Place: Ruler, Landscape and Ritual Space at The Sanctuaries of Labraunda and Mamurt Kale in Asia Minor

Christina Williamson

Landscape is a determining factor in the numinous power of a place. The emotions which certain kinds of landscapes arouse are often channeled through religion, evident at sacred woods or rivers, for example, and especially at peak sanctuaries, commonly dedicated to a deity of supreme power. Ritual is key to tapping this power. Ritual space is equally important, as it shapes the participants' actions and frames their experiences (e.g., Dwyer and Alderman 2008; Parkin 1992; Smith 1987). Spectator events, such as sacrifices or games, take place in areas with a fixed focal point. Mobile practices such as processions, on the other hand, connect successive places of significance and require a linear kind of ritual space, such as sacred roads, but also lines of sight. Landscape and architecture thus work together to heighten awareness of place while directing the public gaze; both are powerful tools of ritual, especially in the hands of those capable of leveraging their potential.

Two sanctuaries for supreme deities in Asia Minor each underwent a metamorphosis under the authority of regional rulers: at Labraunda in Karia, the sanctuary of Zeus was completely overhauled by the Hekatomnids in the mid-fourth century B.C.; just a few generations later Philetairos of Pergamon radically changed the sanctuary of Meter Theon at Mamurt Kale (Figure 6.1). Despite their differences, both places began as open-air shrines centered on a natural phenomenon in a relatively isolated area, yet both were transfigured into monuments of power, where self-representation was intertwined with cult as the new focus. Although little is known of the actual ritual that took place at either sanctuary, its footprint may be traced, in part, through the internal space created by architecture and the locations which they occupied in the external environment, natural and human.

Taken together, topographical location and architectural layout can be indicative of how these ritual spatial contexts were used to embed ruler

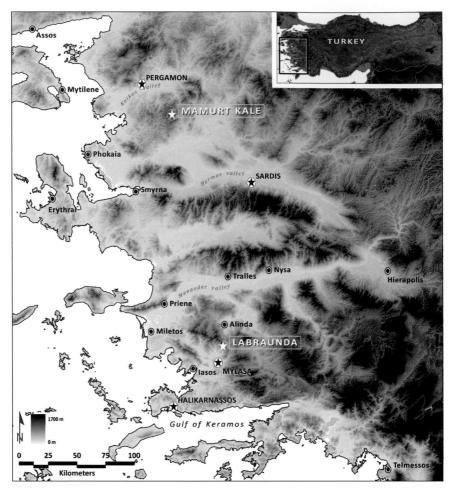

Figure 6.1   Map showing the areas of Mamurt Kale and Labraunda (Christina Williamson)

ideology in the minds of people. This paper uses ideas principally drawn from
ritual studies to give an interpretation of the intended effect underlying the
changes at these two sanctuaries.

Spectacle, focus, and ritual space

Ritual, with its emphasis on focus, memory, and repetition, and especially its
compulsory attitudes regarding rules, is one of the best means of creating a
sense of group identity and a continuity of community (Connerton 1989: 52,
70–71; McCauley and Lawson 2002: 83, 2007: 220). Public ritual typically

relies on the spectacle, the creation of vivid "flashbulb memories" that heighten the senses and thus trigger accurate recall (McCauley and Lawson 2002: 56–64). Successful rituals, then, are those that embed themselves in social memory. By making a lasting impression through ceremonies and performances, they create a common focus for the community (Connerton 1989: 41–71; Tambiah 1985). Michael Chwe refers to such public ceremonies as "rational rituals," since they generate common knowledge which is at the root of any kind of collective identity or cooperative activity (Chwe 2001). Common knowledge may consist of shared experiences, opinions, or goals, but the classic problem in rational choice theory is how common knowledge is generated, and how one can be sure that these things are truly shared. Chwe believes that public rituals are the key: by capturing everyone's attention at once, everyone understands that what they experience is experienced by all – this in itself creates common knowledge, thereby the conditions for group identity, and thereby cooperation (Chwe 2001: 3–4, 26–30).

If ceremony is central to ritual, then space is critical to its success. Parkin describes ritual as "formulaic spatiality," a physical "performance-for-someone" requiring space in which to move and spectators to witness the event (Parkin 1992: 17). Concerning Greek sanctuaries, Mylonopoulos (2006: 92–103) asserts that their architecture was indeed built for audiences to observe ritual mimetic actions, such as sacrifices or mystery rites. According to Durand, "to celebrate a rite is to do something… the spatial distribution of actors and actions, the layout of the space itself, the unfolding and organization of the series of movements, the atmosphere and geography of the rite – all are critical" (1989: 119, cited in Mylonopoulos 2006: 92 n.95).

In considering the optimal setting for "rational rituals," Chwe discusses on the one hand "inward-facing circles," such as theaters or the kivas of the Pueblos, where everyone can actually observe the main event as well as each others' reactions to what is going on (Chwe 2001: 30–33), and on the other, "progresses," or ceremonial processions, which he interprets as "saturation advertising" since the focus of the spectacle travels around to reach the widest possible audience (Chwe 2001: 20–21). This infers two kinds of ritual space relative to the nature of ritual action: concentric space, which creates a focus with an audience for stationary public rituals, such as sacrifices, prayers, or re-enactments, and linear space, which allows for kinetic rituals along trajectories, such as processions following a sacred route.[1] Defined sightlines may also be included in this category, since they literally create a shared point of view, linking the place of observation with a distant object, e.g., a natural, astronomical, or socially significant feature (Boutsikas and Ruggles 2011; Fehr 1970).

Sanctuaries are often located in places that were intuitively felt to be sacred due to some natural phenomenon (e.g., Agelidis 2009: 53; Pedley 2005: 3; Scully 1962). Using linear ritual space, via processions or sightlines, to approach or connect to these often remote places must have heightened their sensory value. Concentric ritual space, on the other hand, defined by architecture at the sanctuary, would have created both a focus for ritual and an arena for spectacle and group introspection.

The sanctuaries at Labraunda and Mamurt Kale clearly show both of these properties, albeit in different ways. Each sanctuary was devoted to a deity whose supreme authority was reflected in the setting of the cult. Each sanctuary was also radically transformed by a ruler who understood this power and the potential of space to capture the attention of their communities and channel it towards their own goals. The next section examines how concentric and linear ritual space was developed as a tool at each sanctuary, and how this may be interpreted in light of these theories.

Power and Place at Labraunda

Labraunda is located in southwest Asia Minor at the southeastern tip of the heavily eroded Beşparmak Dağları (Figure 6.1). Some 13 km north of Mylasa (modern Milas) and 14 km south of Alinda (modern Karpuzlu), the sanctuary is situated along the passage through the mountains, nestled in the southern slope at the top of a valley that overlooks Mylasa and the wider region to the south.

A large boulder dominates the cult place; split from top to bottom, the boulder has a niche on its western side, facing another large rock with steps (Figure 6.2a). This area was in all probability the original locus of a cult for Kybele, as recent excavations indicate (Karlsson in Henry et al. 2013: 298–300; Karlsson 2013). The many springs in the area, the splendid view to the south, and the strategic setting would have further added to the numinous qualities of the location. Herodotus (V.119) describes this sanctuary of Zeus as a sacred "grove of sycamore trees," where the Karians took refuge from the Persians during the Ionian revolt in the early fifth century B.C. Nothing remains of this grove, although archaeological evidence does show that there was at least a small Archaic temple, dating from the late sixth century B.C. (Thieme 1993), with a terrace just to the east. Pottery found in this area goes back to the mid-seventh century B.C., and the terracottas dating from the sixth to fourth centuries indicate the popularity of the cult even before the expansion of the sanctuary under the Hekatomnid dynasty (Karlsson 2014).

Figure 6.2 Labraunda a) View of the sanctuary with Andron A (Idrieus' andron) to the
left and the split rock to the right; b) View from Andron A with Mylasa seen
through the middle window (Christina Williamson)

Hekatomnid transformation of Labraunda

The Hekatomnids governed Karia in the fourth century B.C. as satraps
under Achaemenid (Persian) rule. Maussollos, who ruled from 377–353
B.C., and his brother Idrieus, extensively reorganized Karia: the capital was

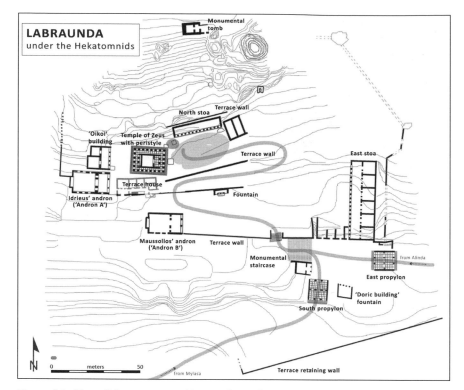

Figure 6.3   Plan of the sanctuary of Zeus Labraundos in the fourth century B.C.; the
            shaded line shows the path of ascent as indicated by Hellström 1991: Figs. 1, 4
            (map after Karlsson, et al. 2008: Fig. 2)

removed from Mylasa to Halikarnassos, several local communities were
consolidated into towns and construction work took place throughout the
region (e.g., Carstens 2009; Hornblower 1982). One of their most prestigious
achievements in this dynamic period was the transformation of Labraunda
into a monumental Karian sanctuary.

Through tremendous excavations, the hillside around the temple was
carved into cascading terraces to support a new ensemble of structures,
accessed via various staircases leading up to the top (Figure 6.3). Rather than
following the natural topography, the sanctuary was systematically aligned
with the cardinal points and the hill styled accordingly (Pedersen 1991: 101–
102). Maussollos' reorganization of ritual space coincided with his expansion
and lengthening of the festival for Zeus to five days, explicitly opening it
to all Karians (cf. Crampa 1969/1972 (abbreviated as *I.Labraunda*) 53–54
and 67, an incomplete list of names, interpreted as envoys to the festival).

The complex was clearly built to impress the worshipers as they were guided through paths and staircases along several stately buildings before they were "permitted" to approach the main ritual space before the temple (Pedersen 1991: 114–115). The sacred way led onto the first terrace, supported by an imposing retaining wall, which leveled the ground near the formal *propylaia*, or gateways, for those coming either from Mylasa (South Propylon) or Alinda (East Propylon). Beyond this, one moved up the grand staircase onto the next terrace to the west, and then immediately through a much smaller staircase to the north; this bottleneck must have created some congestion, heightening the anticipation of reaching the next level.

This next terrace in particular expanded the area of sacred space at Labraunda by some 4,200 m² in addition to the 3,000 m² of the original upper terrace (Pedersen 1991: 99). Characterized by dining facilities, the middle terrace is closed off to the east by a portico with six banqueting rooms at the back (East Stoa); each room could accommodate 11 diners in symposium. Along the northwest end was a retaining wall with a large fountain, and at the opposite, western end of this terrace was the first of two *androns*, as labeled on the architrave; these were spacious banqueting chambers, which Carstens suggests served simultaneously as reception halls (Carstens 2009: 89).[2] Andron B was built by Maussollos and would have been one of the first visible structures from the sacred way. A second *andron* (Andron A) was later built by Idrieus higher up on the terrace behind the temple; it is still visible today (Figure 6.2a). Practically overshadowing the temple itself, these grand structures each had a large niche in the back, presumed to hold statues of Zeus and dynasty members, with room for 20 dining couches (Hellström 2007: 90, 132). It has been calculated that over 100 people could have dined in symposium at Labraunda (Hellström 1989, 1996, 2007: 97–99); many more people (e.g., women and children) were probably served outside or in other areas. The quantities of tableware – both local fabrics and fine Attic black-glazed – unearthed during the excavations of the East stoa underscore this picture of widespread formal dining (Karlsson 2006). The presence of several lamps (Hellström 1965) and the ample supply of fresh water show that a large gathering could easily have camped out at the sanctuary for the greater part of a week.

While the middle terrace was designed for formal ritual dining, the upper terrace immediately east of the temple remained the core ritual space at Labraunda. One might envision the ensemble below as a grand prelude towards this climax, a concept more typical of the Hellenistic period (such as the Asklepieion on Kos, Pedersen 1991: 114–115). The upper terrace could hardly have been seen from the terraces below, heightening the sense of anticipation as one made the final approach from the east and enjoyed a full view of the temple with Idrieus' *andron* in the background. The northern area was enlarged by another retaining wall, concealed by the North Stoa. The columns of this *stoa* visually guided the eye towards the ritual center of the sanctuary – the altar and the temple, now fitted with a peristyle which continued the visual rhythm of columns. In this way the upper terrace was framed at least on these sides (the chronology and function of the building on the east side is as of yet uncertain [Hellström 2007: 103–105]). Architecturally enclosing the area in this way defined a space for an audience and provided a clear focus for the main events. This spatial arrangement created a concentric ritual space, like Chwe's "inward-facing circles," albeit not strictly in the round.

The location of monuments also help identify the critical spots, and in this period these were clustered around the temple – in fact, the space framed by the temple and the North Stoa held a statue of Hekatomnos, founder of the dynasty, and another of Ariarames, the son of Maussollos (*I.Labraunda* 27 and 28, respectively – the area is shown in dark grey on Figure 6.3). The two other inscriptions from this period were also found on the temple terrace (*I.Labraunda* 67 and 83). With its focus on ritual, but also on dynastic members, this terrace was certainly the primary ritual and public space of this sanctuary (Williamson 2011).

This combination of cult and dynasty reverberates throughout the sanctuary, as nearly all of the new or renovated structures were marked with dedicatory inscriptions by either Maussollos or Idrieus on their architraves, above the entrances where everyone could see them. Of particular interest is Maussollos' dedication: *Maussollos son of Hekatomnos gave the andron and what is inside to Zeus Lambraundos* (*I.Labraunda* 14). Like Andron A (Figure 6.2b), Maussollos' *andron* was certainly a "room with a view" as it was atypically fitted with large windows, yet on the south side alone, framing the breathtaking panorama across Mylasa and a large part of Hekatomnid territory including the mountains near Halikarnassos; surely this view was one of the most valuable things inside the *andron*.

The same panorama could be enjoyed from most of the sanctuary, but it is significant that it was occasionally framed, as was literally the case through the *andron's* windows. The linear space provided by this view, visually connecting sanctuary with city and landscape, was thus put to use in a ritual context – in this case, the act of dining by the elite who probably controlled much of Mylasa. In a broader sense, the view was also framed by the terrace architecture in general, a concept more commonly applied in the Hellenistic period.[3] Visitors at Labraunda would already find themselves surrounded by walls except for the open south side towards Mylasa. Visually accenting the view in these contexts is an example of linear ritual space in action.

Linear ritual space may also be used kinetically in processional routes, as space and perspective constantly change during travel. The sacred way, which physically connected the city and sanctuary, was also the main route of passage through the mountains. A monument in itself, this road was 7–8m wide and appears to have been paved for much of its extent, although most of it lies beneath the modern asphalt road (Baran 2011; Dursoy and Bilgin-Altınöz in Henry et al. 2013: 342–350). Running north from Mylasa, the road crossed the cultivated plain of the Sarıçay valley en route to the foothills, where it makes a gentle ascent via a north-south ridge. From here it continues up into the rocky wilderness where it was lined with tombs and punctuated by springs near the sanctuary but also beyond to the north. Being roughly midway between Alinda and Mylasa, Labraunda may well have intersected the borders of both towns' territories. The road may also have delimited the territory belonging to Mylasa and that of Olymos, on the west side of the ridge. Five watchtowers protected the route at various points along the way; most of them had sight-lines with each other and the sanctuary. A fortress was built on the hill above the sanctuary as well, reinforcing the power and strategic importance of this place.

The monumental sacred way thus transported the Mylasan community across the critical economic and political areas of their territory, giving them a wide perspective of their own place in the world and in Karia, carrying them past the tombs of those who had gone before, and affording them a spectacular view across their territory upon arrival. Usage of linear ritual space in this way surely provided a clear focus, a strong sense of identity and place, strengthening the communal bond.

Interpreting power and place at Labraunda

Ritual space was thus used at Labraunda in various ways. The construction of extensive terraces created space for a large crowd to gather, feast, and to observe the main ritual events. The view across this part of Karia created a common outlook, while the processional route literally created a locative goal shared by all as they moved together towards the sanctuary. In short, concentric and linear space was shaped to provide a ritual focus for the entire community.

Architecture played a critical role in creating this focus, as it defined and framed ritual space, guiding the actions but also the thoughts of the masses who passed through this sanctuary. It is therefore highly significant that nearly all of the structures that defined this space were conspicuously labeled with the name of either Maussollos or Idrieus. Hekatomnid identity was merged with that of Zeus Labraundos and it is difficult to discern which may have been more prominent during the rituals.

Still, why this sanctuary? Zeus Labraundos, with his signature double axe, was a militant and supreme deity with a sanctuary in a commanding position over the region. These factors must have been decisive when Maussollos began to turn the place of cult into a showcase of Hekatomnid rule. Pontus Hellström (2009), the excavator, interprets the sanctuary as a "memory theater"– everywhere one looks, one is reminded of the power of the Hekatomnids together with that of Zeus. Its garden-like setting, zigzag complexity of approach with hidden views, and large "reception halls" lead Annemarie Carstens (2009: 100) to an even more intimate interpretation of the sanctuary as an "extended palace" for the Hekatomnids, analogous to Persepolis.

Labraunda thus became a landmark of earthly and divine power. Ritual space was radically transformed to allow for ceremonial spectacle, putting this sanctuary at the center of the public eye. Following Chwe, this would have been the most effective means of generating common knowledge, thereby creating cooperation among the Karians.[4] In any event, the formula was used again a few generations later, at another sanctuary in northwest Asia Minor, that of the Mother of the Gods at Mamurt Kale.

Power and Place at Mamurt Kale

The sanctuary of Meter Theon is situated roughly 30 km southeast of the ancient town of Pergamon, in northwest Asia Minor, on Mamurt Kale, at 1066 m asl the highest peak of the Yünd Dağ massif, known in antiquity as the Aspordenon mountains. Perched on an elongated plateau, Mamurt Kale offers a breathtaking panorama of this corner of Asia Minor (Conze and Schazmann 1911: 8–9). Today the view is mostly obscured by the oak forest at the top, but between the trees one can still get a glimpse of the spectacular view.

Mamurt Kale is in itself a landmark visible from all around. The peak is a natural watershed, marking the boundaries between the modern provinces of Kınık, Manisa, and Saruhanlı. It is the source of several streams and rivers; some of the larger ancient cities that skirt the fringes of the Yünd Dağ, e.g., Gambreion, Apollonis, and Aigai, are located near heads of these valleys (Figure 6.4).

Unlike Labraunda, this sanctuary and the mountain range on which it resides is not on the way to anywhere in particular. In fact, Alfred Philippson (1910: 71) found the entire Yünd Dağ to be a massive obstacle in the region, with scarcely any population or culture. Strabo (13.2.6) describes the Aspordenon mountains in the first century B.C. as "rocky and barren," although it is full of springs and now sustains various crops, orchards, livestock, and villages.

The first clear archaeological evidence for the cult of the Mother Goddess here dates from the fifth and fourth centuries B.C. These are the several terracotta fragments, found under the temple, that show Meter on her throne within an Ionic *naiskos*, or small temple-like alcove (Töpperwein-Hoffmann

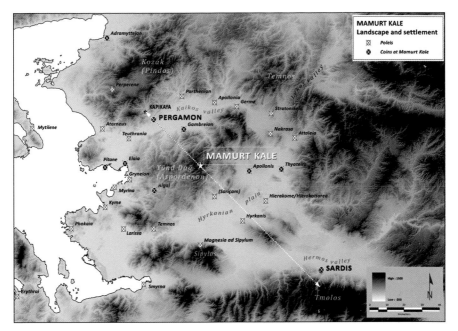

Figure 6.4   Map of Pergamene territory. The line shows the 46° angle of intervisibility
between Kapıkaya, Pergamon, and Mamurt Kale, with the Tmolos mountains
to the southeast (Christina Williamson)

1978). A *naiskos*, probably similar to those in the terracottas, actually existed
at the sanctuary for the cult image; this *naiskos* faced southeast, towards
an altar. The altar however faced northeast, perhaps reflecting an older
orientation (Schalles 1985: 27–28). A few hundred meters to the south was
a small settlement, although the chronology of this, as well as of the *naiskos*
and altar is unclear.

Philetairos' transformation of Mamurt Kale

Despite its apparent remoteness, it is precisely this peak sanctuary of Meter
that was targeted by Philetairos, the first ruler of Pergamon (282–263 B.C.)
and founder of the Attalid dynasty, for his extensive building program. This
began in town and included the temple of Athena on the acropolis and the
sanctuary of Demeter just outside the new city walls (see in general Radt
1999; Hansen 1971; Allen 1983). Philetairos was able to considerably expand
Pergamene territory under the aegis of Seleukos I, who controlled most of
Asia and Syria, including Lydia immediately to the east. In order to stabilize
the area, Philetairos patronized several communities and sanctuaries in the

region (Aigai, Kyzikos, Pitane) and abroad (Delos, Delphi, Thespiai). He furthermore transformed the open-air cult place of Meter Theon at Mamurt Kale into a monumental complex.

Philetairos' design for the sanctuary respected the existing structures and was planned around them: the altar retained its northeast orientation but was enlarged and given steps, and a complete temple encased the small *naiskos* that held the cult image (Conze and Schazmann 1911: 28–30, 33; Schalles 1985: 29–30). Surrounding this ritual center was a stoa complex in the shape of a Π (Figure 6.5a). These halls enclosed the sanctuary on the southwest, northeast, and northwest sides, creating an internal space of roughly 50 × 60 m. Meter's temple interrupted the northwest section of the stoa complex with an open gap of 2.5 to 3m on either lateral side (Conze and Schazmann 1911: Taf. I). This curious feature has been interpreted as allowing for an uninterrupted visual connection with Pergamon, as will be discussed below.

The stoa complex would have served various purposes. In the first place, it had inner chambers which could have been used for storage, or to provide shelter for the overnight stay of pilgrims. The northeast wing extended further than the southwest and the long, closed walls would also have protected the new inner space of the sanctuary, built around the altar, from the harsh north wind. This type of space, closed off on three sides, is reminiscent of the terraces at Labraunda, although the ensemble at Mamurt Kale is more rectangular; it also foreshadows the terrace architecture that would be so skillfully deployed at Pergamon nearly a century later under Eumenes II (e.g., Lehmann 1954; Radt 1993; and note 3 above). Nonetheless, as at Labraunda, the complex created concentric ritual space as it provided room for a reasonably large gathering with a clear focus on the altar and the temple rising above it.

The temple played an important role in this definition of space. Perched before the altar, it was entered by four steps that were flanked with wings, similar to the podium temples common in the Roman period (e.g., the temple of Divine Julius Caesar in Rome). Schazmann reasons that the raised front was to make up for the difference in ground levels (Conze and Schazmann 1911: 17, Taf. IV). In any event, it would have made the temple look even taller and more imposing upon approach, aided by the massive, unfluted Doric columns in the pronaos. The choice of the Doric order echoes the design of the temple of Athena on top of the Pergamene acropolis (Pedersen 2004: 417; Schalles 1985: 26), although Meter's temple had neither peristyle nor opisthodomos. Meter's pronaos was quite deep, slightly larger than the cella, and was unusually fitted with benches on all three sides, possibly for (elite) observers of the sacrifices at the altar.

Ritual space thus clearly focused on the area before the temple and around the altar, but the question remains as to the nature of the ritual itself (besides sacrifice). Pottery is not particularly helpful here since it has not yet been adequately studied as to chronology or function. It is clear, however, that despite Pergamon being one of the main ceramic centers in the region, there was a surprising scarcity of fine tableware; most of the ceramics seem to have been storage or cooking vessels (Conze and Schazmann 1911: 41). Unlike at Labraunda, formal banqueting does not seem to have been part of the ritual practice here.

The terracottas may be more informative. More than 150 specimens were found in the area of the northeast gap between the temple and the stoa. These consisted of a mixture of coarse figurines of animals, and fine depictions of Meter, usually enthroned and with lions, but also dancers, tympanum players, and actors with masks, plus a few draped figurines, mostly female – all typical for the cult of Meter/Kybele, (Töpperwein-Hoffmann 1978: 79). Ohlemutz believes that these reflect orgiastic cult practices commonly associated with Kybele (Ohlemutz 1940: 178–179). The high number of Roman lamps at the sanctuary may indicate a later shift towards more nocturnal activities, but for the Hellenistic period the terracottas and the altar are our main evidence of ritual activity.

One other source of information of what went on in this concentric ritual space concerns the honorific monuments. Although little remains of the actual dedications, at least eight rectangular rock-cut bases survive which once held stelai, probably bearing inscriptions. Two other honorific monuments were recovered: one was a statue base dedicated by Philetairos' nephew Attalos (father of Attalos I) for his wife Antiochis (Conze and Schazmann 1911: 38–39); the other was a dedication by the priestess to Attalos I, who reigned from 241–197 B.C. (Conze and Schazmann 1911: 6–7). One of the most significant inscriptions, however, is that on the architrave of the temple. Above the entrance one could clearly read: *Philetairos, son of Attalos, Mother of the Gods* (Conze and Schazmann 1911: 10, 20). Beginning with Philetairos, the Attalids were at least as prominent at Mamurt Kale as they were at sanctuaries within the city (Ohlemutz 1940: 178). As at Labraunda, ritual space here clearly served as a podium for ruler identity, at least through to the time of Attalos I (Pirson 2008: 36–37).

Concentric ritual space was thus created by this Π-shaped stoa ensemble. As mentioned above, this type of complex is particularly suitable for hillside terraces where it simultaneously articulates space while framing specific views. On the summit of Mamurt Kale, however, the architecture effectively blocked most of the view, confining the grand 360° panorama to just the open side on the southeast, and the narrow gaps left on either side of the temple. The open-air cult place at the highest point in the entire region underwent a metamorphosis that transformed it into an interior space that was largely isolated from the world – the severe blankness of the stoa walls, uninterrupted by columns, may even have had an oppressive effect. This ritual space was thus even more of an "inward-facing circle," as Chwe (2001: 30) describes it than at Labraunda.

Yet besides underscoring the focus on the altar and the temple rising above it, this effect would have added emphasis to the openings to the outside world that were available, especially on the northwest side where it was literally framed by the gaps left between the temple and the stoas. This view extended along the angle between the temple and the altar (Figure 6.5b). At 46° west of north, this was observed by the excavators to correspond exactly with the angle towards Pergamon which lay 30 km further in this same direction (Figure 6.4). This angle obviously existed already between the early *naiskos* and the altar, yet Philetairos' constriction of the view on this side through these gaps may well indicate an intentional use of linear ritual space, visually emphasizing the link with Pergamon (Agelidis 2009: 53; Fehr 1970: 31, 64; Ohlemutz 1940: 174; Schalles 1985: 26–27).

This visual line in fact continues beyond Pergamon (Figure 6.4), where it crosses the temple of Athena on the acropolis, to another sanctuary of Meter – that of Kapıkaya, located on a rocky outcrop 6 km northwest of the city (Nohlen and Radt 1978: 71; Wulf 1999: 41). Seen from Kapıkaya, Mamurt Kale truly appears to hover above the acropolis. Schalles (1985: 21) proposes that this axis was created to link Athena, the newer urban goddess, with the popular rural goddess Meter. Wulf (1999: 41–44) further suggests that this axis was even used to determine the orientation of the street grid of Philetairos' city plan for Pergamon (but see Pirson 2008: 36 for a critical note).

The goddess at Mamurt Kale is, however, actually facing the opposite direction, where the large southeast side of the sanctuary was left open. Extending the line in this direction draws it towards Mount Tmolos, just southwest of Sardis, in Lydia (Figure 6.4). On a clear day, Sardis is perceptible from Mamurt Kale, even though it is some 70 km away. Sardis had been the capital of the area under the satraps only a few generations before, and was now the seat of Seleukid rule in Lydia. Philetairos, who relied on Seleukid support, may well have used visual linear space to extend the existing orientation towards Lydia in the opposite direction, linking it to Pergamon as well.

Part of the sacred road to the sanctuary can be traced on the hill – it ascended via a broad gully along the western side, turning due north near the top where it entered the sanctuary, which would not have been visible up until this point (Figure 6.5b). From here, the worshiper would suddenly be drawn into the inner space, within the walls of the stoa, along a paved path towards the altar with the temple towering above it. Beyond this, however, precious little is

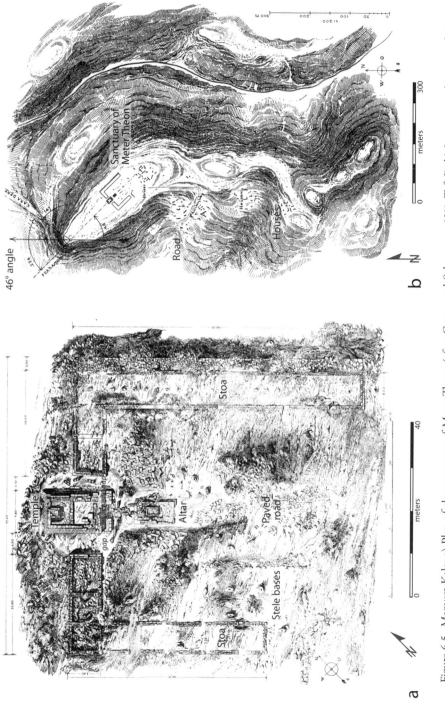

Figure 6.5   Mamurt Kale: a) Plan of the sanctuary of Meter Theon (after Conze and Schazmann 1911: Taf. I): b) Location and setting of the sanctuary, showing the 46° angle of the sanctuary (after Conze and Schazmann 1911: 11)

known about how people reached the sanctuary. Ancient roads have not yet been identified, nor is it clear whether people travelled in mass processions or individual pilgrimages. The kinetic integration of the landscape with the sanctuary through linear ritual space remains an open question, depending on the various origins of the worshipers of Meter on this mountain top.

Interpreting power and place at Mamurt Kale

As at Labraunda, ritual space was clearly put to work at Mamurt Kale. Concentric space here had an even sharper focus – the symmetry and almost abstract geometry of the blank stoa complex would have heightened the sensory effect of the temple and altar, while providing room for a sizeable crowd. Linear space was used for the sacred route, although the trajectory of this beyond the hilltop is unknown. Linear space, however, also seems to have been used to connect the sanctuary visually with Lydia, on the one hand, and Pergamon, on the other. Ritual space was thus applied in different ways to include the ruler at the center of its focus.

The location of the sanctuary of Meter Theon, at the top of the Aspordene massif and visible from all around, was surely the source of its power (on the psychological association of high places with power, see Tuan 1977: 40; Lehmann 1954). This was in itself reason enough for Philetairos to mark his presence here, beside the supreme goddess. But the political-territorial implications of his act deserve further consideration. The mountains had obviously become part of Pergamene territory, otherwise "claiming" such a commanding place would not have gone without consequences. The sanctuary crowns the horizon of several communities in the area, not just Pergamon, and many of these continued to be involved in the cult. This is indicated by the terracottas, which were made elsewhere (Töpperwein-Hoffmann 1978: 80–81), but especially by the coins found at the sanctuary – ranging from Classical to Roman, they show its scope from Adramytteion in the northwest to Sardis in the southeast, shown on Figure 6.4 (Allen 1983: 15–16; Conze and Schazmann 1911: 41–43).

The sanctuary was thus part of a wider communal network. Philetairos may well have used this sovereign cult of Meter to leverage the support, or at least goodwill, from the surrounding communities that frequented the sanctuary at the mountain top that they all had in common. In exploring this issue, Schalles observes that Philetairos' endorsement of Meter's cult, held in great esteem throughout the region, flows from his *Religionspolitik*: he brought the sanctuary into close association with Pergamon, through the visual axis, and with himself, by associating his name with hers, in the hope of connecting with the several, multifarious communities who suddenly found themselves under his rule (Schalles 1985: 29–30). This promotion may even explain the ensuing rise in Meter's popularity throughout Pergamene territory: at Kapıkaya mentioned above, on the hill just east of Pergamon (Dörpfeld 1910: 400), the 'Megalesion' just outside the city walls (Ohlemutz 1940: 181–190; Schalles 1985: 30–31), and possibly in the area on the east slope that was recently excavated (Pirson 2009: 208).

Ritual space was thus used at Mamurt Kale as a platform for ruler identity, but also for regional politics. With the several monuments for the Attalids, Mamurt Kale was certainly as much a "memory theater" as Labraunda was; the sanctuary may not have functioned as an "extended palace" but it was at least as representational as the urban public spaces in Pergamon, if not more. Philetairos' decision to present his name side-by-side with that of the Mother of the Gods in a place where all could see it for generations to come was a way to ensure his own position, literally at the highest point in the region, under her divine authority. But it was also a way of introducing himself and Pergamon as the new center of power for this region. By intertwining this ideology with the existing focus which the community already had on this cult for the Mother of the Gods, he was using one of the best advertising means available, thereby generating common knowledge.

Power of place: location, architecture, and ritual space

These two case studies show that ritual space was in itself a powerful tool that could be leveraged by rulers to create a central focus for the communities that they wished to address. For Philetairos, the peak sanctuary of Meter Theon was the fulcrum to influence the *poleis* in the newly defined territory of Pergamon, while the Hekatomnids used the sanctuary of Zeus at Labraunda to stage a spectacle for the Karian people. Yet such ritual space could not just be conjured up anywhere or at any sanctuary. Its effectiveness depended on location and architectural design.

Location was a prime consideration since both sanctuaries were already interpreted as sacred to a sovereign deity, intuitively experienced as places of power. Their commanding views over the wider environment were a central part of this and would also have held a magnetic attraction for ruling forces. At the same time they were remote for most of the participants; even just getting to the sanctuary would already have been a memorable event, whether through grand civic processions or individual pilgrimages (Chaniotis 1995: 158–160; Graf 1996; Mylonopoulos 2006: 103–108). The many bodily and emotional experiences en route – periods of rest, the springs and the tombs, natural beauty and sublime views, etc. – would have sharpened the senses and so the accuracy of the memories which would have been shared among family and friends (Connerton 1989: 41–71; Tversky 1993). The isolated location of the cult places was thus also critical to the success of what went on at them. Being far removed from urban distractions, they provided added emphasis to the ritual and gave the participants ample mental room to absorb the events during their sojourn.

Processional routes thus extended ritual space along a trajectory, marking the "correct" approach to the common place of cult and thus integrating the sanctuary with the social and physical environment. This kinetic kind of linear ritual space, moving the spectacle through the landscape for all to see or join in, was surely one of the best means of "publicity," as Chwe (2001: 20–21) indicates, creating a common focus which gave definition to the community.

Secondly, the use of architectural design was critical to the success of this association of ruler with deity. Besides giving it a representational grandeur that was suitable to the god and reflective of the ruler, monumental architecture also provided the sanctuary with additional verticality, increasing its visual function as a landmark. The vertical dimension of the architecture was further used to create spaces that were either hidden or gradually revealed at the sanctuary, as one moved towards or through it; the element of surprise was skillfully deployed in the architecture of both sanctuaries – the spatial climaxes surely enhanced the effect of "flashbulb memories" (McCauley and Lawson 2002: 56–64), and it is precisely in these spaces that one reads the name of the ruler joined to that of the deity. Signing their names to imposing architecture provided yet another mnemonic device, triggering associations and creating impressions that were carried over from generation to generation. In this sense, these sanctuaries truly were "memory theaters" (Hellström 2009).

Architectural design was thus critical for the transformation of ritual space – the goals of the ruler could thus determine the "formulaic spatiality" of ritual (Parkin 1992). As shown in the case studies, architecture was used to define spaces that, like Chwe's "inward-facing circles," had a focus which everyone could see, and which allowed everyone to observe each other's reactions (2001: 30–33). While open-air cult places would have provided the same function, the architecture of enclosure introduced by the rulers deliberately articulated this space while creating the center of attention. More than just the footprint of the festival, or public performance, these "concentric ritual spaces," as I have designated them, served to shape it and give it impetus.

Finally, architecture at the sanctuary combined with its location created a third kind of ritual space – the view. This optical kind of "linear ritual space" connected the place of cult with places of significance in the wider environment by defining the perspective through which they were seen. Architecture was used to frame these views, showing the right thing to see and the right way of seeing. In this way, a common focus was literally created as the gaze of the public eye was fixed on points of meaning to the rulers who designed architectural space.

Shaping the memorial landscape in this way of course depended on audience participation (Dwyer and Alderman 2008: 171, 174); the inherent attraction of ritual helped to ensure this. Location, architecture, and ritual space were thus all instrumental in fusing the ideology of the ruler with the identity of the sovereign deity, and forging the mental representation of the sanctuary in the minds of the community.

Conclusion

Sanctuaries such as those of Zeus at Labraunda and Meter Theon at Mamurt Kale have a natural sovereignty in the minds of their communities. Maussollos and Philetairos tapped into this energy to channel the imagination of their public towards a common focus in which they themselves were at the center of power, right next to the gods. Besides self-representation, however, ritual was used to give shape to their ideology as well. Although we may lack details on the festivals and ceremonial actions, this ideology can still be traced through spatial analyses of the architecture in combination with the landscape. The image that then appears shows that the metamorphosis of these sanctuaries was all about creating a common public focus, using several different means.

Chwe's "rational ritual" is about the way in which common knowledge was generated, and this is exactly what the rulers at both sanctuaries did: besides creating landmarks, they literally staged ritual space at these remote places. Processional routes, inward-facing spaces, and pre-defined vistas were designed for a captive audience with nowhere else to go and nothing else to distract them. Their ultimate goal was surely to harness the force of ritual combined with the power of place to create a shared identity for the community with themselves at the center. More than just a display or legitimization of power, these transformations were an attempt to actively solidify power by making it central to the cohesion of society.

Acknowledgments

I would like to thank the editors, Cecelia Feldman and Claudia Moser, for inviting me to join in this session and its inspiring discussions. Several of the results here were obtained during a research trip to Turkey in September 2010; I am grateful to the Stichting Philologische Studiefonds in Leiden for making this trip possible, as well as Felix Pirson of the DAI Istanbul for his support in Pergamon, and to Lars Karlsson and Pontus Hellström for sharing preliminary results from Labraunda. I greatly appreciate their comments on an earlier draft, as well as those by Peter Attema, Onno van Nijf, Marianne Kleibrink, and especially the editors of this volume. Any remaining errors here are entirely my own.

Notes

1 The concepts of concentric and linear space as used here are drawn from the "nodes" and "paths" described in Lynch 1960 as two of the five main elements of civic space (along with "regions", "boundaries", and "landmarks").

2 Carstens (2009: 85–89, 94–100) draws an analogy between Labraunda and Near Eastern palaces, noting the importance of royal receptions combined with banqueting, which she aptly calls "dining in paradise" (Carstens 2009: 88).

3 Pedersen (1991: 114–115) explores the possibility of Hekatomnid terrace architecture, creating a setting becoming to gods and rulers, as a conceptual prototype for Hellenistic architecture, such as the terraced Asklepeieon on Kos and the layout of Pergamon. See also Lehmann 1954.

4 The overall success of this, however, was qualified by the assassination attempt on Maussollos' life that took place during one of the festivals (Blümel 1987 [abbreviated as *I.Mylasa*] 3).

References

Agelidis, Soi
   2009 Cult and Landscape at Pergamon. In *Sacred Landscapes in Anatolia and Neighboring Regions*, edited by Charles Gates, Jacques Morin, and Thomas Zimmermann, pp. 47–54. British Archaeological Reports, International Series 2034. Archaeopress, Oxford.

Allen, Reginald Edgar
   1983 *The Attalid Kingdom. A Constitutional History*. Clarendon Press, Oxford.

Baran, Abdulkadir
   2011 The Sacred Way and the Spring Houses of Labraunda Sanctuary. In *Labraunda and Karia. Proceedings of the International Symposium Commemorating Sixty Years of Swedish Archaeological Work in Labraunda: The Royal Swedish Academy of Letters, History and Antiquities, Stockholm, November 20–27, 2008*, edited by Lars Karlsson and Susanne Carlsson, pp. 51–98. Acta Universitatis Uppsaliensis: Boreas (Uppsala Studies in Ancient Mediterranean and Near Eastern Civilizations) 32. Uppsala Universitet, Uppsala.

Blümel, Wolfgang
   1987 *Die Inschriften von Mylasa. Inschriften griechischer Städte aus Kleinasien*, Band 34–35. Rudolf Habelt, Bonn.

Boutsikas, Efrosyni, and Clive Ruggles
   2011 Temples, Stars, and Ritual Landscapes: The Potential for Archaeoastronomy in Ancient Greece. *American Journal of Archaeology* 115: 55–68.

Carstens, Annemarie

   2009 *Karia and the Hekatomnids: The Creation of a Dynasty.* British Archaeological Reports, International Series 1943. Archaeopress, Oxford.

Chaniotis, Angelos

   1995 Sich Selbst feiern? Städtische Feste des Hellenismus im Spannungsfeld von Religion und Politik. In *Stadtbild und Bürgerbild im Hellenismus. Kolloquium, München, 24. Bis 26. Juni 1993*, edited by Michael Wörrle and Paul Zanker, pp. 147–172. Vestigia 47. Beck, München.

Chwe, Michael Suk-Young

   2001 *Rational Ritual. Culture, Coordination, and Common Knowledge.* Princeton University Press, Princeton, NJ.

Connerton, Paul

   1989 *How Societies Remember.* Cambridge University Press, Cambridge.

Conze, Alexander, and Paul Schazmann

   1911 *Mamurt-Kaleh, Ein Tempel der Göttermutter unweit Pergamon,* Jahrbuch des Kaiserlich Deutschen Archäologischen Instituts. Ergänzungsheft 9. Deutschen Archäologischen Instituts, Berlin.

Crampa, Jonas

   1969 *Labraunda. Swedish Excavations and Researches. Vol. III, Part 1. The Greek Inscriptions Part I. 1–12 (Period of Olympichus).* Acta Instituti Atheniensis regni Sueciae, Series in 4°, V, III, 1. Gleerup, Lund.

   1972 *Labraunda. Swedish Excavations and Researches. Vol. III, Part 2. The Greek Inscriptions Part II. 13–133.* Acta Instituti Atheniensis regni Sueciae, Series in 4°, V, III, 2. Gleerup, Lund.

Dörpfeld, Wilhelm

   1910 Die Arbeiten zu Pergamon 1908–1909, I. Die Bauwerke. *Mitteilungen des Deutschen Archäologischen Instituts, Athenische Abteilung* 35: 346–400.

Durand, Jean-Louis

   1989 Ritual as Instrumentality. In *The Cuisine of Sacrifice among the Greeks*, edited by Marcel Detienne and Jean-Pierre Vernant, pp. 119–128. University of Chicago Press, Chicago.

Dwyer, Owen J., and Derek H. Alderman

   2008 Memorial Landscapes: Analytic Questions and Metaphors. *GeoJournal* 73: 165–178.

Fehr, Burkhard

   1970 Plattform und Blickbasis. *Marburger Winckelmann-Programm* 1969: 31–67.

Graf, Fritz

   1996 'Pompai' in Greece: Some Considerations about Space and Ritual in the Greek Polis. In *The Role of Religion in the Early Greek Polis. Proceedings of the Third International Seminar on Ancient Greek Cult, Organized by the Swedish Institute at Athens, 16–18 October 1992*, edited by Robin Hägg, pp. 55–65. Skrifter Utgivna av Svenska Institutet i Athen. 8°, Vol. 14. Paul Åströms Förlag, Jonsered.

Hansen, Esther V.

   1971 *The Attalids of Pergamon.* Cornell University Press, Ithaca and London.

Hellström, Pontus

  1965 *Labraunda. Swedish Excavations and Researches. Svenska Forskningsinstitutet i Athen.*
        Vol. II. Part 1. Pottery of Classical and Later Date, Terracotta, Lamps and Glass.
        Gleerup, Lund.

  1989 Formal Banqueting at Labraunda. In *Architecture and Society in Hecatomnid Caria.*
        Proceedings of the Uppsala Symposium 1987, edited by Tullia Linders and Pontus
        Hellström, pp. 99–104. Acta Univ. Upsaliensis. Boreas 17. Almqvist and Wiksell,
        Stockholm.

  1991 The Architectural Layout of Hekatomnid Labraunda. *Revue archéologique* 1991:
        297–308.

  1996 The Andrones at Labraynda: Dining Halls for Protohellenistic Kings. In *Basileia:*
        Die Paläste der Hellenistischen Könige. Internationales Symposion in Berlin vom
        16.12.1992 bis 20.12.1992, edited by Wolfram Hoepfner and Gunnar Brands, pp.
        164–169. Phillip von Zabern, Mainz am Rhein.

  2007 *Labraunda: A Guide to the Karian Sanctuary of Zeus Labraundos.* Ege Yayınları,
        Istanbul.

  2009 Sacred Architecture and Karian Identity. In *Die Karer und die Anderen, Internationale*
        Kolloquium an der Freien Universität Berlin, 13. bis 15. Oktober 2005, edited by
        Frank Rumscheid, pp. 267–290. Habelt, Bonn.

Henry, Olivier, Lars Karlsson, Jesper Blid, Ragnar Hedlund, Baptiste Vergnaud, Pontus
Hellström, Thomas Thieme, Agneta Freccero, Elifnaz Durusoy, Ayşe Güliz Bilgin-Altınöz,
Fatma Bağdatlı-Cam, Axel Frejman, and Pascal Lebouteiller

  2013 Labraunda 2012: rapport préliminaire. *Anatolia Antiqua* 21: 285–355.

Hornblower, Simon

  1982 *Mausolus.* Oxford University Press, Oxford and New York.

Karlsson, Lars

  2006 *Labraunda: Preliminary Reports. The 2006 Season,* Electronic document, http://www.
        labraunda.org/Labraunda.org/ Report_2006_eng.html, accessed September 30,
        2010.

  2013 The Sanctuary of the Weather God of Heaven at Karian Labraunda. In *Perspectives*
        on Ancient Greece: Papers in Celebration of the 60th Anniversary of the Swedish
        Institute in Athens, edited by Ann-Louise Schallin, pp. 173–189. Skrifter utgivna av
        Svenska Institutet i Athen, Stockholm.

  2014 The Terracottas from Labraunda. In *Figurines de terre cuite en Méditerranée orientale*
        grecque et romaine: Production et diffusion, iconographie et fonction. Colloque
        international, Izmir 2–6 juin 2007, edited by Ergun Lafli and Arthur Muller, in press.

Karlsson, Lars, Olivier Henry, and Jesper Blid

  2008 A Preliminary Report on the Swedish Excavations. *Istanbuler Mitteilungen* 58:
        109–133.

Lehmann, Phyllis Williams

  1954 The Setting of Hellenistic Temples. *The Journal of the Society of Architectural*
        Historians 13: 15–20.

Lynch, Kevin

  1960 *The Image of the City.* Technology Press, Cambridge, MA.

McCauley, Robert N., and E. Thomas Lawson

2002 *Bringing Ritual to Mind: Psychological Foundations of Cultural Forms*. Cambridge University Press, Cambridge.

2007 Cognition, Religious Ritual, and Archaeology. In *The Archaeology of Ritual*, edited by Evangelos Kyriakidis, pp. 209–254. Cotsen Institute of Archaeology, University of California at Los Angeles, Los Angeles.

Mylonopoulos, Joannis

2006 Greek Sanctuaries as Places of Communication through Rituals: An Archaeological Perspective. In *Ritual and Communication in the Graeco-Roman World*, edited by Eftychia Stavrianopoulou, pp. 69–110. *Kernos* Supplement. Centre International d'Étude de la Religion Grecque Antique, Liège.

Nohlen, Klaus, and Wolfgang, Radt

1978 *Kapıkaya: Ein Felsheiligtum bei Pergamon*. Walter de Gruyter, Berlin.

Ohlemutz, Erwin

1940 *Die Kulte und Heiligtümer der Götter in Pergamon*. Giessen, Würzburg.

Parkin, David

1992 Ritual as Spatial Direction and Bodily Division. In *Understanding Rituals*, edited by Daniel de Coppet, pp. 11–25. Routledge, London and New York.

Pedersen, Poul

1991 *The Maussolleion at Halikarnassos. Reports of the Danish Archaeological Expedition to Bodrum, 3: The Maussolleion Terrace and Accessory Structures*. Aarhus University Press, Aarhus.

2004 Pergamon and the Ionian Renaissance. *Istanbuler Mitteilungen* 54: 409–434.

Pedley, John Griffiths

2005 *Sanctuaries and the Sacred in the Ancient Greek World*. Cambridge University Press, Cambridge and New York.

Philippson, Alfred

1910 Reisen und Forschungen Im Westlichen Klein-Asiën. *Petermanns Mitteilungen Ergänzungsheft* 167. Gotha, Justus Perthes.

Pirson, Felix

2008 Das Territorium der hellenistischen Residenzstadt Pergamon: Herrschaftlicher Anspruch als raumbezogene Strategie. In *Räume der Stadt: Von der Antike bis Heute*, edited by Cornelia Jöchner, pp. 27–50. Reimer Verlag, Berlin.

2009 Pergamon. *Archäologische Anzeiger* 2009/1 Beiheft: 206–214.

Radt, Wolfgang

1993 Landscape and Greek Urban Planning: Exemplified by Pergamon and Priene. In *City and Nature: Changing Relations in Time and Space*, edited by Thomas Møller Kristensen, pp. 201–209. Odense University Press, Odense.

1999 *Pergamon: Geschichte und Bauten einer antiken Metropole*. Wissenschaftliche Buchgesellschaft Darmstadt, Darmstadt.

Schalles, Hans-Joachim

1985 *Untersuchungen zur Kulturpolitik der Pergamenischen Herrscher im dritten Jahrhundert vor Christus*. Wasmuth, Tübingen.

Scully, Vincent Joseph

    1962   *The Earth, the Temple, and the Gods: Greek Sacred Architecture*. Yale University Press, New Haven.

Smith, Jonathen Zittel

    1987   *To Take place: Toward Theory in Ritual*. Chicago Studies in the History of Judaism. University of Chicago Press, Chicago.

Tambiah, Stanley Jeyaraja

    1985   *Culture, Thought, and Social Action: An Anthropological Perspective*. Harvard University Press, Cambridge, Mass.

Thieme, Thomas

    1993   The Architectural Remains of Archaic Labraunda. In *Les grands ateliers d'architecture dans le monde égéen du VIᵉ siècle av. J.-C.: actes du colloque d'Istanbul, 23–25 mai 1991*, edited by Jacques des Courtils and Jean-Charles Moretti, pp. 47–55. Varia Anatolica 3. De Boccard, Paris.

Töpperwein-Hoffmann, Eva

    1978   Die Terrakotten von Mamurt Kale. In *Kapıkaya: Ein Felsheiligtum bei Pergamon. Altertümer von Pergamon XII*, edited by Klaus Nohlen and Wolfgang Radt, pp. 77–89, Taf. 34–37. Walter de Gruyter, Berlin.

Tuan, Yi-fu

    1977   *Space and Place: The Perspective of Experience*. University of Minnesota Press, Minneapolis.

Tversky, Barbara

    1993   Cognitive Maps, Cognitive Collages, and Spatial Mental Models. In *Spatial Information Theory: A Theoretical Basis for GIS*, edited by Andrew U. Frank and Irene Campari, pp. 14–24, Lecture Notes in Computer Science. Springer Verlag, Berlin.

Williamson, Christina

    2011   Public Space Beyond the City: The Sanctuaries of Labraunda and Sinuri in the Chora of Mylasa. In *Public Space in the Postclassical City*, edited by Chris P. Dickenson and Onno M. van Nijf, pp. 1–36. Caeculus: Papers on Mediterranean Archaeology and Greek and Roman Studies 7. Leuven, Peeters.

Wulf, Ulrike

1999   Vom Herrensitz zur Metropole. Zur Stadtentwicklung von Pergamon. In *Stadt und Umland: Neue Ergebnisse der Archäologischen Bau- und Siedlungsforschung. Bauforschungskolloquium in Berlin vom 7. bis 10. Mai 1997 Veranstaltet vom Architektur-Referat des DAI*, edited by Ernst-Ludwig Schwandner and Klaus Rheidt, pp. 33–49. Phillip von Zabern, Mainz.

Transforming the Surroundings and its Impact on Cult Rituals: The Case Study of Artemis Mounichia in the Fifth Century

Chryssanthi Papadopoulou

The Sanctuary of Artemis Mounichia

The sanctuary of Artemis Mounichia was constructed on a limestone hill to the southwest of the harbor of Mounichia, the smallest of the three Piraeus harbors (Figure 7.1), and was in use from the ninth century B.C. until the second or third centuries A.D. (Palaiokrassa 1991). Its main cult was that of Artemis Mounichia, while a secondary cult of Mounichos, an Athenian hero, might have also been housed there (Palaiokrassa 1991: 91). The entrance to the sanctuary was on the northwestern side (Palaiokrassa 1991: 50). Two roads led to that entrance: one from the agora of the Piraeus, which was adjacent to one of the most densely populated areas of the Piraeus, and the second road led from the harbor (Figure 7.1). There was also another entrance – possibly dated to the fifth century B.C. – that led to the sanctuary directly from the harbor (Palaiokrassa 1991: 34).

Artemis Mounichia and Initiation Rites

The Attic months were named after Attic festivals. Mounichion, one of the four Attic months named after Artemis' festivals, attests to the existence of a festival for Artemis Mounichia dated to at least the seventh century B.C., when this Attic month was possibly "baptised" (Trümpy 1997: 18–19).

The cultic persona of Artemis Mounichia and the character of her festival can be inferred from textual evidence mentioning a cult and votive offerings from her sanctuary in Mounichia. According to later sources (Pausanias, Ἀττικῶν ὀνομάτων συναγωγή; Suda), the Athenians harmed a bear in the sanctuary of Artemis Mounichia and a plague fell on the city as punishment. In order for the plague to stop, someone had to sacrifice his daughter to Artemis. Embaros hid his daughter in the sanctuary and sacrificed a goat,

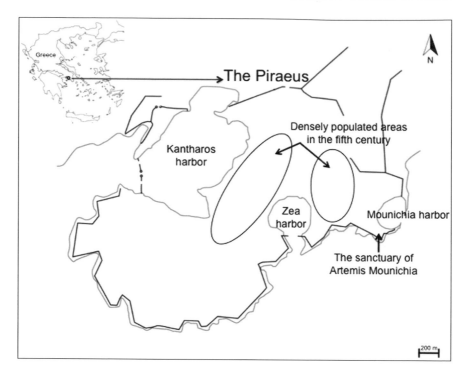

Figure 7.1   The Piraeus peninsula with its three ports, the location of the sanctuary of
             Artemis Mounichia, the wall circuit and the area that was densely populated in
             the fifth century.

which he dressed up as his daughter, in her place. This *aition* (justification)
for the sacrifice is similar to the myths connected to Brauron and the festival
of the *Arkteia*, which also mention the killing of a bear and Artemis' anger at
this act. It has therefore been argued that the rites performed in Mounichia
were similar to those performed in the sanctuary of Artemis in Brauron
(Cole 2004: 204–205; Giuman 1999: 186–190; Hollinshead 1980: 59–60;
Palaiokrassa 1991: 92–93; Parker 2005: 238–239; Perlman 1983: 120; Scanlon
1990: 90; Sourvinou-Inwood 1988: 112; Vernant 1991: 215–216). Also, a
scholiast of Aristophanes (*Scholia in Aristophanem, Scholia in Lysistratam* verse
645) wrote that the *arktoi*, the girls that participated in the *Arkteia*, sacrificed
to both Artemis Brauronia and Mounichia, thus verifying that similar rites
were performed in both sanctuaries, at least for a time.

The connection between the rites for Artemis Brauronia and Artemis
Mounichia is enhanced by the similarity of the votive offerings excavated
in their two sanctuaries (Kahil 1963: 13–14, 1965: 24; Palaiokrassa 1991:

77). Fragments of statues and statuettes of young boys and girls found in Mounichia are very similar to those from Brauron and date from at least the sixth century B.C. and continue until Roman times (Palaiokrassa 1991: 51–53, 54, 58). Also, miniature kraters (*krateriskoi*), votive offerings characteristic of Artemis, have been excavated in both these sanctuaries with similar iconographic schemata (Palaiokrassa 1991: 77). These small pots were often decorated with scenes of young girls dancing or running towards an altar (Giuman 1999: 44; Hamilton 1989: 449–458; Hollinshead 1980: 42; Kahil 1965: 20–22, 1983: 237; Palaiokrassa 1991: 77–78). These types of offerings are connected to rites performed by maidens and in particular initiation rites – scholars have even suggested that they depict the rite of the *Arkteia* – and have thus been employed in the identification of the rites performed in Mounichia and the nature of the deity housed there (Giuman 1999: 185; Kahil 1965: 24; Palaiokrassa 1991: 92–94; Parker 2005: 231 n.59; Scanlon 1990: 75; Sourvinou-Inwood 1988: 68–69 n.7). It should be noted that these *krateriskoi* come from the first half of the fifth century B.C., which has led scholars to believe that, even in this century, Artemis Mounichia was connected to initiation rites. Thus, textual evidence and votive offerings connect Artemis Mounichia with Artemis Brauronia and its initiation rites. Nonetheless, the date and duration of this cultic function are not clear and it may not have been practiced in the fifth century.

Artemis, like her brother Apollo, was a deity who looked after the transition of children into adulthood (Parker 2005: 231, 427–428; Vernant 1990: 152–157, 1991: 198–201) and, in particular, she was very closely connected to the transition of maidens into womanhood (Cole 2004: 209–212; Schachter 1992: 49–51; Vernant 1990: 152–157). In Athens, Artemis Brauronia oversaw the transition of maidens to a marriageable stage and her major festival in Brauron, the *Arkteia*, became a central polis festival in the Classical period (Parker 2005: 245; Sourvinou-Inwood 1988: 116–117). Thus, in Athens this prominent Artemisian function further underscores the interpretation of Artemis Mounichia as an *ephebic* deity (a deity presiding over the transition of children to adulthood).[1]

The location of her sanctuary on the hill of Mounichia further strengthens this hypothesis. As mentioned above, the sanctuary could be dated as early as the ninth century B.C. From that time, we have no archaeological traces of a settlement area in the Piraeus peninsula (Garland 2001: 14; Travlos 1988: 341–342). This lack of evidence for early habitation may be a by-product of the fact that this location has been densely inhabited from the Classical period onwards and is currently overbuilt, thus preventing a thorough understanding of its architectural past. Nonetheless, an excavated Geometric cemetery in Palaia Kokkinia, to the north of the peninsula, indicates that settlement in the wider Piraeus area was in decline from the late Geometric period and until the sixth century B.C. (Garland 2001: 11). Thus, at the time that the sanctuary in Mounichia was established, in the ninth century, and continuing into the subsequent three centuries, signs of habitation in the Piraeus are limited and suggest that the peninsula was a non-urban area (Dowden 1989: 32). Of importance is also the fact that, at that time, the peninsula was unfortified and therefore susceptible to an attack from the sea.

The oldest generation of sanctuaries, such as that of Artemis Mounichia, were located in borderland areas and quite often near the sea (de Polignac 1995: 38–39; 1994: 6). Artemis was the deity most frequently worshipped in such suburban sanctuaries, and often in areas vulnerable to enemy attacks since she was a deity who overlooked boundaries and points of contact (Cole 1998: 27–29; de Polignac 1995: 36, 44; Redfield 1990: 129). Besides, it was often the case for a sanctuary's location to be in accordance with the function of the divinity housed in it (Cole 2004: 15). Thus, Artemis' cults in these borderland sanctuaries were of similar character and the rites performed within these sanctuaries were suitable to take place in marginal areas. Rites taking place in liminal areas, otherwise called *eschatiai*, were commonly connected to *ephebes* and maidens and marked their initiation to adult life (de Polignac 1995: 38–39, 56; Vernant 1991: 209; Vidal-Naquet 1981: 150).

Girls before reaching womanhood and a marriageable age, were perceived as wild, untamed, and thus ritually liminal (Endsjo 2000: 351). It was therefore appropriate for them to hold a festival in a liminal place, void of social order, such as the uncultivated borders of a city-state.[2] The remoteness of the surroundings mirrored the marginal state of the participants in the festival. In this context, the word marginal denotes the state prior to social acceptance, in other words, the state preceding that of a wife and a mother who are subordinate to a husband (Osborne 1985: 168; Scanlon 1990: 106; Sourvinou-Inwood 1990: 54). Also these sanctuaries, located at a city-state's boundaries, were vulnerable to enemy attacks and implicated in accounts of boundary disputes (Herodotus 6.138.1; Cole 2000: 472). The lack of safety of the young "untamed" girls performing those rites in "dangerous" areas effectively contradicted the security inside of the walls of the city, where social order prevailed and the women were integrated into society (Cole 1998: 28). It should also be noted that women at a marriageable age were considered sick, unless they got married. Hippocrates wrote that virgins can get headaches (*Prorrheticon* 2.30.33–36), suffer from their liver (*De natura muliebri* 3.3–5; *De mulierum affectibus* 127.3–5), or even go insane (*De superfetatione* 34.1–6). It was natural for such strange, sickly creatures to perform their rites in borderland places. This was an indirect way for the girls to experience the consequences they would face if they refused to be initiated into womanhood.

In sum, the location of the sanctuaries of Artemis near borders and in marginal areas was appropriate to the character of the girls' rites performed there. Thus, the ancient sources regarding the *aition* for a sacrifice to Artemis Mounichia, the votive offerings found in her sanctuary, and the location of that sanctuary, all point in the same direction regarding the cultic function of Artemis Mounichia. She presided over the transition of maidens into womanhood and initiation rites would take place in her sanctuary (Burkert 1985: 263; Hollinshead 1980: 59–60; Palaiokrassa 1991: 92–93; Parker 2005: 209; Sourvinou-Inwood 1988: 23, 112, 116).

However, what has not yet been examined is the duration of this cultic function and any restrictions that might have been imposed on it in the course of the sanctuary's operation. Scholars imply that the rites taking place in the sanctuary remained unaltered for the whole of the sanctuary's life. However, this sanctuary was unsuitable to house such cults after the sixth century B.C. Until the sixth century B.C. the sanctuary was placed at the border of Attika, near the sea, where it would have been susceptible to enemy attacks, and where the rites performed by the young girls would have been out of sight, maintaining their initiatory and thus secret character. I argue that the cult persona of Artemis Mounichia changed drastically in the fifth century B.C. Therefore, this century needs to be examined separately in regard to the cultic needs that this deity was required to fulfil.

Evidence of Change in the Sanctuary of Artemis Mounichia

In the fifth century B.C. the habitation pattern of the Piraeus peninsula changed drastically, altering completely the surroundings of the sanctuary of Artemis Mounichia. As mentioned above, for the first three centuries of the life of the sanctuary, there are few indications of a nearby settlement. Firm evidence regarding the habitation of the Piraeus peninsula dates to the end of the sixth century B.C. Thus, at the time of the Kleisthenic reforms, in the last decade of the sixth century, the Piraeus was represented in the *Boule* (Council) by nine *bouleutai*, which indicates that the Piraeus was one of the most populated Attic *demes* (Garland 2001: 59). Yet the real boost in its population came after the Persian Wars, with settlement increasing rapidly towards the middle of the fifth century. During that time, the Piraeus may have been as densely populated as the entire Athenian *asty* (city-center) (Garland 2001: 58–61). In the middle of the fifth century, Perikles assigned the architectural organization of the Piraeus to Hippodamus of Miletus (Aristotle *Politics* 1267b). Unlike evidence from the previous periods, excavated remains of houses attest securely to the habitation of the peninsula in the Classical period (Von Eickstedt 1991: 97–112; Travlos 1988: 342). Also, a number of *horoi* (boundary markers), contemporary with the Hippodamian development of the Piraeus, testify to the existence and extent of the inhabited area (Garland 2001: 140–141). *Horoi*, akin to modern street signs, were placed on the exact location that they were defining. *Horos IG I² 894*, located by the Mounichia hill, informs us of the hill's extent, thus implying that the area beyond the boundary marker, to the northwest of this hill, was not marked as sacred territory. This indicates that this region either was inhabited or, due to its secular nature, available for habitation (Garland 2001: 225).

It is only natural for the population in the Piraeus to have increased considerably in the fifth century. The development of the three harbors turned Piraeus into a trade hub, which in turn lured foreigners to emigrate there in order to make the most of their trading operations. Besides, Athens had ensured the monopoly of grain from the Black Sea which would have established the Piraeus as one of the most visited ports in the Aegean (Hopper 1979: 74). At the same time that the peninsula was becoming densely populated, walls were constructed to protect the harbors, their facilities, and the population. These walls also encompassed the sanctuary of Artemis (Palaiokrassa 1991: 43). In the fifth century, the sanctuary turned from an extra-urban place of worship into a central sanctuary for the polis of the Piraeus. The sanctuary of Artemis Mounichia was now located within the Piraeus walls and on a hill overlooking the developed harbor of Mounichia and the settlement area, which possibly extended as far as its northwestern slope (Figure 7.1). The area where the sanctuary was located could no longer be considered liminal or an *eschatia*, because the wall circuit integrated it in the Piraeus *asty* (Endsjo 2000: 358–359). As a result, in the fifth century, the location of the temple, which would have been visible to the population of the Piraeus, elevated Artemis Mounichia's cult to one of the primary Piraean cults (Garland 2001: 104). This fifth-century location was clearly no longer suitable to accommodate initiation rites.

Results of the Transformation of the Piraeus

The Mounichia Harbor and Hill

The harbor of Mounichia was the smallest of the three Piraeus harbors, housing 82 shipsheds in the fourth century B.C. (Garland 2001: 95–96). Excavations in this harbor have shown that such structures were already present in the fifth century (Lovén 2011: 45–50). The sanctuary of Artemis on Mounichia hill, which prior to the Kleisthenic reforms overlooked an un(der)developed bay, in the fifth century acquired a view of possibly extensive naval facilities. Additionally, this military harbor was identified with the epithet of the deity, since it was called Mounichia harbor. According to ancient authors (Aelius Herodianus, *De prosodia catholica* 3.1; Hellanicus, *Fragmenta Jacoby* 1a, 4, F 42a), the entire area of the sanctuary took its name from Mounichos, while Pausanias (I.1.4) suggests that the area took its name from Artemis Mounichia, after the goddess had acquired that cult epithet from Mounichos. Regardless of the origin of the toponym, it is clear that the Athenians identified the deity with the same epithet with which they identified a military harbor.

The hill of Mounichia, where the sanctuary of Artemis was also located, was of strategic importance for both the Piraeus and Athens. Plutarch (*Solon* 12.10) wrote that when Epimenides of Phaestos saw Mounichia he remarked that "if the Athenians knew the troubles that this area could cause to the city of Athens, they would eat it out with their own teeth." Perhaps the obviousness of this observation was the reason behind Hippias' attempt to fortify the hill at the end of the sixth century B.C. – for which attempt we only have literary evidence. Instead, material evidence securely attests to Mounichia's fortification in the fifth century by Themistocles (Travlos 1988: 340). The hill of Mounichia is high enough to have provided views over a large part of the Piraeus peninsula and the Athenian *asty*. The functionality of this hill was obviously noted by the Athenians, since the hill was occupied by their enemies, the Megarians, and later on used as an Athenian garrison (Diodorus Siculus 14.33.1).

The sanctuary of Artemis Mounichia in the fifth century did not only overlook naval facilities, but it also occupied a location of strategic importance. Additionally, after the fifth-century development of the Piraeus, this location became of even greater importance. Apart from Athens, the Mounichia hill also provided views of the densely populated Piraeus peninsula, the well-used narrows between the Piraeus and Salamis and a large part of the entrance to Athens by ships sailing north from the Saronic Gulf. The location of her sanctuary could not have gone unnoticed by the Athenians and it played a part in the new attributes she was given in the fifth century.

Artemis Mounichia and the Harbor

According to Demosthenes (18.107), *trierarchs* (commanders of the triremes) would make petitions or supplications "in Mounichia." Not mentioning the goddess Artemis in these dedications suggests that it was unnecessary to do so, because her sanctuary by the fourth century B.C. was the most prominent landmark of this harbor, and the goddess a well-known patron of the Athenian navy and its officials. Also, it shows that there was a close link between the area and the sanctuary, since the former was enough to define the latter. This connection is enhanced by Kallimachos, who in his third-century *Hymn to Artemis* (line 259), called Artemis Mounichia *limenoskopos* (observer of the port), textually linking Artemis Mounichia to the military port. Naturally, these testimonies might reflect primarily fourth century functions and notions which were not known in the fifth century. Nonetheless, they are indications of the dynamic changes in the cult of Artemis Mounichia throughout the time of the function of her sanctuary.

The Persian Wars

The changes in the prominence of Artemis Mounichia's sanctuary and cult in the fifth century are also related to the general popularity of Artemisian cults in fifth-century Athens. Artemis Agrotera was one of the deities to whom the Athenians sacrificed prior to the battle of Marathon (Garland 1992: 55, 70; Mikalson 2003: 30; Parker 2000: 308–309). They also promised to sacrifice one goat for every Persian they would kill in battle. However, the number of dead Persians was so unexpectedly high that the Athenians could not find enough goats and, instead, instituted an annual festival on the sixth of the month of Boedromion, during which goats were sacrificed to Artemis as a commemoration of her assistance in their military victory (Aristotle, *Athenaion Politeia* 58.1; Plutarch, *De Herodoti malignitate* 862B.9–13). Artemis also helped the Athenians in the naval battle of Salamis; according to Plutarch (*De gloria Atheniensium* 349.f), Artemis shone with a full moon and thus helped the Greeks win the *naumachia* (naval battle), because they were able to see the Persian fleet and estimate its size. Her intervention was celebrated annually by the Athenians on the sixteenth of Mounichion at her sanctuary in Mounichia, which overlooked Salamis and thus the battlefield (Garland 1992: 72; Vernant 1991: 247–248). Again, according to Plutarch (*Themistocles* 22.1), after the battle of Salamis, Themistocles invented a new cult epithet for Artemis. That epithet, *Aristoboule* (of the best judgement), reflected her successful advice in the Persian Wars and Themistocles' foresight in choosing Salamis as a suitable battleground.

As a hunting goddess, Artemis was closely connected to war and the Athenians associated her powers with their own victories in the Persian Wars (Burkert 1985: 151–152; Parker 2005: 400; Vernant 1990: 165–166, 1991: 203–204, 244–257). As a result, Artemis became a very popular deity in fifth-century Athens (Shapiro 1989: 65; Simon 1983: 86). During this period, her sanctuary on the Akropolis was repaired and enlarged (Giuman 1999: 55; Hurwit 1999: 158, 195, 197–198; Travlos 1971: 124). Additionally, older, major, extra-urban temples of Artemis were restored and extended after the damages they suffered by the Persians, because of the increased popularity of the cults they housed.[3] Finally, new temples were constructed honouring the goddess.[4] During this phase of reassessment of Artemis' persona, the deity's sphere of influence was expanded so as to include the Athenian navy; a new festival was instituted for Artemis Mounichia, commemorating the naval victory in Salamis, and thus, for the first time in Athens, a maritime *aition* was invented for a festival honoring Artemis.

The Fifth-century Rites of the Mounichia Festival

The new festival instituted for Artemis Mounichia commemorated the fact that she shone with a full moon over the Greek and Persian navies in Salamis. The evidence we have for the rites taking place during this festival comes from ancient authors. Thus, we know that on the sixteenth of Mounichion the Athenians would hold a procession to the sanctuary of Artemis Mounichia and offer her round cakes with a candle in the middle called ἀμφιφῶντες (shining all around), which symbolized the moon (Pausanias, Ἀττικῶν ὀνομάτων συναγωγή: ἀμφιφῶντες; Plutarch, *De gloria Atheniensium* 349.f). While the sources mentioning this festival date from the first and second centuries A.D., the *aition* for this festival is nonetheless connected to the battle of Salamis. Therefore, this festival should be dated to the early fifth century. Garland (1992: 176) writes that this festival was instituted in 479 B.C. and this date is indeed plausible, since it follows the Persian Wars.

The battle of Salamis, which was commemorated in this procession, had taken place in the month of Boedromion, seven months earlier than the time of its annual celebration (Simon 1983: 81). Yet the Athenians chose to celebrate it in the month of Mounichion. Therefore, I argue that the sixteenth of Mounichion was chosen because there was a pre-existing festival for Artemis Mounichia on that day, possibly the Mounichia, which was reinterpreted or even reorganized to incorporate this new protecting facet of the deity – her assistance in the battle of Salamis (Garland 1992: 72; Mikalson 2003: 76; Parker 1996: 187). Thus, the disassociation between the chosen date and the battle of Salamis is a clear indication that the Athenians wished to reinterpret and alter the character of the previous festival of Artemis Mounichia. As a result, in the fifth century, the state festival of Artemis Mounichia changed from one involving initiation rites into one celebrating the naval battle of Salamis. It was a festival celebrating a naval victory over which the Athenians had presided and the deity who influenced its outcome.

Inscriptions attest that the festival of the Mounichia included rites with ships (*IG* II² 1006; Hesperia 16: 170, 67; *IG* II² 1011; *IG* II² 1028; *IG* II²

1030). In particular, five inscriptions mention *ephebes* sailing around the port of Mounichia on the occasion of the Mounichia festival. Unfortunately, these inscriptions are not contemporary with the period in concern, since they date to the late second and early first centuries B.C. Also, these rites are not connected to an *aition* related to a dated historic event, which could indicate a *terminus post quem* for their institution. While, the fifth century might appear as a reasonable date for the institution of this rite, we lack the necessary evidence to establish this. Therefore, we cannot exclude the possibility that this rite was instituted in the second century B.C., the earliest date attested to by the inscriptions. Garland's (2001: 114) assertion that the rites with the ships should have been a later addition to the Mounichia is indeed plausible. Thus, due to the lack of substantial evidence regarding its contemporaneity, this rite, despite its relevance to the Athenian navy, will not be used in my assessment of the cultic persona of Artemis Mounichia in the fifth century.

The Rites Excluded from the Fifth-Century Mounichia Festival

So far, I have examined the rites performed in Mounichia prior to the fifth century, the transformation of Artemis Mounichia's sanctuary in the fifth century and the new festival that was instituted for the deity in the same century. Now I shall return to both the *aition* mentioned above, which connects Artemis Mounichia with Artemis Brauronia and initiation rites, and to the votive offerings that highlight this connection, in order to show that both these forms of evidence do not reflect the character of the fifth-century Mounichia festival, which was the celebration of the naval victory in Salamis.

The sources mentioning the *aition* for Embaros' goat-replacing-daughter sacrifice do not offer us the name of the festival with which this rite was associated. Nonetheless, because the Embaros story could date as early as the Mounichia festival, since at least the seventh century B.C., it is fitting to connect this rite with this festival. This conclusion is enhanced by the character of the rite (substitution of a human with an animal sacrifice), which clearly points to a festival of an early date (Garland 2001: 113; Parke 1977: 138). However, this association was interrupted in the fifth century, since Plutarch (*De gloria Atheniensium* 349.f) states that the Mounichia festival celebrated the victory in the battle of Salamis. Therefore, it is reasonable to assume that since the battle of Salamis, in the early fifth century, the Mounichia festival was re-considered and altered. Nonetheless, the rites connected to Embaros' sacrifice come to us from sources postdating the fifth century and the reinterpretation of the Mounichia festival. I argue that these sources are describing the older festival on the sixteenth of Mounichion, which was abandoned in favour of the new, fifth-century cult for Artemis Mounichia. This is the reason why the name of the festival at which these rites were performed is nowhere mentioned. Yet the *aition* of the older, abandoned cult survived and was attested in the sources because of its resemblance to the Artemisian cult in Brauron, which remained unaltered in the fifth century. Summing up, the survival of the *aition* of the old Mounichia festival cannot, on its own, lead us to interpret the fifth-century festival of the Mounichia as an initiation festival.

Similarly, even though the previously mentioned miniature kraters depicting young girls walking or running towards an altar are dated to the first half of the fifth century (Palaiokrassa 1991: 80–81), we should not interpret this as an indication that initiation rites took place in Mounichia in this century. It was often the case that there was a lack of differentiation of offerings for certain goddesses such as Hera and Artemis (de Polignac 1995: 26). This means that the dedications were often not indicative of the nature of the state or local cult of the recipient deity. These *krateriskoi* seem to be a characteristic offering for Artemis and were found in most of her Attic sanctuaries, regardless of the rites performed there. It has also been suggested that these *krateriskoi* could be dedications by families who did not have their girls participate in the *Arkteia*. Instead, these families would dedicate these offerings as a substitute service, because their girls were not there in person (Parker 2005: 234). If this were the case, then the spread and popularity of these offerings is most effectively explained. We should not read more into them; these offerings cannot indicate the precise rites that took place in all of the sanctuaries in which they were found. It was common for an individual to make a personal offering to a deity regardless of the specific cult housed in that particular sanctuary. Women and their families made dedications to Artemis prior to marriage and before and after giving birth, and their offerings would be welcomed in all sanctuaries of Artemis. Thus, in the fifth century, these *krateriskoi* could have been offerings reflective of the previous cult function of Artemis Mounichia or even of the current cult function of Artemis Brauronia. Proof of that is the fact that these *krateriskoi* have also been found on the Akropolis, in the Athenian Agora and in the cave of Pan, places where we know that no initiation rites were performed (Kahil 1965: 23–24, 1977: 87–87, 1979: 79, 1981: 261, 1983: 237).

In summary, the fifth-century dating of the miniature kraters found in Mounichia and the stories of the *aition* of Embaros' sacrifice do not contradict the character of the fifth-century Mounichia festival, as attested by Plutarch and analysed above. The *krateriskoi* and the *aition* related to Embaros' sacrifice cannot overshadow the fact that the state cult of Artemis

Mounichia was reinterpreted in the fifth century, owing to the drastic change in the surroundings of her sanctuary and the contemporary reassessment of Artemis' persona due to her successful involvement in the Persian Wars.

Conclusions: The Cult of Artemis Mounichia in the Fifth century

In the fifth century, the surroundings of the sanctuary of Artemis Mounichia changed completely: the sanctuary became intra-mural and one of the central sanctuaries of the Piraeus *asty*. The habitation of the Piraeus peninsula increased considerably, possibly extending as far as the sanctuary's northwestern slope. The harbor of Mounichia developed into a military harbor with naval installations. These changes in its surroundings necessarily affected the rites performed in the sanctuary, rendering it an inappropriate place for the accommodation of initiation rites, the cultic activity that possibly took place there prior to the Persian Wars. Because of the fifth-century changes in the cityscape of the Piraeus, these rites would have been visible from the Piraeus *asty* and the Mounichia harbor, that is in plain view of the nearby inhabitants and mariners (Figure 7.2). The initiatory and thus private character of these rites, which included nudity, would have been jeopardized. Also, initiation often involved ritual death (de Polignac 1995: 61; Redfield 1990: 120). It is unlikely that such rites would have been performed within the city's walls, when graves – even of notable Athenians – were carefully placed outside the Long Walls (the walls connecting Athens with the Piraeus). Perhaps this was one of the reasons that the festival of the *Arkteia* performed in the sanctuary of Artemis in Brauron became a central polis cult in the fifth century and its importance was elevated (Sourvinou-Inwood 1988: 115–116). It was a countermeasure for the fact that the sanctuary of Artemis in Mounichia could no longer house this festival.

Nonetheless, the archaeological record points to a fifth-century connection between Artemis Mounichia and maidens. The finds from the Piraean sanctuary continue to be rich in offerings related to marriage. The miniature kraters disappeared in the second half of the fifth century and the figurines decreased in number, but some of the offerings that replaced them were also connected to marriage, for example *lebetes gamikoi* (Palaiokrassa 1991: 53, 59, 66–68, 81–82). However, in this case, the dedications made in Mounichia by maidens should be viewed similarly to those found in the Brauronion on the Akropolis. They were related to the *Arkteia*, but they were not an indication of the performance of this festival in these locations. In the sanctuary of Artemis Mounichia, these offerings belong in the sphere of popular cult and perception and not state cult. They were indications of the prominence of the Panhellenic persona of Artemis as patron deity of initiation, as well as the prominence of the Athenian state cult of the *Arkteia*. They underscore the

Figure 7.2 Image from a boat entering the modern port of Mounichia (Mikrolimano). The
area of the temple of Artemis Mounichia, which was located at the exact place,
where the white building (Yacht Club of Greece) on the top of the hill stands
today, is clearly visible as it would have been in antiquity (I. Sapountzis)

individual's choice and convenience for the dedication of a private offering,
but do not represent a state institution. Therefore, these offerings were not
indications of the state cult of Artemis Mounichia, the rites performed at the
Mounichia festival, and thus the full extent of the cultic persona of Artemis
Mounichia in fifth-century Athens.

In sum, the fifth-century transformation of the surroundings of the
sanctuary created a gap in the sanctuary's role in Athenian state cult. This gap
could be filled only through the acquisition of new attributes by the occupant
of the sanctuary. This meant that different aspects of the cultic persona of
Artemis Mounichia needed to be brought to the foreground, so that a new
state festival could be instituted for this deity. According to Sourvinou-
Inwood (2000: 20), historical circumstances could change the religious
system of a polis. Artemis' persona in Athens after the Persian Wars acquired
a new meaning. Until then, Artemis was a deity with the potential to assist in
battle. After 480 B.C., having proven herself in practice, Artemis was elevated
to a trustworthy protector of Athens. Artemis Mounichia was connected to
the naval battle of Salamis in particular. This event was used as an *aition* for
the institution of the new festival that filled the gap of the cultic function
of her sanctuary. Thus, the historical circumstances in the period after the
Persian Wars directed the reinterpretation of Artemis Mounichia's persona
and the placing of emphasis on her patronage of the Athenian navy.

Sourvinou-Inwood (2000: 18) also noted that the connection between a
deity and a place could lead to placing emphasis on a particular and most

relevant aspect of this deity. Artemis Mounichia was connected to the harbor of Mounichia, which was named after her. The location of her sanctuary led the Athenians to emphasize her connection to the newly developed military harbor and the nearby-stationed Athenian navy; they might have even constructed a new entrance to the sanctuary, which led there directly from the harbor so that it could be visited by disembarking mariners (Palaiokrassa 1991: 34). As mentioned above, the hill where the sanctuary was located was of strategic importance. It offered a view to the new fifth-century naval installations, the entrance to the harbor, and a large part of the Saronic Gulf. The mariners on board the triremes entering the Piraeus would see her sanctuary from a distance, and at the same time the deity would have a view of her protégés. This location, which prior to the fifth century was remote, extra-mural and of limited political importance since there was no military harbor under it, suddenly became a look-out point for both the Athenians and Artemis. Thus, the transformation of the place called for a shift in emphasis to a newly-invented maritime aspect of Artemis Mounichia and, in particular, to a contemporary connection between the deity and the Athenian navy. According to Feld's (1996: 91) insightful remark that "as places make sense, senses make place," Mounichia no longer made sense for housing initiation rites and the senses (views to and from the military harbor, sounds of mariners hauling and launching triremes, the sound of the *auletes* [piper] keeping the pace of the rowers on board the triremes, etc.) of fifth-century Athenians rendered this place appropriate for the accommodation of a naval cult instead.

Acknowledgments

I would like to thank the panel organisers and volume editors Claudia Moser and Cecelia Feldman. I am very grateful to Dr. Karim Arafat (King's College London) and Dr. Hugh Bowden (King's College London) for their comments and advice.

Notes

1   For a different opinion regarding the connection between the *Arkteia* and initiation, see Burkert (1996: 75).

2   For an opposite opinion regarding liminal spaces, see Faraone (2003: 46) and Polinskaya (2003: 91–93).

3   See Hollinshead (1980: 32–39) and Travlos (1988: 55) for Brauron, Hollinshead (1980: 70, 73) for Halai Araphenidai, and Palaiokrassa (1991: 49) for Mounichia.

4   See Travlos (1971: 112–113) and Camp (2001: 105–106) for the temple of Agrotera, and Garland (1992: 73, 77) for the temple of Aristoboule.

References

Burkert, Walter

  1985   *Greek Religion.* Harvard University Press, Cambridge.

  1996   *Creation of the Sacred: Tracks of Biology in Early Religions.* Harvard University Press, Cambridge.

Camp, John McKesson

  2001   *The Archaeology of Athens.* Yale University Press, New Haven.

Cole, Susan Guettel

  1998   Domesticating Artemis. In *The Sacred and the Feminine in Ancient Greece,* edited by Sue Blundell and Margaret Williamson, pp. 27–43. Routledge, London.

  2000   Landscapes of Artemis. *The Classical World* 93: 471–481.

  2004   *Landscapes, Gender, and Ritual Space: The Ancient Greek Experience.* University of California Press, Berkeley.

de Polignac, François

  1994   Mediation, Competition and Sovereignty: The Evolution of Rural Sanctuaries in Geometric Greece. In *Placing the Gods: Sanctuaries and Sacred Space in Ancient Greece,* edited by Susan E. Alcock and Robin Osborne, pp. 3–18. Clarendon Press, Oxford.

  1995   *Cults, Territory and the Origins of the Ancient Greek City-State.* Chicago University Press, Chicago.

Dowden, Ken

  1989   *Death and the Maiden: Girls' Initiation Rites in Greek Mythology.* Routledge, London.

Endsjo, Dag Øistein

  2000   To Lock Up Eleusis: A Question of Liminal Space. *Numen* 47: 351–386.

Faraone, Christopher A.

  2003   Playing the Bear and the Fawn for Artemis: Female Initiation or Substitute Sacrifice? In *Initiation in Ancient Greek Rituals and Narrative: New Critical Perspectives,* edited by David B. Dodd and Christopher A. Faraone, pp. 43–68. Routledge, London.

Feld, Steven

  1996   Waterfalls of Song: An Acoustemology of Place Resounding in Bosavi, Papua New Guinea. In *Senses of Place,* edited by Steven Feld and Keith H. Basso, pp. 91–135. School of American Research, Santa Fe.

Garland, Robert

  1992   *Introducing New Gods: The Politics of Athenian Religion.* Duckworth, London.

  2001   *The Piraeus from the Fifth to the First Century B.C.* Bristol Classical Press, London.

Giuman, Marco

  1999   *La dea, la vergine, il sangue: Archeologia di un culto femminile.* Longanesi, Milano.

Hamilton, Richard

  1989   Alkman and the Athenian Arkteia. *Hesperia* 58: 449–472.

Hollinshead, Mary Brooks Berg
  1980 Legend, Cult and Architecture at Three Sanctuaries of Artemis. Ph.D. dissertation, Bryn Mawr College, Pennsylvania. University Microfilms, Ann Arbor.

Hopper, Robert John
  1979 *Trade and Industry in Classical Greece.* Thames and Hudson, London.

Hurwit, Jeffrey M.
  1999 *The Athenian Acropolis: History, Mythology and Archaeology from the Neolithic Era to the Present.* Cambridge University Press, Cambridge.

Kahil, Lilly Ghali
  1963 Quelques vases du sanctuaire d'Artemis à Brauron. *Antike Kunst* Supplement 1: 5–29.
  1965 Autour de l'Artémis attique. *Antike Kunst* 8: 20–33.
  1977 L'Artémis de Brauron, rites et mystère. *Antike Kunst* 20: 86–98.
  1979 La déesse Artémis: mythologie et iconographie. In *Greece and Italy in the Classical World. Acta of the XI International Congress of Classical Archaeology*, edited by Nicholas John Coldstream and Malcom A.R. Colledge, pp. 73–87. The National Organizing Committee, London.
  1981 Le "cratérisque" d'Artémis et le Brauronion de l'Acropole. *Hesperia* 50: 253–263.
  1983 Mythological Repertoire of Brauron. In *Ancient Greek Art and Iconography*, edited by Warren G. Moon, pp. 231–244. University of Wisconsin Press, Wisconsin.

Lovén, Bjørn
  2011 *The Ancient Harbours of the Piraeus: The Zea Shipsheds and Slipways.* 1.1: *Architecture and Topography. Monographs of the Danish Institute at Athens* 15.1.1. Aarhus University Press, Aarhus.

Mikalson, Jon D.
  2003 *Herodotus and Religion in the Persian Wars.* University of North Carolina Press, Chapel Hill.

Osborne, Robin
  1985 *Demos: The Discovery of Classical Attika.* Cambridge University Press, Cambridge.

Palaiokrassa, Lydia
  1991 *Το ιερό της Αρτέμιδος Μουνιχίας. Αρχαιολογική Εταιρεία*, Athens.

Parke, Herbert William
  1977 *Festivals of the Athenians.* Thames and Hudson, London.

Parker, Robert
  1996 *Athenian Religion: A History.* Clarendon Press, Oxford.
  2000 Sacrifice and Battle. In *War and Violence in Ancient Greece*, edited by Hans van Wees, pp. 299–314. Duckworth, London.
  2005 *Polytheism and Society at Athens.* Oxford University Press, Oxford.

Perlman, Paula
  1983 Plato *Laws* 833c–834d and the Bears of Brauron. *Greek, Roman and Byzantine Studies* 24: 115–130.

Polinskaya, Irene
  2003 Liminality as Metaphor: Initiation and the Frontiers of Ancient Athens. In *Initiation*

in Ancient Greek Rituals and Narrative: New Critical Perspectives, edited by David B. Dodd and Christopher A. Faraone, pp. 85–106. Routledge, London.

Redfield, James

1990   From Sex to Politics: The Rites of Artemis Triklaria and Dionysos Aisymnetes at Patras. In *Before Sexuality: The Construction of Erotic Experience in the Ancient Greek World*, edited by David M. Halperin, John J. Winkler and Froma I. Zeitlin, pp. 115–134. Princeton University Press, Princeton.

Scanlon, Thomas Francis

1990   Race or Chase at the Arkteia of Attika? *Nikephoros* 3: 73–120.

Schachter, Albert

1992   Policy, Cult, and the Placing of Greek Sanctuaries. In *Le sanctuaire grec: huit exposés suivis de discussions*, edited by Albert Schachter, Emily Kearns, Birgitta Bergquist, Fritz Graf, Madeleine Jost, Folkert T. van Straten, Roland Etienne, and Richard Allan Tomlinson, pp. 1–57. Vandœuvres, Genève.

Shapiro, H. Alan

1989   *Art and Cult Under the Tyrants in Athens*. Philipp von Zabern, Mainz.

Simon, Erika

1983   *Festivals of Attica: An Archaeological Commentary*. The University of Wisconsin Press, Wisconsin.

Sourvinou-Inwood, Christiane

1988   *Studies in Girls' Transitions: Aspects of the Arkteia and Age Representation in Attic Iconography*. Kardamitsas, Athens.

1990   Lire l'*arkteia* – lire les images, les textes, l'animalité. *Dialogues d'histoire ancienne* 16: 45–60.

2000   What is *Polis* Religion? In *Oxford Readings in Greek Religion*, edited by Richard Buxton, pp. 13–37. Oxford University Press, Oxford.

Travlos, John N.

1971   *Pictorial Dictionary of Ancient Athens*. Thames and Hudson, London.

Travlos, John N.

1988   *Bildlexikon zur Topographie des antiken Attika*. Ernst Wasmuth Verlag, Tübingen.

Trümpy, Catherine

1997   *Untersuchungen zu den altgriechischen Monatsnamen und Monatsfolgen*. C. Winter, Heidelberg.

Vernant, Jean-Pierre

1990   *Figures, idoles, masques*. Julliard, Paris.

1991   *Mortals and Immortals: Collected Essays*. Princeton University Press, Princeton.

Vidal-Naquet, Pierre

1981   The Black Hunter and the Origin of the Athenian *Ephebeia*. In *Myth, Religion and Society*, edited by Richard Lindsay Gordon, pp. 147–162. Cambridge University Press, Cambridge.

Von Eickstedt, Klaus Valtin

1991   *Beiträge zur Topographie des antiken Piräus*. Αρχαιολογική Εταιρεία, Athens.

The Sacred Houses in Neolithic Wansan Society

CHIH-HUA CHIANG AND YI-CHANG LIU

This paper explores the multifaceted meanings of the houses in Neolithic Wansan society in Taiwan. We argue that the houses in the Wansan society might provide an example with which to challenge the common approach in archaeological research of viewing sacred and profane spaces as distinct from each other (Bradley 2003). The Neolithic Wansan society is situated in the northeastern part of Taiwan (Figure 8.1). The excavation of the site reveals the presence of houses and numerous utilitarian artifacts related to people's daily lives. More importantly, archaeological evidence of the mortuary practice, the burials, has also been recovered in proximity to these residential houses. Based on ethnographic research, mortuary rituals are often closely associated with the practice of ancestral worship (Bloch 1995; Waterson 1990). The Wansan example thus offers archaeologists an opportunity to explore possible ritualistic meanings of the houses.

The perspective which regards sacred space as being set apart from domestic areas in the landscape not only distorts scholars' understandings of prehistoric society by projecting current social conditions on the past, but also impedes scholars from exploring the process of how people interact with the landscape and construct their sense of the place both through ritual and daily practices in the domestic sphere. Increasingly, investigations of several ancient societies have revealed that the domestic sphere was often imbued with sacred power by the performance of the so-called "domestic rituals" (Bradley 2003, 2005; Gonlin and Lohse 2007; Plunket 2002). Richard Bradley argues about prehistoric domestic spaces in Europe that:

> This scheme is entirely a product of modern assumptions about the past in which ritual and religious belief are separated from the everyday. As the settlements of the British Iron Age show, that need not be the case. There seems no reason to insist that shrines should have been set apart from domestic buildings or that they should have been located at conspicuous points in the landscape [Bradley 2003: 11].

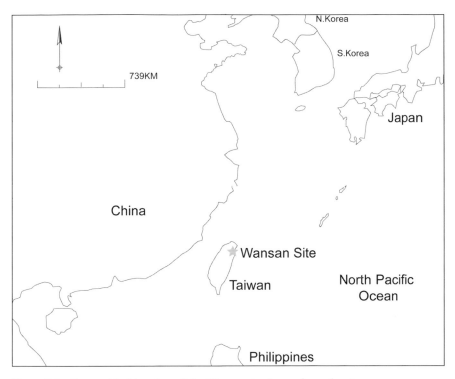

Figure 8.1   Geographical location of the Wansan site (image by authors)

In this paper, we use the example of Wansan society to illustrate that houses play important roles both in peoples' daily and ritual lives. First, we introduce the concept of house society (developed from rich ethnographic research) to demonstrate that, in some societies, houses can be more than simply physical structures for providing protection. Houses can also be places where important ritual activity is practiced and where the ancestors reside. A house also constitutes a focal point of economic, social, ritual, and political life. The ample ethnographic work conducted in these house societies offers archaeologists an interpretive framework with which to explore the possible ritual meanings of residential houses (e.g., Carsten and Hugh-Jones 1993; Fox 1993; McKinnon 1991; Waterson 1990). We utilize these ethnographic examples, especially the discussion of the close link between mortuary rituals and ancestral worship, to explore sacred aspects of houses in prehistoric Wansan society through examining the spatial association of possible house structures, mortuary practices, and utilitarian artifacts. Our research on this small-scale Neolithic settlement is a testament to the fact that the separation of domestic and sacred needs to be re-examined and cannot be automatically assumed in archaeological research. To the Wansan people, the landscape they engaged with on a daily basis consisted of both profane and sacred meanings where ritual and daily practices were spatially and conceptually intertwined.

House Society: the Sacred House

The concept of the house society developed within socio-cultural anthropology is both the inspiration of our study of prehistoric Wansan society and simultaneously its point of departure. Originally proposed by Lévi-Strauss in the 1970s, a house is defined as:

> a corporate body holding an estate made up of material and immaterial wealth, which perpetuates itself through the transmission of its names, its goods, and its titles down a real or imaginary line, considered legitimate as long as this continuity can express itself in the language of kinship or of affinity and, most often, both [1982: 174].

Although Lévi-Strauss' original attempt is to offer another social form to categorize societies without clear kinship systems, his proposal opened up a new field of research. This new understanding of the importance of physical houses in the process of social formation has redirected anthropologists' attention toward exploring the various roles that houses can play in human social and ritual life (Beck 2007; Carsten and Hugh-Jones 1995; Gillespie and Joyce 2000; Sparkes and Howell 2003). The most promising research for this study is a series of ethnographic work conducted in the Austronesian-speaking societies[1] in Southeast Asia.

In these Austronesian-speaking societies, the house is the prominent feature of the landscape in terms of both its social function and its ritual significance. As defined by Lévi-Strauss (1987: 152), the house possesses a domain consisting of material and immaterial wealth and even includes goods of supernatural origin. As in the Kalauna houses in Papua New Guinea, the fist-sized black stones stored inside the house are considered to be inhabited by ancestral spirits (Young 1993). In several Austronesian-speaking societies, the house is thus often regarded as a "repository of ancestral objects that provide physical evidence of a specific continuity with the past" (Fox 1993: 1). More specifically, as Fox (1993) illustrated, certain structures inside the house, such as certain posts, beams, altars, and platforms are activated as "ritual attractors" where rituals are routinely performed to signify their close connection with the ancestors of the houses (see also McKinnon 1987, 1995).

In addition, the Austronesian houses are often regarded as living things, and the characteristics of the house are often expressed in anthropomorphic terms in local languages (Ellen 1986: 26; Fox 1993; Waterson 1990). As a living entity, the house passes through different stages of the life cycle, which is emphasized in terms of various ritual ceremonies. In the Iban longhouse in Indonesia, for example, "space is transformed by rituals of birth and death from the familiar mundane setting of everyday social life to a symbolically organized landscape, displaying basic social distinctions and mirroring a series of superimposed realities, both seen and unseen" (Sather 1993: 103). In other words, this physical house structure becomes more than a shelter for people's daily activities. It is also a place infused with multiple meanings and where rituals are constantly performed.

The house is viewed as incorporating multiple facets of human daily life (e.g., economic, ritual, social, and political) (Carsten and Hugh-Jones 1995; Fox 1993; McKinnon 1991; Sparkes and Howell 2003), this challenges traditional assumptions that the uses and meanings of residential houses are always excluded from the sacred realm. Based on ethnographic research, various activities closely related to the formation and continuation of social house groups can be recognized as ritual actions which can be observed archaeologically – the placement of deceased ancestors associated with residential structures (e.g., Chesson 1999; Düring 2007; Lopiparo 2007), the building and rebuilding processes of house structures (e.g., Gerritsen 2007; Tringham 2000), and objects possibly related to rituals such as ceramic vessels (e.g., Chiu 2003; 2005; Heitman 2007; Lopiparo 2007).

Among these house-related practices mentioned above, in this paper we focus on the relationship between the space of people's daily activities and the place where they bury their ancestors. The ethnographic work conducted in the house societies indicates that one of the most significant ritual activities is the one that emphasizes the connection to the house ancestors, especially mortuary rituals. Ethnographic research on several Austronesian-speaking societies reveals how the ritual recognition of ancestors is tied to the construction of social identity and the delimitation of a corporate group. These rituals can occur at the level of an entire community, but also for individual residential groups (Adams 2005; Waterson 1990). Waterson (1990: 209) also observes that in several societies, the sense of closeness between the living members with the house ancestors is prominent. One of the common practices was to bury the deceased house members inside or in close physical association with domestic houses. For the house members, the deceased were often transformed into ancestors; and burials in close proximity to the domestic sphere can serve as a reference point to maintain the spatial continuity between the living house members and their ancestors

(Grove and Gillespie 2002: 13). Gillespie concludes that:

> The deposition of burials or parts of human remains on house land, with or
> without the building of elaborate tombs, and the use of heirloomed costume
> ornaments and other valuables that are indexical signs of ancestral personages are
> means by which archaeologists can demonstrate the perpetuation of the house
> [Gillespie 2007: 35].

The continuous existence of the social house-group is reinforced by the
group's claim of connection with the house ancestors. Through referencing
these indexical signs, this strong presence of ancestors in the house, thus, can
transform an ordinary house into a place with sacred power.

Sacred Houses in Taiwan

The close relationship between residential houses and burials is evident in
most of the archaeological sites in Taiwan. This particular relationship has
survived for thousands of years in Taiwan. The distribution of burials in
several prehistoric societies is closely associated with the houses – either under
the house floors, such as at Peinan (Lien 2008) and Ciyubing sites (Chen
1994), or around the houses, such as at the Wansan site (Liu 2000, 2002).

In addition, the practice of burying the deceased family members inside
or close to the house has also been an important tradition in most of the
indigenous societies of Taiwan until the early twentieth century. The earliest
evidence of this practice in Taiwan can be traced back to the first Neolithic
culture, the Tapenkeng culture, around 5,000 years ago (Tsang et al. 2006).
Although the deeper meaning and significance of this practice in prehistoric
Taiwanese societies has not yet been explored, ethnographers have already
pointed out the apparent relationship between the house and burials in
several Taiwanese indigenous societies. As in the contemporary Bunun
society in central Taiwan, Huang (1986: 380) argues that "family members
confirm their right to inherit the land by burying their deceased members
inside the house. Their house represents the society, and the acquiring of
the house signifies their identity in the society." His observation resonates
with the understanding of other Austronesian-speaking societies in Southeast
Asia where the ritual recognition of the ancestor is connected with the
demarcation of a corporate group and the creation of social identity.

Furthermore, the members of contemporary Paiwan society, another
indigenous society in Southern Taiwan, also connect with the past by
burying their deceased members inside the houses in which they are still
living (Chiang 1999: 383). These house members demonstrate their claim to
house property ownership by making the connection with its past through

the burying of deceased relatives inside the house floor. Thus, the continuity of the house and the lineage of the family that resided in the house are sealed through this process.

These aforementioned archaeological and ethnographic examples clearly demonstrate a close connection between houses, burials, and ancestors in Taiwan. The house society concept thus offers a framework within which to explore the possible multifaceted meanings of houses in prehistoric Wansan society. In the following sections, we examine the importance of the ritual and domestic roles that the houses play in prehistoric times. As discussed above, burials associated with houses signify important ritualistic practices that are intended to highlight the connection between the living and the dead. More importantly, this act of placing the deceased house members around Wansan houses enhances the sanctity of the houses themselves and possibly transforms the residential houses into "holy houses" (e.g., Kirch 2000).

The second role of the house that we will analyze is its domestic aspect. The artifacts associated with daily life include various tools and ceramic vessels at the Wansan site. The discovery of these utilitarian objects on the site implies that this is where the occupants conducted their daily lives. Thus, it is now necessary to examine the types of activities the residents of each house might carry out regularly.

The Wansan Society

The Wansan site is located on an isolated hill in the northeastern part of Taiwan facing the Pacific Ocean. The main habitation area, where an abundance of artifacts were concentrated, is towards the top of the hill where the terrain is flatter. The site has been excavated several times in the 1990s, generating 39 radiocarbon dates which suggest that it was occupied from 3,700 to 2,700 years ago (Liu 2000, 2002).[2]

The Sacred Houses

At the Wansan site there is no definitive evidence for standing structures which can be identified as houses. Therefore, we established the presence of houses based on the distribution of the postholes as indicators of dwellings at the Wansan site. According to ethnographic work conducted on indigenous architecture in Taiwan, there are three types of residential dwellings: the pile-dwelling, the ground building, and the semi-subterranean dwelling (Chijiiwa 1960). Regardless of which of the three common types of residential houses are constructed, wooden posts are the basic, common, consistent component of all the three types of domestic architecture. After setting up the wooden posts as the main structure, different materials are used to assemble each dwelling. Therefore, when clusters of postholes are uncovered from archaeological sites, they are considered to be indications of the existence of houses.

Two possible mortuary practices have been uncovered from the Wansan site (both practices involving exotic goods). One practice was to place the corpse inside a box-shaped container made out of slate. The second type of practice was to position the body of the deceased in a large jar. Although only two forms of burial practices have been identified, there are variations within these practices in terms of the shape and size of the object used for deposition. The slate used to construct the container is imported from neighboring mountains, and the source of the clay to make the jar burial is also located outside of the Wansan hill. Both of the materials for creating slate coffins and jar burials were exotic to the local Wansan people. Consequently, the preparation and actual burying activities required certain efforts for the arrangement and organization of the mortuary practice. Also, the presence of certain grave goods carrying symbolic meanings further enhanced the importance of this process, such as the presence of a jade zoo-anthropomorphic object. As mentioned above, the dead person was probably converted into an ancestor as a result of mortuary rituals, and the burials within or adjacent to the houses could create spatial proximity between the living house members and their ancestors (Grove and Gillespie 2002; Waterson 1993, 2000). Therefore, we argue that the burials at the Wansan site could serve as a significant place for ancestral ritual activity.

In order to examine the relationship between the houses and burials, we superimposed the distribution of postholes, stone coffins, and jar burials on the same map (Figure 8.2). Since the presence of postholes can be used to argue for the presence of house structures, several posthole clusters can be identified as areas where a group of ancient house structures might have been constructed. Once the location of houses has been established, it is possible to identify a pattern of burials positioned to encircle the houses.

The lack of standing architecture for house structures impedes archaeologists from examining whether people practiced any intentional house modification or demolition at the Wansan site. Nevertheless, the spatial association of posthole clusters with burials illustrates that prehistoric Wansan people not only utilized the same location for constructing the houses over hundreds of years, but also intentionally placed their deceased members in close proximity to their houses. In other words, houses were not building structures meant to provide the living inhabitants with shelter. The houses were also places for connecting the ancestors to the living members of the house.

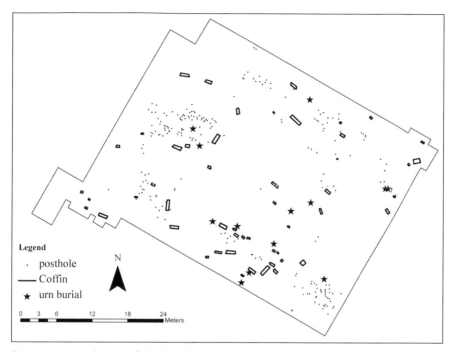

Figure 8.2 Distribution of the burials and postholes at the Wansan site (image by authors)

Furthermore, assembling slate coffins and making jars for the dead suggests a series of decision-making processes and negotiations between individuals and groups. For example, the materials to make the coffins and jars are not locally available; thus, the descendents of the deceased had to travel and exchange with other societies to acquire the proper materials. The time and energy spent on preparing and conducting the mortuary rituals signified the importance of the ancestral veneration in the society. Unlike their houses built from perishable materials, these stones and jars used for burials were made from durable materials which lasted much longer than the houses. While these houses might deteriorate after abandonment, the permanent marker, burials, served as enduring evidence of the presence of the ancestors. In prehistoric Wansan society, a house must have been a prominent feature of the landscape for the living like it is in other Austronesian societies in Taiwan and Southeast Asia. These houses, which members could encounter on a daily basis, not only stood out in the landscape, but also the mortuary rituals conducted around the houses further infused this landscape with spiritual power where the ancestors were omnipresent.

The Residential Houses

The excavation of the Wansan site not only uncovered several burials and postholes, but also unearthed abundant pottery and lithic artifacts, including storing, cooking, and serving vessels and a variety of weaving, hunting, fishing, farming, and tool production equipment. All of these artifacts are closely related to daily activities. Based on the lithic assemblages, the Wansan people practiced hunting, fishing, wood-working, land clearing, and harvesting activities. Also a variety of ornaments, such as bracelets, earrings, and necklaces played an important role in their daily life. Moreover, the concentration of artifacts implies that prehistoric Wansan people discarded their broken vessels and tools in certain areas close to the houses. Even though these "dumping" areas were probably outside of the houses, they are still quite near the houses. The types of discarded artifacts associated with each house revealed the possible activities that occurred within the houses. To explore whether these identified localities for house construction are also where people conducted the activities of their daily lives, we distinguished and compared the concentrations of lithic and ceramic artifacts (Figure 8.3). Each artifact concentration is associated with the different possible house localities (identified in the previous section) and is named according to locality – I, II, III, IV, V, and VI, respectively. Figure

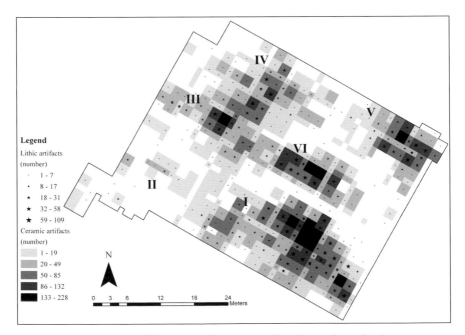

Figure 8.3   Distribution of the lithic and ceramic artifacts (image by authors)

8.3 illustrates the six main artifact concentrations in association with the postholes. Based on the distribution of postholes and burials, it seems that the area in the southwest corner (II) probably can be identified as one locality where houses might exist. However, recent road construction removed most of the cultural layer in this area. Therefore, the following analysis excludes the data from this locality.

Table 8.1 shows the numbers and relative frequencies of ceramic artifacts from each locality. Table 8.2 demonstrates the numbers and relative frequencies of lithic artifacts from each locality. Lithic artifacts associated with tool production and ceramic vessels are the most common artifact type in each location, clearly demonstrating that each locality consists of similar types of artifacts.

The presence of similar artifact types associated with these identified house localities suggests that similar activities occurred in each space. Most artifact types – ground and chipped stone tools and ceramic vessels and tools – are present in every locality. These artifacts indicate that the daily activities conducted by prehistoric Wansan people included hunting, fishing, land clearing, woodworking, tool production, harvesting, and weaving. Even though similar activities were practiced in the majority of places, emphasis on specific activities in particular places can be determined. Lithic tool production and maintenance is the most general activity; artifacts associated with tool production, such as whetstones, lithic debitage, and preforms, were predominant in each locus.

In conclusion, the repeated occurrence of basic activities indicates that the inhabitants of each house probably organized themselves as an independent social and residential unit to carry out certain repetitive activities necessary for daily life. Crafting activities, such as weaving or ornament making, and

		Vessel	Spindle whorl	Bracelet	Figurine	Knife	Unclear	Total
Locality I	Number	10,733	52	7	1	1	165	10,959
	RF	97.9%	0.4%	0.0%	0.0%	0.0%	1.5%	100.0%
Locality III	Number	4890	40	21	3	1	52	5007
	RF	97.7%	0.8%	0.4%	0.0%	0.0%	1.0%	100.0%
Locality IV	Number	1595	21	25	-	-	23	1664
	RF	95.9%	1.2%	1.5%	-	-	1.4%	100.0%
Locality V	Number	3,686	18	5	2	-	38	3,749
	RF	98.5%	0.4%	0.1%	0.0%	-	0.9%	100.0%
Locality VI	Number	4,538	27	6	-	-	22	4593
	RF	98.8%	0.5%	0.1%	0.0%	0.0%	0.8%	100.0%

Table 8.1   Number and relative frequencies of ceramic artifacts. (RF refers to the relative frequencies in each locality)

Possible function unfunction	Tool		Locality I	Locality III	Locality IV	Locality V	Locality VI
Cutting	Knife	Number	98	32	12	33	20
		RF	3.4%	2.6%	3.1%	4.6%	3.0%
Earth-clearing	Hoe-axe	Number	163	69	26	37	44
		RF	6.0%	8.3%	6.6%	12.3%	7.0%
Expedient	Scraper	Number	26	8	2	1	5
		RF	1.2%	1.0%	0.5%	0.3%	0.8%
Fishing	Net Sinker	Number	147	78	33	36	57
		RF	5.3%	9.4%	8.4%	12.0%	8.6%
Harvesting	Multiperforated Tool	Number	274	52	24	44	65
		RF	9.5%	6.3%	6.1%	5.8%	10.0%
	Polished Perforated Disk	Number	57	13	7	22	7
		RF	1.9%	1.6%	1.8%	7.3%	1.0%
	Polished Disk	Number	11	1	3	1	2
		RF	0.4%	0.1%	0.8%	0.3%	0.3%
	Sickle	Number	12	2	2	2	2
		RF	0.5%	0.2%	0.5%	0.6%	0.3%
Hunting	Arrow	Number	101	37	24	22	39
		RF	3.3%	4.5%	6.1%	2.1%	6.1%
Ornament	Bracelet/earring	Number	175	82	49	38	73
		RF	7.4%	9.9%	12.5%	7.9%	11.8%
Others	Chopper	Number	23	6	1	1	5
		RF	0.7%	0.7%	0.3%	0.3%	0.7%
	Pointer	Number	7	2	2	1	3
		RF	0.3%	0.2%	0.5%	0.3%	0.5%
	Disk	Number	101	40	12	39	22
		RF	3.7%	4.8%	3.1%	1.3%	3.4%
Processing	Anvil	Number	15	4	1	1	4
		RF	0.6%	0.5%	0.3%	0.3%	0.6%
	Hammer	Number	12	3	1	1	3
		RF	0.4%	0.4%	0.3%	0.3%	0.5%
	Mortar	Number	3	1	1	-	-
		RF	0.1%	0.1%	0.3%	-	-
	Pestle	Number	3	2	-	2	1
		RF	0.2%	0.2%	-	0.7%	0.1%
Tool-making	Unfinished Artifacts, Debitage	Number	938	271	95	278	166
		RF	32.0%	32.7%	24.3%	28.1%	25.9%
	Whetstone	Number	435	92	67	140	76
		RF	15.3%	11.1%	17.1%	19.3%	11.9%
	Perforated disk	Number	93	10	14	26	18
		RF	3.3%	1.2%	3.6%	5.1%	2.8%
Woodworking	Adze-axe	Number	117	34	15	30	28
		RF	4.5%	4.1%	3.8%	7.0%	4.3%
Total	Total	Number	2811	829	391	755	640
		RF	100.0%	100.0%	100.0%	100.0%	100.0%

Table 8.2   Number and relative frequencies of lithic artifacts. (RF refers to the relative frequencies in each locality)

the production of useful implements, such as lithic tools, occurred in every locality. Added to this mix of activities and interactions that were tied to economic production and social reproduction was an emphasis on important mortuary rituals. Burials were found in every locality, and the participation in ritual necessarily reinforced the solidarity of these residents.

Conclusion

The concept of house society suggests that the house can have multiple meanings in human social life. The rich ethnographic work conducted in contemporary house societies offers numerous examples for archaeologists to explore these meanings from archaeological remains. In this paper, we have argued that the residential house in Neolithic Wansan society was also a sacred place where ancestral rituals were constantly performed. Furthermore, due to the practice of these rituals, the houses were transformed into a sacred space.

Through the analysis of the distribution of features and artifacts, we illustrate that hunting, fishing, and certain level of agricultural activities were probably the Neolithic Wansan community's main subsistence activities. The presence of large amounts of broken potsherds, such as cooking, storing, and serving vessels, suggests that the house structures at the Wansan site were places in which people carried out the ordinary activities of daily life. Weaving and tool production also played an important role in their lives. Based on the undifferentiated types of artifacts concentrated outside of the houses, the residents of each house probably conducted similar activities on a daily basis. Nevertheless, the burials surrounding the houses prove that these houses were not purely domestic structures for daily life. The house residents also made an effort to execute proper mortuary rituals, acquiring materials for the coffins from other places, assembling slate coffins or molding specific mortuary jars, and preparing particular grave goods to inter with the corpses, then interring the deceased around the house.

The extensive ethnographic research in house societies provides numerous examples to demonstrate that the houses can be both secular and sacred places where mundane and ritualistic activities can be carried out simultaneously. We have also shown how Neolithic Wansan people created their connection with the place through building their residential houses on specific locations within the landscape and conducting their everyday lives in and around the houses. At the same time, they imbued their residential houses with sacred power by interring their deceased members in the areas surrounding the houses. The houses were more than roofed areas for the living; they were also places where the deceased resided. This exploration of the significance of houses in Wansan society thus testifies that no such separation between their domestic and sacred spaces existed. On the contrary, for the Wansan people the landscape in which ritual and daily practices were conducted was both secular and sacred.

Acknowledgements

We would like to express our appreciation to Cecelia Feldman and Claudia Moser for organizing the session "Locality of Sacrality" in the TAG conference and their valuable comments on our paper. To Mr. Shuei-jin Chiou and Ms. Chen-ying Li for conducting the preliminary data cataloguing and providing a friendly working environment in Ilan Cultural Center in Taiwan. Most importantly, to all the people who worked on the rescue excavation at the Wansan site in 1998.

Notes

1 The Austronesian languages form a single language family and it is the most widespread language family in the world. The distribution of the Austronesian-speaking peoples covers almost half of the globe, including the indigenous peoples of Taiwan, Philippines, Malaysia, Indonesia, Madagascar, and all of the peoples in the Oceanic Islands.

2 The data employed in this paper was primarily collected from the rescue excavation conducted in 1998. The 1998 excavation was initiated due to a pagoda-tower construction. The local government asked the archaeologist, Yi-chang Liu, from the Institute of History and Philology to conduct a rescue excavation. This excavation uncovered an area about 2,225 m².

References

Adams, Ron L.
  2005 Ethnoarchaeology in Indonesia: Illuminating the Ancient Past at Çatalhoyuk? *American Antiquity* 70: 181–188.

Beck, Robin A. Jr. (editor)
  2007 *The Durable House: House Society Models in Archaeology.* Occasional Paper 35. Center for Archaeological Investigations, Southern Illinois University, Carbondale.

Bloch, Maurice
  1995 The Resurrection of the House amongst the Zafimaniry of Madagascar. In *About the House: Levi-Strauss and Beyond*, edited by Janet Carsten and Stephen Hugh-Jones, pp. 69–83. Cambridge University Press, Cambridge.

Bradley, Richard
  2003 A Life Less Ordinary: the Ritualization of the Domestic Sphere in Later Prehistoric Europe. *Cambridge Archaeological Journal* 13(1): 5–23.
  2005 *Ritual and Domestic Life in Prehistoric Europe.* Routledge, New York.

Carsten, Janet, and Stephen Hugh-Jones (editors)
1995   *About the House: Lévi-Strauss and Beyond.* Cambridge University Press, Cambridge.

Chen, Chung-yu
1994   *Ciyubin.* Institute of History and Philology, Academia Sinica, Taipei.

Chesson, Meredith S.
1999   Libraries of the Dead: Early Bronze Age Charnel Houses and Social Identity at Urban Bab edh-Dhra', Jordan. *Journal of Anthropological Archaeology* 18(2): 137–164.

Chiang, Bien
1999   Mu Zangyu Xi Min: Paiwan de Lianggejiyijizhi. In *Time, History and Memory,* edited by Ying-Keui Huang, pp. 381–422. Institute of Ethnology, Academia Sinica, Taipei.

Chijiiwa, Suketaro
1960   *Taiwan Takasagozoku no Jūka.* Maruzen, Tokyo.

Chiu, Scarlett
2003   The Socio-Economic Functions of Lapita Ceramic Production and Exchange: A Case Study From Site WKO013A, Kone, New Caledonia, Unpublished Ph.D. Dissertation, Department of Anthropology, University of California, Berkeley.
2005   Meanings of a Lapita Face: Materialized Social Memory in Ancient House Societies. *Taiwan Journal of Anthropology* 3(1): 1–47.

Düring, Bleda S.
2007   The Articulation of Houses at Neolithic Çatalhöyük, Turkey. In *The Durable House: House Society Models in Archaeology,* edited by Robin A. Beck Jr., pp. 3–24. Occasional Paper 35. Center for Archaeological Investigations, Southern Illinois University, Carbondale.

Ellen, Roy F.
1986   Microcosm, Macrocosm and the Nuaulu House: Concerning the Reductionist Fallacy as Applied to Metaphorical Levels. *Bijdragen Tot de Taal, Land en Volkenkunde* 142: 1–30.

Fox, James J.
1993   Comparative Perspectives on Austronesian Houses: An Introductory Essay. In *Inside Austronesian Houses: Perspectives on Domestic Designs for Living,* edited by James J. Fox, pp. 1–29. The Australian National University, Canberra.

Gerritsen, Fokke A.
2007   Relocating the House: Social Transformations in Late Prehistoric Northern Europe. In *The Durable House: House Society Models in Archaeology,* edited by Robin A. Beck Jr., pp. 3–24. Occasional Paper 35. Center for Archaeological Investigations, Southern Illinois University, Carbondale.

Gillespie, Susan
2007   When is a House? In *The Durable House: House Society Models in Archaeology,* edited by Robin A. Beck Jr., pp. 25–50. Occasional Paper 35. Center for Archaeological Investigations, Southern Illinois University, Carbondale.

Gillespie, Susan, and Rosemary A. Joyce (editors)

2000   *Beyond Kinship: Social and Material Reproduction in House Societies.* University of Pennsylvania Press, Philadelphia.

Gonlin, Nancy, and Jon C. Lohse (editors)

2007   *Commoner Ritual and Ideology in Ancient Mesoamerica.* University Press of Colorado, Boulder.

Grove, David C., and Susan D. Gillespie

2002   Middle Formative Domestic Ritual at Chalcatzingo, Morelos. In *Domestic Ritual in Ancient Mesoamerica*, edited by Patricia S. Plunket, pp. 11–19. Cotsen Institute of Archaeology, University of California at Los Angeles, Los Angeles.

Heitman, Carrie C.

2007   Houses Great and Small: Reevaluating the House in Chaco Canyon, New Mexico. In *The Durable House: House Society Models in Archaeology*, edited by Robin A. Beck Jr., pp. 3–24. Occasional Paper 35. Center for Archaeological Investigations, Southern Illinois University, Carbondale.

Huang, Ying-keui

1986   Two Types of the Taiwanese Aboriginal Social Organization. In *The Studies on Taiwanese Aborigines' Social Culture*, edited by Ying-Keui Huang, pp. 3–43. Lingking Books, Taipei.

Kirch, Patrick V.

2000   Temples as "Holy Houses": Transformation of Ritual Architecture in Traditional Polynesian Societies. In *Beyond Kinship: Social and Material Reproduction in House Societies*, edited by Susan D. Gillespie and Rosemary A. Joyce, pp. 103–114. University of Pennsylvania Press, Philadelphia.

Lévi-Strauss, Claude

1982   *The Way of the Masks.* University of Washington Press, Seattle.

1987   *Anthropology and Myth: Lectures, 1951–1982.* Blackwell, Oxford.

Lien, Chao-mei

2008   *Studies on the Stratified Mortuary Data of Peinan in Neolithic Taiwan.* National Taiwan University, Taipei.

Liu, Yi-chang

2000   *Yi Lan Xian Wansan Yizh Qiang Jiu Fa Jue Zi Liao Zheng Li Ji Hua* (Part I). Ilan County Government, Yilan.

2002   *Yi Lan Xian Wansan Yizh Qiang Jiu Fa Jue Zi Liao Zheng Li Ji Hua* (Part II). Ilan County Government, Yilan.

Lopiparo, Jeanne

2007   House Societies and Heterarchy in the Terminal Classic Ulua Valley, Honduras. In *The Durable House: House Society Models in Archaeology*, edited by Robin A. Beck Jr., pp. 3–24. Occasional Paper 35. Center for Archaeological Investigations, Southern Illinois University, Carbondale.

McKinnon, Susan

1987   The House Altars of Tanimbar: Abstraction and Ancestral Presence. *Art Tribal*: 3–16.

1991   *From a Shattered Sun: Hierarchy, Gender, and Alliance in the Tanimbar Islands.* University of Wisconsin Press, Madison.

1995 Houses and Hierarchy: The View from a South Moluccan Society. In *About the House: Levi-Strauss and Beyond*, edited by Janet Carsten and Stephen Hugh-Jones, pp. 174–188. Cambridge University Press, Cambridge.

Plunket, Patricia S. (editor)

2002 *Domestic Ritual in Ancient Mesoamerica*. Cotsen Institute of Archaeology, University of California at Los Angeles, Los Angeles.

Sather, Clifford

1993 Post, Hearths and Thresholds: The Iban Longhouse as a Ritual Structure. In *Inside Austronesian Houses: Perspectives on Domestic Design for Living*, edited by James J. Fox, pp. 65–115. Research School of Pacific Studies, Australian National University, Canberra.

Sparkes, Stephen, and Signe Howell (editors)

2003 *The House in Southeast Asia: A Changing Social, Economic and Political Domain*. Routledge Curzon, New York.

Tringham, Ruth

2000 The Continuous House: A View From the Deep Past. In *Beyond Kinship: Social and Material Reproduction in House Societies*, edited by Susan D. Gillespie and Rosemary A. Joyce, pp. 115–134. University of Pennsylvania Press, Philadelphia.

Tsang, Cheng-hwa, Kuang-ti Li, and Chung-i Chu

2006 *The Archaeological Discovery in the Southern Taiwan Science Park Tainan*. Tainan County Government, Tainan.

Waterson, Roxana

1990 *The Living House: An Anthropology of Architecture in South-East Asia*. Oxford University Press, Singapore.

1993 Houses and the Built Environment in Island South-East Asia: Tracing Some Shared Themes in the Uses of Space. In *Inside Austronesian Houses: Perspectives on Domestic Designs for Living*, edited by James J. Fox, pp. 227–242. Research School of Pacific Studies, Australian National University, Canberra.

2000 Houses, Place, and Memory in Tana Toraja. In *Beyond Kinship: Social and Material Reproduction in House Societies*, edited by Susan D. Gillespie and Rosemary A. Joyce, pp. 177–188. University of Pennsylvania Press, Philadelphia.

Young, Michael W.

1993 The Kalauna House of Secrets. In *Inside Austronesian Houses: Perspectives on Domestic Designs for Living*, edited by James J. Fox, pp. 185–199. Research School of Pacific Studies, Australian National University, Canberra.

Putting Religious Ritual in its Place:
On Some Ways Humans' Cognitive Predilections Influence the Locations and Shapes of Religious Rituals

Robert N. McCauley

The cognitive science of religion brings the methods and findings of cognitive sciences to the study of religion. *Maturationally natural systems* are perceptual, cognitive, and action systems that arise in human development and that are intuitive, instantaneous, automatic, domain specific (by the end of their development), woefully underdetermined by evidence and, thus, sometimes subject to illusions. Cognitive by-product theorists hold that much religious belief and practice turns on engaging maturationally natural systems, which arise in human minds on the basis of considerations that have nothing to do either with religion or with one another. Introducing minor variations in the outputs of maturationally natural systems produces modestly counter-intuitive representations, which are attention-grabbing, memorable, inferentially rich, and communicable. Some even motivate people to transmit them. These are characteristics of culturally successful representations. Humans' *Hazard Precaution System* includes maturationally natural systems for avoiding environmental contaminants and for producing ordered environments. Both include principles that cut across cultures, however particular cultures may tune the systems in question. Religious rituals routinely exploit these predilections in ways that have implications for their shapes and locations. They cue participants' contamination avoidance systems, and they take advantage of human preoccupations with environmental order and vertical symmetry.

The cognitive sciences study the mind/brain from multiple analytical levels, ranging from molecular neuroscience all the way up to the ethnographies of cultural anthropology. They employ at least three types of theories that explore (1) systems' structures, (2) systems' operations in the short term (which can extend at least as far as the life span of individual human beings), and (3) processes in extremely large-scale systems over long periods of time such as the evolution of mind/brains over a few million years (McCauley

2009). Darwinian gradualism suggests that the brains of *Homo sapiens sapiens* have not undergone any especially radical or rapid transformations, certainly at the level of gross anatomy, over the last 60,000 years even though the archaeological findings do demonstrate both radical and rapid transformations in human cultures during that time. Although substantial changes in the frequencies of some traits in human populations (e.g., lactose tolerance) have occurred within the last 10,000 years, any modifications in the standard cognitive machinery with which human beings come equipped have probably been minor and few during the period in question. Consequently, cognitive scientists have reason to hold that the *natural* features of human minds that influence the shapes and locations of cultural forms, including religious ritual, have probably changed little since human prehistory.

In the first and longest section of this paper I will lay out a general account of some natural features of human cognition that a variety of cognitive theorists have maintained undergirds religious rituals. In the second section I will then examine one example of a maturationally natural system that religions enlist, and in the final section I will briefly explore how such features of human cognition affect the shapes and locations of religious rituals.

Maturationally Natural Cognition and the By-Product View

Natural Cognition

What Aspects of Cognition Come to Us Naturally? By "natural" cognition, I refer to perceptions, beliefs, and actions that arise in an instant and are familiar, intuitive, and accomplished without reflection. I have in mind here the wide range of things that we think, so to speak, without thinking. We know about someone's emotional state from his or her facial expression, bodily comportment, or tone of voice. We know that an utterance is linguistically ill-formed even though we are often incapable of articulating any principles that would show why. We have no problem inferring that people who have come into contact with some contaminant may themselves be contaminated. Such knowledge is grounded in assumptions and inferences that seem to occur to us effortlessly, immediately, and automatically. In fact, they are so effortless, immediate, and automatic that we tend not to notice them. We find them the unremarkably *normal* ways that we see, understand, and act in the world.

Natural cognition is so familiar that our presumptions about its soundness are usually *un*apparent to us. *What* we seem to know and *that* we seem to know it are *so transparent* that we take no notice of either. Research in moral psychology has yielded the phenomenon known as "moral dumbfounding"

(Haidt 2001, 2006; Thagard 2010). Presented with scenarios that elicit strong moral intuitions, participants in experiments find themselves incapable of supplying even what *they* take to be persuasive arguments in support of their moral convictions. When forced to ponder various intuitive beliefs, we not only realize that we possess them, we often are surprised to learn, our initial confidence in them notwithstanding, that they are false. For example, human beings' intuitions about many aspects of basic mechanics, for example, the path of a ball that is being dropped by someone who is walking, are typically false (McCloskey 1983; McCloskey et al. 1980, 1983).

It is no more obvious to us how *many* of these things we know, in no small part because we have known them for so long. These natural expectations that we have about the world leap into consciousness when they are violated. Consequently an easy way to reveal how plentiful these assumptions are is to begin to catalogue our negative knowledge. Human beings know that water does not retain the shape of its container when it is poured out, that hand tools do not indulge in midnight snacks, that we do not breathe through our elbows, that skunks have no opinions about America's balance of payments deficit, that it is not fair for one person to get all of the food when many have come to share a meal, and on and on and on.

Natural Cognition Comes in Two Varieties. Much natural cognition results from extensive training, education, or practice in some domain or another. After a good deal of practice, most drivers become so skilled at maneuvering their automobiles around that the act of driving becomes largely automatic. One minute with a novice driver in a moving car in traffic will suffice to remind experienced drivers how much they have come to take for granted. The *practiced* naturalness they have acquired in driving is a cultural feat through and through.

Cognitive predilections that enjoy a practiced naturalness regularly result in domains where skilled teachers have, quite consciously, provided repeated lessons, often in specially designed environments that are structured to facilitate novices' acquisition of some skill or knowledge. Piano teachers help to gradually instill a practiced naturalness in the perception, cognition, and action of their pupils. For pupils much about attaining such practiced naturalness is a conscious achievement too. Initially, pupils must not merely attend to the tasks at hand, they must concentrate. With considerable practice or experience, though, ways of perceiving, or thinking, or acting often become *second nature*.[1]

Practiced naturalness is the naturalness that comes with expertise. Experts not only have ready familiarity and developed intuitions in some domain; they also possess enhanced perceptual acuity, inferential efficiency, and memory for that domain (Chase and Simon 1973). Expertise in many domains, however, can be quite widespread. Although very few people in any city are expert pianists, tens of thousands of people will possess expertise with regard to that city's subway system. Many know how to operate fare machines and how to get from one location to another by way of the various subway lines. If such mundane knowledge does not seem to rise to the level of expertise, then reflect for a moment about the challenges you faced the last time you had to use the subway system in a major city with which you were not familiar. One of the newcomer's prominent impressions in such circumstances is how swiftly all of the experienced riders do everything.

Humans remember when they acquired skills and knowledge for which they have obtained a practiced naturalness. People remember when they learned how to read and write and when they learned how to ride a bike. By contrast people do *not* remember when they learned how to comprehend and produce speech or when they learned how to chew food or walk. These are just some of the many considerations that distinguish practiced naturalness from ways of perceiving, thinking, and acting that I call *maturationally* natural. It is the maturationally natural variety of our natural cognition that will be the focus in the remainder of this paper.

Maturationally Natural Cognition

Humans Undertake Maturationally Natural Matters on Their Own. Humans pursue maturationally natural ways of perceiving, thinking, and acting, spontaneously – unlike reading, writing, and riding a bicycle. No one teaches human beings how to distinguish human faces from one another or how to talk, or crawl, or walk, or chew food. Older people regularly exhibit their competencies with such matters, but they rarely, if ever, *instruct* children (let alone consciously instruct them) about how to manage such perceptual, cognitive, and practical tasks. Again, unlike reading, writing, or riding a bicycle, no one invented these maturationally natural abilities, and their acquisition relies no more on artifacts than it does on instruction or consciously prepared environments.

Maturationally natural capacities generally appear early in life, and humans typically have command of most of them by school age. That people do not recall when they acquired such capacities is, largely, a function of the fact that most develop during the period of childhood amnesia, when humans show little long-term declarative memory for anything. But the criterion still holds for maturationally natural capacities that develop after the period of childhood amnesia, such as the tuning of the human visual system in carpentered environments to have a particular sensitivity to corners (McCauley and Henrich 2006).

Culture Tunes Maturationally Natural Capacities. Culture certainly infiltrates and tunes other maturationally natural capacities in addition to the visual system. If a baby is raised in a French-speaking community, the baby will learn to speak French. But if that same baby were raised in a Hindi-speaking community, it would learn to speak Hindi. A child's learning to speak a particular language, however, is distinguishable from the more general preparedness of infants the world over to acquire a natural language in the first few years of life. Diverse cultural arrangements have no important impact on the schedule for children's mastery of maturationally natural capacities, which occur in *every* culture (see, e.g., Callaghan et al. 2005 for suggestive evidence on this point pertaining to theory of mind). Throughout our species' history, children have learned to walk, to speak some language, to understand others' mental states, and, eventually, to identify potential mates, no matter how culture cloaks such items and activities. Maturationally natural capacities, in short, arise regardless of cultures' peculiarities.

Maturationally Natural Capacities Address Problems Closely Connected to Human Survival. The pervasiveness of such maturationally natural capacities across cultures probably turns on the fact that they address problems that are fundamental to human survival – such as distinguishing agents from other things in the environment, understanding the syntax of an utterance, and knowing what to do in the face of an environmental contaminant. The matters that maturationally natural capacities address are so fundamental to human survival that their acquisition virtually defines the course of what we take to be *normal* development. Parents of children who fail to manifest these maturationally natural capacities will take those children to medical professionals, if such resources are available, to find out what is wrong. Many maturationally natural capacities, such as locomotion, are fundamental to the survival of a wide range of species, not just *Homo sapiens sapiens*. That at least introduces the plausibility of an extended phylogenetic heritage for some of these capacities.

Maturationally Natural Capacities End Up as Domain Specific. Maturationally natural capacities constitute domain-specific systems at the end of their development, if not at the beginning. Considerable controversy surrounds the origins of these capacities and the principles of learning by means of which people acquire them. Evolutionary psychologists (e.g., Cosmides and Tooby 1994) maintain that the appearance of many of these capacities in human development results from the operations of innate, domain-specific, mental modules that evolved to handle just those tasks. By contrast, what might broadly be called "learning theorists" (e.g., Tomasello 1999) hold that humans come by most of what they know on the basis of general inductive abilities supplemented, perhaps, by but one task-specific module in particular, viz., theory of mind, which is concerned with understanding the contents of other humans' mental states. Armed with a natural appreciation of others' communicative intentions and fed input from culture, humans and human cultures have progressively ratcheted themselves up to steadily more impressive intellectual achievements.

Regardless of which of those accounts captures the correct etiology for the acquisition of various maturationally natural capacities (each theory may capture some of the truth about nearly all maturationally natural capacities or all of the truth about some of them), developmental psychologists differ little about what children seem to know by the time they reach school age (i.e., around seven years of age). They may not even know that reading and writing exist, but all normal seven-year-old children know how to speak their communities' languages. They may have never seen a bicycle, but they all know how to walk and even how to adjust their gait, without the slightest thought, as they walk over uneven terrain. They may have no idea how to deal with the dangers of electricity, but they are quite confident about how to conduct themselves around an environmental contaminant.

It is not just the principles of learning that guide the acquisition of one maturationally natural capacity or another that may vary. Again, developmental psychologists do not disagree about the fact that children, or adults for that matter, deploy different principles of inference for the various domains that maturationally natural capacities address. Children carry out inferences on the basis of different substantive principles about linguistic form, about how uneven terrain must be for them to change their mode of locomotion from walking to climbing, and about the handling that is required for managing solids as opposed to liquids. Intriguing experimental evidence suggests that even adults have different conceptions of inferential norms when they carry out inferences pertaining to social contracts compared to inference in other domains (Stone et al. 2002).

Maturationally Natural Systems Operate on the Basis of Distinctive Cues. Maturationally natural systems engage automatically on the basis of detecting a few particular cues. Because they typically address matters of considerable importance to human survival, maturationally natural systems usually leap to particular perceptions, judgments, or actions and ask questions later. Inputs that satisfy a few cues, which are *reliable enough*, trigger these systems' operations. They kick into gear even when their outcomes are woefully underdetermined by the available evidence (humans rarely act on the basis of demonstrative inferences). And that is the way we would want things most of the time with most of the matters that maturationally natural systems tackle. Issues of conscious recall or conceptual nuances or concerns with coherence or integration with the rest of our knowledge, do not delay these systems' operations. This contributes to their speed. So too do their restrictions on the number of confirmation relations, i.e., on the number of those cues, which are reliable enough, that need to be detected in the process of identifying items from their forms. Jerry Fodor (1983: 70) underscores how useful this can be, citing Ogden Nash's sage advice that "If you are called by a panther / don't anther" (Fodor 1983: 70). Panther identification is something that humans always want accomplished with spectacular efficiency and that we do not wish to have encumbered by numerous cognitive requirements for confirming panther properties mentally as a precondition for us being able to take action.

The sensitivity of maturationally natural systems to but a small subset of all of the potentially relevant information available with regard to some stimulus, in effect, constitutes sets of biases in perception, cognition, and action. Such biases render their owners susceptible to corresponding perceptual, cognitive, and practical illusions. It is easy to recognize the biases and corresponding illusions in other species. Whether it is the moth that is attracted to the flickering candle, the frog who leaps to nab a flying bee-bee, or the males of a variety of species that seem ready for liaisons with just about anything in sight that even vaguely resembles a female, we can readily spot those creatures' biases and their resulting illusions. It is our own biases and illusions that we are less clear about. Humans' responses to motion pictures are probably the best illustration of our own susceptibilities. Coordinating a sound track with variations in patterns of light on a two-dimensional screen can create for us whole new three-dimensional worlds. They are filled with people and events that we effortlessly perceive and make judgments about (including social and psychological judgments) and that elicit our emotions and bodily reactions.

More often than not, both the operations of maturationally natural capacities and their effects take place beneath the level of consciousness. Usually, the detection of critical cues, the inferences drawn, and their mental and practical impacts transpire with little, if any, conscious recognition. The susceptibility to the Müller-Lyer illusion (Figure 9.1) of the overwhelming majority of this paper's readers evinces the (culturally tuned) biases in their visual systems for detecting corners and edges. They cannot help themselves from seeing the line connecting the inverted arrow heads at the top as longer than the line connecting the ordinary arrow heads at the bottom, and this is true even *after* readers measure the lines to confirm that they are, in fact, the same length. Their conscious knowledge of the facts is incapable of eliminating the illusion, indicating that the functioning of the maturationally natural system is cognitively impenetrable. Such *persisting illusions* are sure signs of the functioning of biased maturationally natural systems.

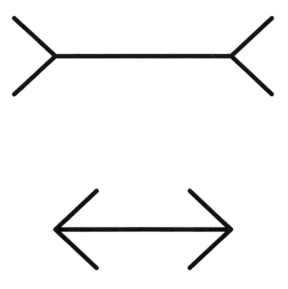

Figure 9.1   The Müller-Lyer illusion (image by author)

For the most part, humans are no more conscious of their cognitive biases and the cognitive illusions that result than they are of their mental operations that exhibit them. For example, researchers found that posting a picture of a pair of eyes on the wall, as opposed to a picture of flowers, elicited significantly more honest behavior from people participating in an honor system for paying for cups of coffee from their otherwise unsupervised office coffee pot (Bateson et al. 2006). It seems that people are far more likely to conform to rules for cooperation when they detect that they are being watched, *even when the detection is unconscious.*

Amos Tversky, Daniel Kahneman, and their colleagues have documented numerous cognitive biases (or "heuristics") that human beings deploy when they undertake tasks calling for probabilistic inference (Gilovich et al. 2002; Kahneman et al. 1982). For example, contrary to the overwhelming majority of participants' intuitive judgments, the probability that Linda, who was a bright, outspoken philosophy major in college and who was active in a variety of causes concerned with questions of justice, is both a bank teller and a feminist cannot be greater than the probability that she is a bank teller. (The probability of a conjunction can never exceed the probability of its least probable conjunct).

Cuing Maturationally Natural Systems Often Involves Powerful Emotions. Often the cuing of such mental systems stimulates powerful feelings in human beings as well as characteristic intuitions and behaviors. Those emotional effects are often transparent not just to observers but sometimes even to the participants themselves. Consider, for example, the feelings and behaviors associated with (a) perceptions of contaminated food, or (b) the inability of an informant who is socially equal to make eye contact, or (c) unfairness in assessments, or (d) the influence of recognized social hierarchies in the distribution of opportunities and resources. All other things being equal, the human beings in each of these scenarios typically experience distinctive feelings that can readily propel them into characteristic behaviors – here, respectively, acts and attitudes of avoidance with (a), wariness with (b), complaint with (c), and deference with (d) – even though they may be completely unable to articulate those judgments or anything about either their emotional responses or the motives for their actions.

Some Candidate Domains. As noted earlier, over the past two decades especially debates have raged anew about the origins of human knowledge. Very roughly, the evolutionary psychologists and their allies have emphasized nature, while learning theorists (who have dominated the social sciences) have stressed nurture. The notion of maturational naturalness circumvents those debates. Distinguishing between our natural cognition and those mental processes that require conscious, effortful thought and careful, time-consuming reflection is a necessary step for further distinguishing between the two types of natural cognition that I have outlined here. Crucially, distinguishing maturationally natural knowledge from the forms of (non-natural) cognition that can only attain cognitive naturalness on the basis of prolonged experience or practice provides a means for characterizing most, if not all, of the cognitive achievements that the evolutionary psychologists wish to highlight without any need for a commitment to either their nativism about the origins of these systems or particularly strong claims about those systems' modularity.

Since maturational naturalness is a more general characterization of perceptual, cognitive, and action systems that does not demand either innate origins or fully modular architectures, most of the candidates that the evolutionary psychologists offer of innate cognitive modules will almost certainly qualify as maturationally natural systems. (It is primarily by eschewing automatic nativist assumptions that maturational naturalness can be distinguished from the evolutionary psychologists' innate cognitive modules, as many of them also reject the full-blown account of modular architecture defended by Fodor [1983: 47–100]).

The scores of domains that the evolutionary psychologists target, then, are probably all candidate domains as maturationally natural systems. The most prominent example is, undoubtedly, natural language, since

Chomsky's claims (e.g., Chomsky 1972) for its innate modularity precede the evolutionary psychologists' proposals by two decades. Others include *perceptual capacities* such as our abilities to recognize and distinguish human faces (Kanwisher et al. 1997; Kanwisher 2000), *cognitive capacities* bearing on topics as diverse as the basic physics of solid objects (Baillargeon et al. 1986; Spelke et al. 1992) and theory of mind (Avis and Harris 1991; Callaghan et al. 2005), and *action capacities* such as the avoidance of environmental contaminants (Hejmadi et al. 2004; Nemeroff and Rozin 1994; Rozin et al. 1993; Rozin et al. 1995; Rozin and Nemeroff 1990).

The By-Product View of (Much) Religious Cognition

The By-Product View Finds No Natural Unity in the Cognitive Foundations of Religion. Cognitive scientists of religion who advocate the so-called "by-product" view of religious cognition hold that religious ideas and forms are *naturally appealing* to the human mind because they are largely rooted in maturationally natural cognitive dispositions. They suggest that religious beliefs and behaviors emerge from routine variations in the functioning of components of our normal mental machinery. Religions variously activate a diverse collection of cognitive inclinations that enjoy neither a logical nor a functional unity. *Cognitively speaking* religions enlist a variety of ordinary, maturationally natural psychological propensities, which are, otherwise, mostly unconnected with one another. The standard features of religious mentality and conduct are cobbled together from various susceptibilities of a compilation of sundry psychological dispositions that develop in human minds on the basis of very different considerations – different both from one another and from anything having to do with the roles they might play in religions.

Latent Susceptibilities of Cognitive Dispositions. Dan Sperber (1996: 66–67) differentiates cognitive *dispositions*, which are adaptive, from the *susceptibilities* for which they are responsible. Dispositions are genuine adaptations and, thus, have what Sperber calls a *"proper domain."* The materials and the problems, which those materials presented, constitute the proper domain that the disposition evolved to manage (well enough). The proper domain of a disposition is, however, but a subset of its *actual domain*. Its actual domain is made up of all of the items and circumstances sufficient to rouse the disposition. Although those additional items and circumstances played no role in either the evolution or the development of the disposition, they are no less capable of exploiting that system's latent susceptibilities, producing what are best understood as intellectual and behavioral *by-products* of that disposition (Tremlin 2006: 44). The moth's attraction to the candle's flame, the frog's consumption of flying bee-bees, and those preoccupied males' interests in anything remotely resembling females are all by-products of the various dispositions of the species in question.

Broadly speaking, the by-product account of religion's cognitive foundations contends that when some cognitive disposition's actual domain exceeds its proper domain, it is capable of erring, in effect, on the side of liberality. It can yield perceptual, cognitive, or practical false alarms. Crucially, cultures and their religions everywhere take forms that manipulate our maturationally natural cognitive predilections (recall the comments about movies above). They have developed all sorts of ways of stimulating false positive responses by activating the relevant perceptual, cognitive, or action systems. The question remains, though, why only some of the resulting representations that these false alarms create persist in populations of human minds.

The proposed answer of by-product theorists is that the persisting representations are the ones that survive the culling wrought by a process of *cultural* selection. What makes representations cognitively and psychologically appealing constitutes some of the most important selection forces here. Cultural selection is based largely on humans' maturationally natural systems, since they include all of the unconscious and automatic dispositions of mind that all humans share.

Features of Culturally Successful Representations. By introducing only minor variations into the operations and outputs of maturationally natural systems, religions produce modestly, often minimally, counter-intuitive representations. The modest counter-intuitiveness of religious representations *attracts attention*. Experimental findings suggest that such modest counter-intuitiveness of representations also facilitates the recollection of those representations (Barrett and Nyhof 2001; Boyer and Ramble 2001). Representations that are *easily remembered* have a clear advantage over those that are not. This is particularly important for understanding cultural transmission in non-literate cultures.

People also have an interest in retaining and transmitting representations that enable them to solve problems. A representation's promise on that front turns largely on its *inferential potential*. The operations of maturationally natural systems include a large body of *default inferences*. If we know, for example, that something is an agent, we know automatically that it has aims and goals, that it desires to accomplish those aims and goals, that it pursues courses of action for bringing about its aims and goals, that it does not desire to be foiled in those pursuits, etc. Their abilities to attract attention, to facilitate recall, and to address problems by means of automatically available inferences help to insure that those representations are *communicable*. These features make them easy to transmit.

It will also aid the cultural success of a representation if it also *motivates* people to transmit it. For example, if part of some idea is that rewards will accrue to those who transmit that idea, all else being equal, that will contribute to that idea's persistence in a population of human minds. Like magic, and music, and civil ceremonies, and superstition, religion largely results from the responses of fallible perceptual, cognitive, and action heuristics, which are enshrined in human minds, to conditions that are not part of those dispositions' proper domains but that elicit their operations, nonetheless.

Modern human minds' maturationally natural dispositions have rendered them susceptible to generating and retaining a variety of representations, beliefs, and practices that presume modestly counter-intuitive arrangements, i.e., representations that do not absolutely conform to our unreflective expectations. These include *representations* of fairy-god-mothers, talking wolves that can plausibly be mistaken for elderly women, and Superman, *beliefs* in everything from Lassie, Santa Claus, elves, and leprechauns to ancestors, angels, and gods, and *practices* such as theater, parades, concerts, and ritual. These variations appear in everything from folk tales, fantasy, and fiction to comic books, commercials, and cartoons. What precise forms these representations, beliefs, and practices take are mostly a function of what is in the air locally and, needless to say, not all of them are religious. So, what I have been describing is only *part* of the story about religion, but it is an important part. In the next section, I explore an illustration of how religions exploit maturationally natural dispositions of mind that can bear on rituals' shapes and locations. In the final section, I will briefly examine some of their possible implications on that front.

Enlisting Hazard Precautions

Hazard Precautions and Contamination Avoidance

Contamination Avoidance as Part of a Hazard Precaution System. Human beings the world over possess a repertoire of tactics for dealing with what they perceive as contaminants in their environments. Pierre Lienard and Pascal Boyer (2006) hold that this concern with contaminants is part of a larger evolved "Hazard Precaution System" (see Szechtman and Woody 2004). This Hazard Precaution System is concerned with a variety of dangers that our prehistoric ancestors faced, such as "predation, intrusion by strangers, contamination, contagion, social offence and harm to offspring" (Lienard and Boyer 2006: 12).

Hazard Precautions as Evolved Systems. The appearance of hazard precautions in human development certainly qualifies as maturationally natural phenomena, and the proponents of an overall Hazard Precaution System maintain that it is an adaptation of the human mind that arose on the basis of natural selection. Evidence for the origins of these Hazard Precaution Systems in the evolution of our species does not depend merely on the fact that caution about these matters seems so transparently adaptive. A number of other considerations point in the same direction. First, humans and monkeys seem to have similar natural fears. Rhesus monkeys' observations of other rhesus monkeys' fear of snakes sufficed on the basis of a single trial to induce such fears in the observers. By contrast, no matter how often rhesus monkeys observed other rhesus monkeys' (apparent) fear of flowers and bunnies, experimenters could not induce those fears in the observers (Blaney and Millon 2008: 123). In short, humans exhibit similar predilections with respect to fearing snakes (Öhman and Mineka 2001; 2003). Second, human beings exhibit facilitated conditional reasoning about hazard precautions (Stone et al. 2002). Third, the fact that hyper-vigilance about such matters (such as repeated hand washing, lock checking, and closet ordering) effectively characterizes the most prominent features of obsessive-compulsive disorder (OCD) suggests that OCD may be malfunctioning of fundamental, maturationally natural systems (Mataix-Cols et al. 2005). In addition, although the Hazard Precaution System seems to outfit us for handling a wide range of dangers, it does not have unlimited scope. Specifically, it does not instill any automatic caution concerning threats to life and limb that have arisen during human history (in contrast to human *prehistory*), such as tobacco, electricity, guns, and automobiles.

Contamination Avoidance as a Principled System. Although some of the items and substances that constitute contaminants differ from one culture to the next, concerns about items and substances associated with animals' bodies (including, of course, human bodies) such as meat, blood, and excrement possess a psychological salience that cuts across cultures. So too does the movement of substances across our bodily borders (Rozin et al. 1995). Regardless of what people in a particular culture take to be contaminating, their conduct with regard to those contaminants seems to be regulated by principles all humans share.

Among those principles are presumptions that contaminants need not be perceptible. In particular, they may be invisible or so small as to be unseen. The imperceptibility of a contaminant makes ascertaining its transmission vectors all the more difficult. Prudence, therefore, dictates maintaining a safe distance from contaminants. A second principle is that *any* contact with a contaminant may introduce risk. Even the slightest contact may suffice to convey the *full* risk associated with the contaminant (Rozin et al. 1993).

Contamination Avoidance as a Principled System – to a Fault. Getting rid of contamination is also tricky business. Recall that maturationally natural cognitive systems fire instantly and automatically and, typically, operate below the level of consciousness. Even when they know that the glass has been disinfected, experimental participants refuse to drink from a glass that they know had earlier contained a cockroach. The point here is that the putatively evolved dispositions in question were adaptations to prehistoric conditions in which the notion of disinfecting was not an option. *Disinfection* is not a computable input to this maturationally natural contamination avoidance system. So, participants remain needlessly cautious (Boyer 2001: 119–120; Rozin et al. 1993). Ample evidence from the ancient world indicates, as the theory would predict, that people possessed the same contamination avoidance principles then and that they acted accordingly. Thus, the maturationally natural systems at stake predate the invention of the germ theory of disease.

Ordered Environments as Hazard Precautions

Ordered Environments as Hazard Precautions. As noted, the Hazard Precaution Repertoire is concerned with more things than just contaminants. In addition to propensities to fear and, thus, avoid contaminants as well as snakes and spiders, it is also hypothesized to include special sensitivities to disruptions or threats to social relations, to off-spring, and to domestic environments. The latter consideration seems particularly likely to bear on spatial features of rituals.

Many young children and Obsessive Compulsive Disorder (OCD) patients display profound concern for the elaborate ordering of personal possessions (Boyer and Lienard 2006). The connections of ordered environments and of having everything in its place with the detection of intruders may provide insight about the emotional reassurance that both children and OCD patients seem to derive from such arrangements. Imposing some order on objects in a domestic environment is a good means for ascertaining whether someone has violated that space. The intruder's movements are almost guaranteed to disturb that order. Violations of visible patterns, alignments, and symmetries make intrusions conspicuous.

The Psychological Prominence of Vertical Symmetry. Symmetries in the ordering of objects in some setting or symmetries in the design of the setting itself enjoy a particular prominence for human minds. The human visual system finds symmetry along a *vertical* axis arresting and manages it with greater efficiency than any other direction of symmetry (Wenderoth 1994). The human penchant for producing symmetry along the vertical axis is manifest in every human culture. Humans manufacture all sorts of tools, structures, buildings, and spaces that are vertically symmetrical. The fact that only one circumstance, viz., facing another animal straight-on, reliably approximates such arrangements in nature again suggests an evolutionary rationale for such a preference. It will always be important to know whether the animal we have spotted (who, incidentally, may also be staring at us) is predator, prey, or conspecific, and it will often be important to know it *fast*.

Another Example of Religions Enlisting Maturationally Natural Systems

Hazard Precautions Do Not Exhaust the Maturationally Natural Systems that Religions Exploit. The final section will focus on some of the implications for ritual of religions enlisting these intuitive hazard precautions. These various hazard precautions, however, are by no means the only maturationally natural systems that religions engage. Space limitations require that one quick further illustration must suffice.

Religions Recruit the Human Penchant to Comprehend and Produce Natural Language. That religions employ natural language is no surprise. Humans talk pretty much all of the time. But *that* is not the question. The question is whether or not religions engage natural language *by virtue of its status as a maturationally natural system*. They do. Christianity is but one of dozens of religions exhibiting glossolalia or speaking in tongues (May 1986). Participants in ecstatic states are alleged to be speaking in unknown languages. With regard to its *production*, whether glossolalia involves more than the simple repetition of a few syllables or not, the by-product theorist predicts that the utterances will overwhelmingly utilize the phonemes of the speaker's native language in utterances that exhibit prosodic features that are quite similar to routine talk. It is on the *comprehension* side, though, that the impact is most direct. When humans hear human voices producing utterances that have these characteristics of linguistic activity, they cannot help themselves from hearing it *as language*. (Try to hear someone else's speech as mere sound without immediately and involuntarily processing it as language.) The point is that when humans hear glossolalia, their minds automatically draw the inference that it is linguistic activity and, thus, that it must mean something, which, of course, instigates a mental search for what it, in fact, means.

Implications for the Shapes and Locations of Religious Rituals

Opportunities for Enlisting Contamination Avoidance in Religious Rituals

Recruited Maturationally Natural Systems Make Some Ritual Arrangements More Probable. None of the considerations that I have reviewed demand some particular ritual arrangement, but they do make some arrangements more probable than others. Following the organization of the previous section, I will take up contamination avoidance first and then turn to ordered environments and symmetry.

Cuing Contaminants and Cleaning Them Up. The two clear implications of the discussion of contamination avoidance for the shapes and locations of religious rituals concern the behaviors for cuing the presence of contaminants and the probable measures required for carrying out ritual cleansings. Although the first are the conditions for the second, in what follows, I will take them up in opposite order.

All of that Washing! Probably the most obvious clue that religious rituals have something to do with cuing contamination avoidance systems is the pervasive concern for purification and for washing things in so many religious rituals (Boyer and Lienard 2006). This stretches from the multiple ritual baths that the sponsors of a performance of an Agnicayana ritual (McCauley and Lawson 2002) take to the relatively perfunctory sprinklings with a few drops of water that many Christians employ in blessings and baptisms (Lawson and McCauley 1990). Religious rituals involve the (ritual) washing and cleaning of people, animals, artifacts, and spaces (such as buildings, cemeteries, and fields). Why are participants in religious rituals all over the world so concerned about the cleanliness of things that, most of the time, it is obvious are not just clean already but have, in fact, been specially cleaned in advance just for the ritual occasion?

Religions Engage the Maturationally Natural Contamination Avoidance System. On the by-product view of religious belief and practice, that preoccupation with cleansing and purifying in religious rituals is the inevitable result of cuing people's contamination avoidance systems. Human beings can employ a variety of means for cuing the presence of contaminants. When people noticeably divert their paths, as if they were walking around some invisible obstacle and then returning and proceeding in the original direction that they were walking, they cue others' contamination avoidance systems. When people repeatedly monitor some location, this too can trigger inferences about contaminants. People may also engage in special motor routines appropriate to a contaminant by using exaggerated care in handling or transporting something or in conspicuously assuring that some liquid does not spill or that some object does not touch others. They may use special protections or shields for substances, artifacts, or spaces. They may stipulate that special, (ritually) qualified religious authorities are the only persons for whom it is safe to approach or handle some items or traverse some spaces. They may also post guards.

A roughly comparable analogy in the secular world is the way that law enforcement officials may demarcate crime scenes with police tape and the forms of conduct that they exhibit and impose on others with regard to that space and the objects in it. Whether with crime scenes or with religious rituals, the point is that once humans' contamination avoidance systems are cued, a wealth of inferences becomes available to them about how to conduct themselves with regard to those items or settings. (Recall the brief review of salient principles informing humans' contamination avoidance systems above.)

Religions Invert the Contamination Avoidance System. In most religious rituals, religions *invert* the system's normal operations, since, if anything, *it is the people themselves who are the contaminants*. Inducing participants' awareness of some sacred object or space creates the need to purify participants ritually. The danger is that they might contaminate the holy artifact or the sacred place. Much of the time the contamination in question is the people's *moral* contamination. That religious participants might need to be cleansed *multiple* times before they are eligible to be near or touch or consume some sacred material squares perfectly well with the fact that ridding oneself or something else of contamination can be a formidable challenge. Because contaminants can be imperceptible, people who have carefully bathed and turned out in their very best attire may, nonetheless, still need to be ritually purified.

Differentiating Reserved Ritual Spaces from Ones that are More Publicly Available. Relevant ritual locations should disclose evidence of demarcating reserved ritual spaces from more publicly available ritual spaces. The border between the two might be directly marked by physical barriers, by changes in height, by changes in light and darkness, by changes in color or patterns, and more. On the other hand as noted above, it might be marked less directly by diverting pathways around some space or by stations for guards. On the safe distance principle, the allocation of space *per participant* between any two areas will probably be disproportionate in favor of the ritual space that is more reserved.

Water, Water Everywhere But Not a Drop to Drink. Humans use water in every culture to clean things, and all of the available evidence suggests that it is nearly as pervasive in ritual cleansings. There is, then, every good reason to expect rituals of purification to have either sources of water conveniently at hand or artifacts and systems designed both to transport and store quantities of water that are sufficient for cleansing ritual objects or participants. The waters would be for cleansing, as opposed to quenching thirst and, presumably, the accompanying artifacts would reflect the first function rather than the second.

Opportunities for Enlisting Ordered Environments in Religious Rituals

Order and Symmetry in Ritual Settings is Patent. That religious ritual settings are ordered and symmetrical very nearly goes without saying. The principle of *everything in its place* applies more directly in ritual than, perhaps, in any other context. In literate societies, ritual manuals explicitly specify spatial arrangements. Purposely designed containers, such as jars, cases, and cabinets, protect and order ritual artifacts. The imposition of order extends not only to objects but to persons as well. People are regularly ordered in ranks and files (e.g., for prayers in mosques). Special clothing, which must also be kept orderly, designates entitled ritual practitioners.

Vertical symmetry is the norm for most religious architecture and icons. Churches, cathedrals, mosques, and temples are so routinely symmetrical vertically that it is where they are not that stands out (such as the spires of Chartres Cathedral). Although icons often involve variations on perfect symmetry, they typically retain a balance in their design along the vertical axis. Hindu icons may have multiple pairs of arms, but they do not have three arms on one side and one on the other. Although the correlation is not perfect (consider, for example, bee hives), human beings tend to regard order and symmetry as a reliable sign of the presence of designing minds.

Acknowledgements

I wish to thank Shiela Shinholster for her aid in the production of Figure 9.1.

Notes

1   I wish to express my gratitude to Tom Kasulis for pointing out to me how naturally the well-worn English idiom to the effect that something has become "second nature" captures my notion of practiced naturalness.

References

Avis, Jeremy, and Paul L. Harris
   1991   Belief-Desire Reasoning among Baka Children: Evidence for a Universal Conception of Mind. *Child Development* 62: 460–467.

Baillargeon, Rene, Elizabeth S. Spelke, and Stanley Wasserman
   1986   Object Permanence in Five Month Old Infants. *Cognition* 20: 191–208.

Barrett, Justin L., and Melanie A. Nyhof
   2001   Spreading Non-natural Concepts: The Role of Intuitive Conceptual Structures in
            Memory and Transmission of Cultural Materials. *Journal of Cognition and Culture*
            1: 69–100.

Bateson, Melissa, Daniel Nettle, and Gilbert Roberts
   2006   Cues of Being Watched Enhance Cooperation in a Real-World Setting. *Biology
            Letters* 2: 412–414.

Blaney, Paul H., and Theodore Millon
   2008   *Oxford Textbook of Psychopathology*. Oxford University Press, Oxford.

Boyer, Pascal
   2001   *Religion Explained: The Evolutionary Origins of Religious Thought*. Basic Books, New
            York.

Boyer, Pascal, and Pierre Lienard
   2006   Why Ritualized Behavior? Precaution Systems and Action Parsing in Developmental,
            Pathological, and Cultural Rituals. *Behavioral and Brain Sciences* 29: 1–56.

Boyer, Pascal, and Charles Ramble
   2001   Cognitive Templates for Religious Concepts: Cross-Cultural Evidence for Recall of
            Counter-Intuitive Representations. *Cognitive Science* 25: 535–564.

Callaghan, Tara, Philippe Rochat, Angeline Lillard, Mary Louise Claux, Hal Odden, Shoji
Itakura, Sombat Tapanya, and Saraswati Singh
   2005   Synchrony in the Onset of Mental-State Reasoning. *Psychological Science* 16:
            378–384.

Chase, Wiliam G., and Herbert A. Simon
   1973   Perception in Chess. *Cognitive Psychology* 4: 55–81.

Chomsky, Noam
   1972   *Language and Mind*. Harcourt Brace Jovanovich, New York.

Cosmides, Leda, and John Tooby
   1994   Origins of Domain Specificity: The Evolution of Functional Organization.
            In *Mapping the Mind: Domain Specificity in Cognition and Culture*, edited by
            Lawrence Hirschfeld and Susan Gelman, pp. 85–116. Cambridge University Press:
            Cambridge.

Fodor, Jerry
   1983   *The Modularity of Mind*. MIT Press, Cambridge.

Gilovich, Thomas, Dale W. Griffin, and Daniel Kahneman (editors)
   2002   *Heuristics and Biases: The Psychology of Intuitive Judgment*. Cambridge University
            Press, Cambridge.

Haidt, Jonathan
   2001   The Emotional Dog and its Rational Tail: A Social Intuitionist Approach to Moral
            Judgment. *Psychological Review* 108: 814–834.

Haidt, Jonathan
   2006   *The Happiness Hypothesis*. Basic Books, New York.

Hejmadi, Ahalya, Paul Rozin, and Michael Siegal

 2004 Once in Contact, Always in Contact: Contagious Essence and Conceptions of Purification in American and Hindu Indian Children. *Developmental Psychology*, 40: 467–476.

Kahneman, Daniel, Paul Slovic, and Amos Tversky (editors).

 1982 *Judgment Under Uncertainty: Heuristics and Biases.* Cambridge University Press, Cambridge.

Kanwisher, Nancy

 2000 Domain Specificity in Face Perception. *Nature Neuroscience* 3: 759–763.

Kanwisher, Nancy, Josh McDermott, and Marvin M. Chun

 1997 The Fusiform Face Area: A Module in Human Extrastriate Cortex Specialized for Face Perception. *Journal of Neuroscience* 17: 4302–4311.

Lawson, E. Thomas, and Robert N. McCauley

 1990 *Rethinking Religion: Connecting Cognition and Culture.* Cambridge University Press, Cambridge.

Lienard, Pierre, and Pascal Boyer

 2006 Whence Collective Rituals? A Cultural Selection Model of Ritualized Behavior. *American Anthropologist* 108: 814–828.

Mataix-Cols, David, Maria Conceição do Rosario-Campos, and James F. Leckman

 2005 A Multidimensional Model of Obsessive-Compulsive Disorder. *The American Journal of Psychiatry* 162: 228–238.

McCauley, Robert, N.

 2009 Time Is of the Essence: Explanatory Pluralism and Accommodating Theories about Long Term Processes. *Philosophical Psychology* 22: 611–635.

McCauley, Robert N., and Joseph Henrich

 2006 Susceptibility to the Muller-Lyer Illusion, Theory Neutral Observation, and the Diachronic Cognitive Penetrability of the Visual Input System. *Philosophical Psychology* 19: 79–101.

McCauley, Robert N., and E. Thomas Lawson

 2002 *Bringing Ritual to Mind: Psychological Foundations of Cultural Forms.* Cambridge University Press, Cambridge.

McCloskey, Michael

 1983 Intuitive Physics. *Scientific American* 248: 122–130.

McCloskey, Michael, Alfonso Caramazza, and Bert Green

 1980 Curvilinear Motion in the Absence of External Forces: Naive Beliefs about the Motion of Objects. *Science* 210: 1139–1141.

McCloskey, Michael, A. Washburn, and Linda Felch

 1983 Intuitive Physics: The Straightdown Belief and its Origin. *Journal of Experimental Psychology: Learning, Memory & Cognition* 9: 636–649.

May, L. Carlyle

 1986 A Survey of Glossolalia and Related Phenomena in Non-Christian Religions. In *Speaking in Tongues: A Guide to Research on Glossolalia*, edited by Watson E. Mills, pp. 53–82. Eerdmans, Grand Rapids, MI.

Nemeroff, Carol J., and Paul Rozin

1994 The Contagion Concept in Adult Thinking in the United States: Transmission of Germs and Interpersonal Influence. *Ethos* 22: 158–186.

Öhman, Arne, and Susan Mineka

2001 Fear, Phobias, and Preparedness: Toward an Evolved Module of Fear and Fear Learning. *Psychological Review* 108: 483–522.

2003 The Malicious Serpent: Snakes as a Prototypical Stimulus for an Evolved Module of Fear. *Current Directions in Psychological Science* 12: 5–8.

Rozin, Paul, Jonathan Haidt, and Clark R. McCauley

1993 Disgust. In *Handbook of Emotions*, edited by Michael Lewis and Jeannette Haviland, pp. 575–594. Guilford, New York.

Rozin, Paul, and Carol J. Nemeroff

1990 The Laws of Sympathetic Magic: A Psychological Analysis of Similarity and Contagion. In *Cultural Psychology: Essays on Comparative Human Development*, edited by James W. Stigler, Richard A. Shweder, and Gilbert H. Herdt, pp. 205–232. Cambridge University Press, Cambridge.

Rozin, Paul, Carol J. Nemeroff, Matthew Horowitz, Bonnie Gordon, and Wendy Voet

1995 The Borders of the Self: Contamination Sensitivity and Potency of the Mouth, Other Apertures and Body Parts. *Journal of Research in Personality* 29: 318–340.

Spelke, Elizabeth S., Karen Breinlinger, Janet Macomber, and Kristen Jacobson

1992 Origins of Knowledge *Psychological Review* 99: 605–632.

Sperber, Dan

1996 *Explaining Culture: A Naturalistic Approach*. Blackwell Publishers, Oxford.

Stone, Valerie E., Leda Cosmides, John Tooby, Neal Kroll, and Robert T. Knight

2002 Selective Impairment of Reasoning about Social Exchange in a Patient with Bilateral Limbic System Damage. *Proceedings of the National Academy of Sciences* 99: 11,531–11,536.

Szechtman, Henry, and Erik Woody

2004 Obsessive-compulsive Disorder as a Disturbance of Security Motivation. *Psychological Review* 111: 111–127.

Thagard, Paul

2010 *The Brain and the Meaning of Life*. Princeton University Press, Princeton.

Tomasello, Michael

1999 *The Cultural Origins of Human Cognition*. Harvard University Press, Cambridge.

Tremlin, Todd

2006 *Minds and Gods: The Cognitive Foundations of Religion*. Oxford University Press, New York.

Wenderoth, Peter

1994 The Salience of Vertical Symmetry. *Perception* 23: 221–236.

— 10 —

The Aptitude for Sacred Space

Ian B. Straughn

A Pilgrimage of Sorts

The essays that comprise this volume are responsible for taking us on a journey that explores the diversity of material and cultural engagements with place that spans millennia and extends from a re-placed Anatolian Nile to the South China Sea. It might be fitting then to consider such a journey to be a pilgrimage, given the concern here with ritual practices and their emplacement. However, despite the centrality of sacred space, this collection works against an analytically stale pilgrimage trope. These studies do not profess nor do they attempt to guide us to some ultimate *topos*, and, at the risk of disappointing the editors, these concluding remarks will similarly fall short. Instead of outlining any paradigmatic hierophany, to borrow Eliade's term for discussing the ontological position of the sacred in "founding" a world (1959: 21–23), what is at stake in *Locating the Sacred* is a set of questions that are both methodological and theoretical. These studies examine the ways in which sacred space and ritual practice operate as analytical categories, as well as what forms of evidence demonstrate the co-constitutive relationship between these two objects of study.

As the editors discuss in their introduction, the social production of sacred space has long been associated with ritual practice as the mechanism by which seemingly ordinary places acquire extraordinary meaning and power to act in the world. They highlight the need for a distinction to be made between the use of the term "sacred" as a descriptor and its employment as an analytical concept. Significant problems arise when it functions in both capacities without adequate discussion. Underlying this distinction is a question that has inspired archaeologists and scholars of religion alike, namely, whether the designation of certain places as sacred is a universal characteristic of all cultures. Is the sacred an *a priori* category of perception for how we understand the world? Are we predisposed to finding sacred in the phenomenal world? What does that do for us? Does it have practical benefits for our social lives or is it purely a matter of our spiritual being?

The articles in this present volume amplify these issues and take them in a set of intriguing directions through a demonstration that the designation of something as either sacred space or ritual practice is not the end point of analysis but rather the point of departure. Our journey does not find its culmination in the sacred. Instead, it initiates investigations into its material conditions, its cognitive patterns, and its political articulations. A prominent assertion of this volume is that practice, ritual or otherwise, is material and that such materiality is necessarily located. What we learn, and here lies the significant contribution to the field, is that this matters; it is not simply epiphenomenal fluff that makes for the pretty PowerPoint slides that archaeologists use to illustrate their talks. Whether it is a line of altars in early Republican Latium or the site where all hell will break loose (Meggido), there is an irreducible relationship among thing, place, and practice that produces the very conditions of possibility for those social engagements of the temporal, spatial, material, cultural, and cognitive elements that constitute ritual. I have purposefully left off "practice" in this previous statement because it is unnecessarily limiting. For the archaeologist in particular, it may well be a red herring that causes us to undermine the value of the evidence that we possess in things like landscapes, votives, or even domestic architecture. This volume has gone far in redressing this problem and what remains for me is perhaps only to suggest some new territory into which it might allow for further exploration.

Cultivation and Argumentation: Towards a Ritual Disposition

The places investigated here are not just things, they are happenings, or in the words of J.Z. Smith (1987) so prominent in this volume, they "take place." Archaeology, as Moser and Feldman have discussed, is well-positioned to examine the event-like nature of such places through both its attention to materiality and its long temporal lens. Such event-places are historically constituted and should not be confined to reified static moments. In order to talk of them in terms of practice, I want to shift the ground slightly and think of them more as "practiced," in the sense of being cultivated through the laborious work of learning, doing, repeating, and improving. At stake in such forms of practice – those activities in which there is a desire to develop excellence – are what the moral philosopher Alasdair MacIntyre (1984: 187–189) describes as the "goods" both internal and external to that activity. MacIntyre offers the example of either the pianist or the chess player, both of whom are open to rewards which may come in the shape of prizes or adulation from fans (external goods), but who are also invested in the satisfaction that comes from the very mastery of the practice and the ever-closer approach to the asymptotic unattainable: perfection (internal goods). In the investigation of the various temples, shrines, and other locations that form the diverse case studies of *Locating the Sacred*, it is important to consider them not as single recitals or individual matches, but as ongoing vehicles for practicing place-making. Sacred space, I will argue, is itself ritual practice and not simply where it happens.

As with any practice of this type, it must happen within the frame of a social world whose cultural referents are often quite outside the individual. But at this point, the analogy with the chess grand master or the piano virtuoso breaks down in important ways. Virtuosity may well be a goal pursued in relation to space, but the mechanisms for evaluating whether it has achieved either internal or external goods operates in a rather different manner. At issue is often the question of the efficacy of place-making in that achievement. It is the basis for argumentation, which, as we have seen, may be the result of powerful ideologies or good old-fashioned imperial muscle. However, its cognitive structure might work quite differently. This is where McCauley's essay in this volume is invaluable for the ways in which it complements the focus on materiality and performativity with its excursion into the realm of cognition. His work reveals how the cultivation of such practices may not only lie in the workings of culture and in the institutions which society has developed for the training of its members, but in the very maturational capacities of the human species and a certain pre-disposition to the sacred.

There is another possibility worth considering in relation to the cultivation of place-making disposition and its effectiveness in bringing about sacred space. This is the position that we might ascribe to the believer, those for whom there is an ultimate authority, in most cases a divinity that can judge these takings-place. The problem in religious traditions has always been how to authorize those judgments, to legitimate them amongst the believers and demonstrate their superiority. If archaeologists are interested in paying attention to the emic nature of belief systems, then they will need to be in dialogue with the scholars of religion, be they theologians, jurists, philosophers, anthropologists, or historians. At the very least it should push archaeologists to pay closer attention to those activities by which individuals and communities lay claim to the authority of god-speech, whether in the form of scripture, mystical experience, sacrificial divination, or whatever other shapes it might take.

The Resurrection of the "Dead Cities"

Let me offer an example from the Islamic world in order to consider three of the prominent overarching themes shared by many of the studies in this volume: identity, memory, and landscape. A critical lens is required in such an endeavor. The mere fact that these three terms have reached such a status within archaeology to have prompted at least one prominent scholar to employ, with not a small hint of sarcasm, the acronym IML as shorthand (Yoffee 2007: 2) should spark some caution. With that warning, however, the analytical value of these concepts may still merit consideration despite their perhaps waning trendiness.

In the year 1203/4 A.D. the ruler of Aleppo commissioned one of his notables, a certain Sadīd al-Dīn Muzaffar, to undertake a cadastral survey of the region of limestone hills west of the city. Prior to leaving for his duty, this official was struck with the flu and upon his arrival to the region his illness intensified and took a turn for the worst. It was here, in the village of Ruhīn that he sought out a ruined shrine, described in the Arabic sources as a *mashhad* (something roughly equivalent to a martyrium in the Christian tradition). Within this rock cut tomb, despite warnings from the villagers,

Figure 10.1 Triple-apsed saints' tomb at Mashhad Ruhin (Ian Straughn)

he sought refuge and sleep. According to the thirteenth-century scholars Ibn Shaddād and Ibn Shihnah who have left us the record of these events, Sadīd al-Dīn vowed that, should he be cured, he would reconstruct the shrine and restore it to its rightful place as a pilgrimage center where people could receive blessings (*baraka* in Arabic) from the individuals who were entombed here.[1] He recovered, attributing it to the efficacy of this place, so Sadīd al-Dīn made good on his promise. He sold all his possessions and rebuilt the shrine and expanded it into a complex that included a bath. The ruler of Aleppo was himself so pleased with this act of piety that he offered his official one-fifth of the revenues from the village to support this effort. Reportedly, other elites, including a prince's daughter and a prominent religious scholar, added structures which included a hostel for pilgrims and second bath. Sadīd al-Din, in fact, was so successful in resurrecting this sacred place that it became the site of a regular festival for the people of Aleppo whose ritual practice was modeled on that of the *hajj* to Mecca. In this account, we are told that, prior to this rediscovery of the site's *baraka*, the shrine had not witnessed many visitors other than the thieves and criminals that sought to prey upon true devotees.

Step back to the early fifth century A.D. when this region of limestone hills hosted a young Syrian monk who, prone to excess in his asceticism, sought to escape interruptions to his devotions by erecting a pillar on which he would pass the rest of his days. For some 36 years this man, who would become known as St. Simeon Stylites, continued to attract crowds of followers who sought his advice and council. His column, which overlooked the rocky landscape of north-western Syria, continued to rise from an original height of just 3 m to more than 15 m. Within a few decades of his death in 459 A.D., the site on which he stood became the locus for one of the most costly and architecturally important monuments of the early Byzantine period. The complex that arose around St. Simeon's column continues today to attract pilgrims, despite the reduction of his lofty abode to a mere nub of marble at the center of a still magnificent cruciform basilica (Biscop and Sodini 1984).

Even before St. Simeon's arrival onto the scene, the region in which he chose to build his career, so to speak, was already well developed as a locus of Christian religious activity. Basilicas, monasteries, and martyria had largely replaced the pagan temples of the classical era throughout this series of limestone hills triangulated between the important cities of Antioch, Aleppo, and Apamea. Archaeologically, the region has come to be known as the "Dead Cities," though this is somewhat of a misnomer. The vast majority of the nearly 1,000 sites with occupation levels largely dating from the early second to the late sixth centuries A.D. were not urban centers.

Rather, they comprised a handful of regional market towns and a much larger number of villages and hamlets. As for their death, this has become a question of persistent archaeological interest ever since their reintroduction into the consciousness of Western historians, classicists, and others in the mid-nineteenth century (Biscop and Sodini 1984; Khoury 1987, 2005; Peña et al. 1987, 1990; Peña et al. 1999, 2003; Tate 1992; Tchalenko 1953). An earlier generation of scholars offered the Muslim conquests as the most likely candidate for the presumed abandonment of the region in the sixth/seventh century A.D. More recently, blame has also been laid at the feet of various others including the Sasanians, the Byzantines themselves, as well as a series of exogenous environmental events ranging from climate change to earthquakes (Foss 1997; Tate 1992).

For the purpose of these remarks, I want to examine the process by which such a religiously charged landscape becomes transferred during the transition of this territory to a series of Muslim polities. Does its connection to a particular sacred tradition prevent its easy incorporation within the logics of territorial sovereignty by those outside this tradition? What are the processes by which such a landscape becomes integrated into the frameworks of a new tradition for the production of sacred space and associated ritual practices? Such processes, I argue, fall along a continuum. On one end of the spectrum is the acceptance that what was sacred in a previous tradition is coterminous with the sacred in the new. In essence, no adjustments were required in order to establish claims to the space, its remembrance, and its representation. Archaeologically, this correlates to the reuse of an already existing sacred space with only slight alterations. On the other end are efforts to efface the sacred of the old tradition, to deny that it ever existed or was ever legitimate. Here the archaeological parallel is not the reuse of old monuments, but rather their destruction and reconstruction. Wherever this particular case may fall in that continuum, arguments about how to cultivate a proper engagement with this space can occur at multiple scales.

These two strategies are, of course, not simply acts of devotion and spirituality. They are intimately connected to politics and the transformation of social relations through the production of sacred space. However, I do not want to over-emphasize the political to the point that any act of devotion is analyzable only in terms of the social and hence disconnected from a relationship with the divine. It would be only too facile to say, for instance, that St. Simeon and those who copied him were either narcissists in search of adulation or savvy politicians looking to influence state policy through the avenues open to them.

While both the process of acceptance and evacuation were employed within the Islamic tradition for laying claims to the sacred nature of the spaces that Muslims came to control, I will argue that neither of these was the primary mode for the material and cultural transformation of the Dead Cities region in the Islamic period. Instead, it appears that change was accomplished through conscious strategies of neglect that pervaded this region in the early Islamic period. The result was the erosion of the specificity of associations while maintaining a general sense of sacredness. In this way, it could become recast within Muslim society through a rediscovery of its *baraka* in more culturally acceptable forms. While such a space does not strictly conform to the notions of liminality elucidated by Victor Turner (1995: 126–127), it no longer remains a place of social structure in order to become a locus that may have the future potential for the spontaneous eruption of "communitas."

The region of the Dead Cities is generally compartmentalized into three sub-districts that are topographically distinguished. In the north is the Jebl Sem'an; in the far south, with Apamea at its tip, is the Jebl Zawiyya; and sandwiched between them are Jebl al-Ala', Jebl Baricha, and Jebl Wastani (Peña et al. 1987, 1990; Peña et al. 1999, 2003; Tate 1992). To the west lies the valley of the Orontes and to the east the fertile plain of Chalcis. The most striking feature of the region is the large number of standing architectural remains constructed from the local limestone. Throughout the twentieth century there were numerous expeditions to catalogue the various sites and provide plans and drawings of this rich local tradition of building and style. More recently, there have been a number of excavations of key sites such as at Dehes and Deir Seta in the Jebl Baricha, as well as Serjila, one of the larger and more urbanized sites in the Jebl Zawiyya (Khoury 1987, 2005). Despite the richness of the archaeology, this was a rural society that survived largely on its agricultural production. The large number of olive presses found throughout the region suggests that this was probably the main economic engine for the region, particularly in late antiquity. However, there is good evidence to suggest a more diversified economy that included stock-raising and cereal grains. Together the wool, meat, oil, and other foodstuffs were part of a well-established trade network with the major cities of northern Syria. It was within this context of general rural prosperity that these peasant farmers also circulated within networks of local pilgrimage that connected the villages with one another and with the larger Christian world through major holy places such as Qal'at Sem'an.

With the arrival of the Muslim armies to Syria in the late 630s A.D., the region of the Dead Cities was soon ceded to the territorial sovereignty of the emerging Islamic polity. Unlike the wealthy elites in many of the larger cities, it is likely that only a small minority of these peasant farmers had the financial wherewithal to relocate to areas still under the control of the Byzantine Emperor. Most stayed in their villages and continued to produce the same agricultural products that had allowed for the original prosperity of the region. The excavations at Dehes and Deir Seta both demonstrate significant occupation of the sites well into the ninth century A.D. Surface ceramics from a number of sites elsewhere in the Jebl Baricha also indicate significant occupation into the early Abbasid period (as late as the early tenth century). Several of the larger sites such as al-Bara and Deir Sem'an (the town located below the famed site of St. Simeon) became important regional centers. The latter, in fact, served for a brief period as the residence of the ascetic and pious Umayyad Caliph 'Umar II (r. 717–720 A.D.) who shunned the luxury of Damascus for this town closer to the frontier with Byzantium.[2] The historical record has yet to offer any explicit suggestion that he sought to draw on the aura of the Christian saint or recast the site in a new light of his own piety, this choice of residence is still a possible indication for some level of re-engagement with a geography of sacred associations.

One aspect of the landscape that we do not encounter is any large-scale destruction of Christian monuments, whether churches, martyria or other shrines. Nor do we find that these structures were transformed in significant ways in order to make them serviceable for Islamic ritual practice. On the one hand, this is an indication that the population of these villages remained largely Christian, while on the other hand this suggests that there was no significant effort to destroy or replace the religious associations already established and invested in this landscape. In fact, there are only a handful of sites that indicate a Muslim presence in this region during the first couple of centuries of its control by Muslim polities. The evidence for this is primarily the construction of mosques. In most instances these mosques were either newly built structures such as at larger sites like al-Bara and Dier Sem'an or they were fashioned by the simple addition of a *mihrab* (prayer niche) in the southern wall of structures that may have originally served as *androns* (e.g., the site of Dier Seta [Khoury 1987]). This is significant because the connotation of such a structure is linked with public/official activities and not with religious ritual practice.

With the exception of a few larger sites, this region of the Dead Cities was largely left to its own devices in the early Islamic period (ca. 650–1000 A.D.). The archaeological evidence suggests that there was little significant building undertaken throughout the region starting as early as the late sixth century, i.e., prior to the Muslim conquests. It is not until the later tenth century that the region re-emerged as something of a frontier between various Muslim states and Byzantium, and then later the Crusader principalities (Cahen 1940). It is only at this point in the twelfth and thirteenth centuries that there were efforts on the part of the Ayyubid dynasty (founded by Salāh ad-Dīn ibn Ayyūb, also known as Saladin in European Christendom) to institute a policy of resettlement for these villages by displaced Muslims. The question to be asked is whether this failed to happen sooner, in part, because the region retained such a strong Christianized topography for which there was little political or social immediacy to necessitate either its effacement or acculturation within the Muslim tradition. However, with the renewed threat that the region might again fall under the control of a Christian power, and one which would presumably have the ability to establish territorial claims based on a sacred substrate invested in sites such as Qal'at Sem'an, political exigencies may well have had a role in how this space could attract attention (Sourdel-Thomine 1954).

It is at this point, somewhere in the twelfth and early thirteenth centuries, that there was a rediscovery or, perhaps better stated, a reattribution of the region's sacrality on the part of Sadīd al-Dīn Muzaffar. Eschewing a lengthy description of the site, Mashhad Ruhīn contains many of the features that are often associated with taking place within such sites of ritual practice.[3] Situated in the southern part of the Jebl Sem'an some 12 km south-west of Qal'at Sem'an, the landscape that forms the site is topographically quite striking. The village is perched nearly 150 m above a seasonal riverbed (*wādī*) and nestled about midpoint in the steep slope is the *mashhad* itself, with its triple arch, carved out of the limestone, jutting out almost imperceptibly as one descends. Without precaution when approached from the top, the visitor could easily misstep and fall three meters into the forecourt. Other dangers included not only the bandits of the medieval period, but also, according to local residents, poisonous asps and the *jinn*, malevolent spirits who often make their home in ruins.

The issue of ruination is particularly significant; it is what attracted attention in the past and what also catches our interest in the present. Despite archaeology's distinctly secular agenda for studying the past, it follows many of the same patterns of rediscovery that mark the activities of someone like Sadīd al-Dīn. Additionally, this site is blessed with a perennial spring which presumably supported the operation of the baths and slaked the thirst of visiting pilgrims. Today, out of the well which was constructed to harness its *baraka* grow magnificent fig trees which serve as home to a family of owls – or perhaps they are *jinn* in their visible form.

There are two elements of formal religious practice apparent at the site. Across the *wādī* a small prayer space (*musallah*) was created, employing a rock cut *mihrāb* that opens out onto a flat limestone surface. A direct site line connects this feature with the shrine on the opposite hillside such that those engaged in prayer would have the inhabitants of the tomb looking down on their backs. At the base of the hill, below the various ruined structures that were part of the thirteenth-century complex, is an extensive

Muslim cemetery that is in continual use by the villagers who inhabit the area above; these villagers have spoliated much of their building material from the former Byzantine settlement on the hilltop and the later-period structures on the slope.

What we have then is the classic archaeological jumble, the palimpsest of structures for ritual practice interspersed with domestic dwellings, all in various states of decay and renovation, and contained within a context of manipulated natural features. In such an instance it seems at best artificial and at worst an analytical injustice to attempt any effort to prioritize landscape over memory, or to insist on identity as causal in the production of either one. At this point, let me say that such a place might be better thought of as largely unscripted, even when it seems to so closely fit well-established patterns for what we have become comfortable labeling "sacred space." There may well exist standard tropes and themes, and IML may legitimately be among them, but lest hubris get the better of us, we should be deferential to all that we do not know and cannot know, no matter how solid and rich our data. Ritual practice and the places where it happens are often as obscure to those who enact and produce them as they are to those who observe and analyze from the sidelines, often several millennia removed.

The Marks of Craftsmanship

In analyzing a place like Mashhad Ruhīn it is necessary to balance the cultivation of strategy with serendipity, to distinguish those elements that make for good story-telling from those that lead to effective policy making. As with the various other case studies in this volume, we see how such places happen not only through the manipulation of the physical environment but through the weaving of narratives; they are at once hewn from stone and carved from story. Are these places, then, works of craftsmanship that transform their raw materials in skillful if not always creative ways? That balance between skill and creativity is an important component in the cultivation of a ritual disposition.

In the context of an Islamic tradition that structures the development of a place like Mashhad Ruhīn there is equivocation on the value of creativity. On the one hand, acts that are considered to be "inventions" (*bida*) find considerable resistance by the claimants to orthodoxy and orthopraxy. The mantra that the ability to create remains solely a divine prerogative carries considerable weight (Meri 1999). At the same time, however, interpretation, flawed as it may be by the incapacities of the human agent, is at the heart of the tradition. Such interpretation, whether it takes a textual, performative, or material form (or as often is the case some combination of all three), is essential to any practical effort to understand and engage with divine creation. The notion of skill, however, is far less problematic. It only curries disfavor when it loses its humility and loses sight of the ultimate creative principle. The ninth-century Baghdadi litterateur and social critic al-Jahiz once chastised the citizens of Damascus when he recorded: "Some of our ancestors said that the Damascenes will not be as attached to heaven as others because they see their Great Mosque" (cited in Bahnassi 1989:73). His implication was that they have become too proud of their mosque to the point that it has become the vehicle for the reverence of their own human ingenuity over that of God.

What then are we to make of the skill and creativity of Sadīd al-Dīn in place-making? It starts with the very sourcing of the raw materials which required a particular faculty for recognizing the potential of place even when this was not part of a conscious effort. His original mission had not been to locate a pilgrimage site. He was a bureaucrat sent to bring order to a long-ignored region in hopes that it might produce some tax revenue or allow for the resettlement of some displaced peoples. However, the circumstances of his illness distracted him. Whatever one might think of the potential for divine intervention in human affairs, it has certainly been a trope within the tradition of medieval Muslim Syria to seek cures in places with the potential for blessing (Meri 2002). Within the tradition, at least, he would be credited for his skill in locating a site that was ultimately efficacious and thereby bringing it to the attention of others.

The historical backdrop is that this limestone massif had long been deemed marginal not only for its productive capacities but also for its historical associations. In a region dominated by Christian asceticism, and even earlier by the cults of the classical pantheon, it was perhaps beyond fortuitous that the shrine in question harkened to a pre-Islamic Arab presence.[4] This was a history that could be more easily incorporated into a notion of Islam that counted amongst its faithful all those who had submitted to God's will despite their having come before the revelation of the Qur'an. There is nothing unique in such a move. It is part of a long established pattern in which the places of the prophets of the monotheistic tradition were legitimate venues for veneration within the Islamic tradition, a practice that drew on the example of the Prophet Muhammad himself for authorizing such visitations (*ziyarat*). It was not without controversy and argument as to who counted, who was a legitimate Muslim of the pre-Islamic era, and whether this practice could also extend to those considered saintly (*al-awliya*) in the post-prophetic age.[5]

It is important then to consider what is not included in the refashioning of Mashhad Ruhīn. While attention focuses on the final resting place of these three pre-Islamic Muslims (*hunafā*, s. *hanīf*), the church and other specifically

Christian structures that are part of the built environment are not mentioned. They are excluded from the re-development plan for the site which is concentrated away from the village and down the slope towards the *wadī*.[6] This selectivity of what can be remembered and what should be forgotten is very much a part of the craft. Those aspects of the landscape that remain in ruins may serve in themselves as reminders and lessons (*'ibar*), something which various medieval Muslim authors have noted in relationship to the decayed monuments of the Pharaohs and others (Colla 2007). Negotiating this narrative of the past and its potential to teach the present is precisely where the creative balance between invention and interpretation must be struck. At Mashhad Ruhīn we are meant to understand that this was particularly successful given the longevity of the pilgrimage that it inspired and its status as *hajj*-like.

This place-event, of course, was not a one-man show. While Sadīd al-Dīn tasked himself with its foundation, the ruling elite apparently knew a good thing when they saw it. Of particular importance in this account is the mention that the local potentate had devoted tax revenues to the development and upkeep of this place. Sustainability and growth was as important as the moment of inauguration. While the reports of Ibn Shaddād (1984), Ibn Shihnāh (1984), and others lack the specifics, we can speculate on fairly firm grounds that a pious foundation (*waqf* in Arabic) was established that designated this site as its beneficiary. In essence, it tied the production of the surrounding fields and the labor of the village's inhabitants to continuation and support of this new establishment. The chain of participation in its taking-place would include not only those engaged in its specific rituals but those threshing wheat and watering animals at its edges.

This last point raises the issue of scale, both the scales of analysis and the scales at which a particular place operates within its contexts. The direct context of Mashhad Ruhīn within the region of the Dead Cities located it within a particular set of geo-political and theo-political discourses with specific nuances in a period that was witnessing the waning years of the Crusades. It would not, however, become the catalyst for so many similar sites in the way that St. Simeon on his column had done centuries earlier. As with the various studies that form this volume, the scalar lens with which the analyst approaches these place-events is determinative of much of what can be said about them. Do we want to include the village peasants in the analysis? How big must we draw the political landscape into which these sites are located? Where does the economic impact or cultural influence of these places end? These and other similar questions bring us closer to understanding what constitutes an aptitude for sacred space. While any individual, community, empire – you pick the scale – may engage in this practice, some will be more practiced than others.

Ultimately, we must be cautious of the potential biases of our samples. With rare exception, the tendency of such studies is to analyze those places that succeeded and were efficacious in that effort to draw attention to the ritual practice which they constituted. The study here by Chiang and Liu of the Neolithic Wansan houses provides a useful counterpoint. In shifting the analysis away from those societies in which ritual practice can only be deemed sacred when compartmentalized or institutionalized in space, we become privy to the arbitrary nature of these scales and the potential to unduly naturalize them. This would be the caution I offer to an archaeology that too rigidly institutionalizes an *Annaliste* approach.

In organizing this volume, the editors have demonstrated that sacred space and ritual practice are not problems, but rather opportunities, for archaeology. These concepts have long suffered from being alienated from their material existence and their contextualization within the scales of analysis with which archaeologists are most comfortable. Their relocation within these frames of analysis forces a renewed attention to the specificity of place, while maintaining an appreciation for its essential role in organizing human experience. That balance, I have argued, is inherently social, and necessarily practiced. As we attempt to locate the sacred, it should almost go without saying that we must first locate ourselves and our own aptitude for engagement with these places.

Notes

1 This mashhad was attributed to an Arabian ḥanīf (one who had accepted monotheism prior to Islam but had not joined either the Christian or Jewish faiths) known as Quss b. Sāʿida and his two companions (Sourdel 1953: 106). This early article by Dominque Sourdel provides the most comprehensive discussion of the site as found in the various Arabic pilgrimage guides and historical chronicles.

2 The piety of ʿUmar II and his personal restraint for the finer things in life are the anomaly for the Umayyad dynasty (r. 661–750 A.D.) and even gains mention for such in the later, usually hostile, chronicles of the Abbasid period.

3 The site has not undergone any extensive archaeological investigation or mapping and is on the private property of a local landowner who manages a fruit orchard in the surrounding area. The author was given permission to make a photo documentation of the site and take some measurements during a visit in 2007.

4 See both Cobb (2002) and Meri (2002) for detailed discussions of the production of the wider sacred landscape of medieval Syria in the periods before and after the Crusades.

5 It is a foundational belief in the Islamic tradition that Muhammad was the last of God's prophets and thus the Qurʾan would be the final revelation for humanity.

6 Today these structures have been repurposed as domestic structures and agricultural facilities. It will await further archaeological investigation to potentially determine whether this was similarly the case for the thirteenth century.

References

Bahnassi, Afif
    1989 *The Great Omayyad Mosque of Damascus: The First Masterpieces of Islamic art.* TLASS, Damascus.

Biscop, Jean-Luc, and Jean-Pierre Sodini
    1984 Qal'at Sem'an et les chevets à colonnes de Syrie du Nord. *Syria* 61: 267–330.

Cahen, Claude
    1940 *La Syrie du nord à l'époque des croisades et la principauté franque d'Antioche.* P. Geuthner, Paris.

Cobb, Paul
    2002 Virtual Sacrality: Making Muslim Syria Sacred Before the Crusades. *Medieval Encounters* 8: 35–55.

Colla, Elliott
    2007 *Conflicted Antiquities: Egyptology, Egyptomania, Egyptian Modernity.* Duke University Press, Durham.

Eliade, Mircea
    1959 *The Sacred and the Profane: The Nature of Religion.* Harcourt Brace, New York.

Foss, Clive
    1997 Syria in Transition, A.D. 550–750: An Archaeological Approach. *Dumbarton Oaks Papers* 51: 189–269.

Ibn al-Shihnah
    1984 *al-Durr al-muntakhab fī tārīkh mamlakat Halab,* edited by Muhammad al Darwīsh. Dār al-Kitāb al-'Arabī, Damascus.

Ibn Shaddād
    1984 *Description de la Syrie du Nord (a translation of al-A'lāq al-Khatīra fī Dhir Umarā' al-Shām wa l-Ghaīra),* edited by Anne-Marie Eddé-Terrasse. Institut Français de Damas, Damascus.

Khoury, Widad
    1987 Deir Seta: prospection et analyse d'une ville morte inédite en Syrie. Ph.D. Dissertation, Université de Genève Faculté des lettres 1985. Dar Tlass, Damas.
    2005 Banassara, un site de pèlerinage dans le Massif Calcaire. *Syria* 82: 225–266.

MacIntyre, Alasdair C.
    1984 *After Virtue: A Study in Moral Theory.* 2nd ed. University of Notre Dame Press, Notre Dame.

Meri, Josef
    1999 Aspects of *baraka* (Blessing) and Ritual Devotion among Medieval Muslims and Jews. *Medieval Encounters* 5(1): 46–69.
    2002 *The Cult of Saints among Muslims and Jews in Medieval Syria.* Oxford Oriental Monographs. Oxford University Press, Oxford.

Peña, Ignacio, Pasquale Castellana, and Romualdo Fernández
    1987 *Inventaire du Jébel Baricha: recherches archéologiques dans la région des villes mortes de la Syrie du nord.* Collectio Minor (Studium Biblicum Franciscanum) 33. Franciscan Printing Press, Jerusalem.

1990   *Inventaire du Jebel el-A'la: recherches archéologiques dans la région des villes mortes de la Syrie du nord*. Collectio Minor (Studium Biblicum Franciscanum) 31. Franciscan Printing Press, Milan.

1999   *Inventaire du Jébel Wastani: recherches archéologiques dans la région des villes mortes de la Syrie du nord*. Collectio Minor (Studium Biblicum Franciscanum) 36. Éditions de la Custodie de T.S., Centro Propaganda e Stampa-Milano, Franciscan Printing Press, Milan.

2003   *Inventaire du Jébel Doueili: recherches archéologiques dans la région des villes mortes de la Syrie du nord*. Collectio Minor (Studium Biblicum Franciscanum) 43. Éditions de la Custodie de T.S., Centro Propaganda e Stampa-Milano, Franciscan Printing Press, Milan.

Smith, Jonathan Z.
1987   *To Take Place: Toward Theory in Ritual*. Chicago Studies in the History of Judaism. University of Chicago Press, Chicago.

Sourdel-Thomine, Janine
1954   Le peuplement de la région des "villes mortes" (Syrie du nord) à l'époque Ayyūbide. *Arabica* 1(2): 187–200.

Sourdel, Dominique
1953   Ruhin, lieu de pèlerinage Musulman de la Syrie du nord au XIII siècle. *Syria* 30: 89–107.

Tate, Georges
1992   *Les campagnes de la Syrie du nord du II au VII siècle: un exemple d'expansion démographique et économique dans les campagnes à la fin de l'antiquité*. P. Geuthner, Paris.

Tchalenko, Georges
1953   *Villages antiques de la Syrie du nord: le massif du Bélus à l'époque romaine*. P. Geuthner, Paris.

Turner, Victor W.
1995   *The Ritual Process: Structure and Anti-Structure*. The Lewis Henry Morgan Lectures, 1966. de Gruyter, New York.

Yoffee, Norman (editor)
2007   *Negotiating the Past in the Past: Identity, Memory, and Landscape in Archaeological Research*. University of Arizona Press, Tucson.

Index